BEYOND DEFEAT

BEYOND DEFEAT

by JAMES E. JOHNSON
with
DAVID W. BALSIGER

Introduction by Charles W. Colson

A Doubleday – Galilee Original
Doubleday & Company, Inc.
Garden City, New York
1978

Library of Congress Cataloging in Publication Data

Johnson, James E 1926–
Beyond defeat.

1. Johnson, James E., 1926– 2. Afro-Americans—
Biography. 3. Christian biography—United States.
I. Balsiger, Dave, joint author. II. Title.
E185.97.J685A33   973.92′092′4 [B]
ISBN 0-385-13486-x
Library of Congress Catalog Card Number 77–16849

to
my parents,
Richard and Veola Johnson
(both deceased),
and my wife,
Juanita

INTRODUCTION

by
Charles W. Colson

In the pages to follow I want you to meet a remarkable man, my friend Johnny Johnson.

When I was an assistant to the President, Johnny was named to a high government post. He soon caught my attention. Many black politicians are Democrats, but Johnny was a lifelong Republican, a conservative one at that. A powerful speaker with a dynamic personality and contagious smile, Johnny is the kind of a man who quickly inspires confidence.

Shortly after the 1972 election, I returned to practice law. Wealth, power, and prestige beckoned. I should have been exuberant. The President's re-election was for me a great personal triumph. But instead, I was experiencing a curious inner deadness. Then ominous dark clouds rolled across the horizon—the burgeoning scandal of Watergate. I forgot about Johnny Johnson, about politics, about almost everything except the all-consuming struggle engulfing those of us caught in the storm's eye.

One night, I was in the Los Angeles Airport on my way home from a business trip. I had been on television so much that my face was instantly recognized by most passers-by. So, I had developed an almost frozen stare, which avoided eye contact. Suddenly out of the crowd appeared a familiar face with a huge warm smile. I couldn't miss it. It was my friend Johnny. We boarded the night flight, affectionately known as the "red-eye," back to Washington. Johnny had a cold and needed sleep. Buffeted by the Watergate hearings, I myself was exhausted. But neither one of us slept. We talked the entire night about the Marine Corps, which both of us had served in and loved, about government, politics, and our friend, President Nixon.

There was something more to Johnny—a warmth, a radiance. In politics, I'd become accustomed to everyone wanting something from me. Johnny didn't. He was simply understanding and concerned about me. My own life was so empty I couldn't know what it was that made a man like Johnny different.

Then, late one summer night in 1973, I discovered what had been missing. I asked Jesus Christ into my life, and immediately I discovered what it was that Johnny Johnson had that I had not been able to recognize.

On the morning of March 2, 1974, I waited in the quiet of my office for the long-awaited announcement of indictments in the Watergate case. My wife, Patty, was at my side. We were hopeful even in those final suspenseful moments that I would not be indicted. Minutes dragged interminably. Then came the shattering news—I was one of seven named. Within seconds my telephone rang. It was Johnny Johnson. "Brother," he said, "I have just gotten the news. Don't worry about a thing. Trust the Lord and know that we love you." Johnny was in California. He had awakened to the first radio broadcast and instantly grabbed his telephone. It may sound like a little thing, but in those dreadful days just the knowledge that a brother cared and stood at my side made all the difference.

Since then we have become close, not as former proud Marines or political comrades, but in the strongest bond ever—as brothers in Christ.

So, you can see why I want you to know him as I know him: a patriot, fiercely loyal to his country and his ideals, a remarkably gifted public servant, and a deeply committed follower of the Lord Jesus Christ.

But even more important than meeting Johnny, I hope as you travel through the pages that follow, you will meet the One who changed Johnny's life and then mine. If you know Him already, sharing Johnny's experiences can only bring you closer.

BEYOND DEFEAT

CHAPTER

1

Three of us were in the house one afternoon during the Depression years of the 1930s. My mother, Veola, was in the kitchen, her long black hair just visible through the curtain separating kitchen from living room. My sister Elisa, two years older than I, was sewing in a chair Dad had nailed together from scrap wood. Mama had made cushions for it out of remnants.

I sat on a square of carpet Mama had patched, holding my little red car with the broken wheel and staring at the new comic strip Mama had pasted on the wall. A fireplace spark had scorched the old "wallpaper."

Someone calling on us was always an event, and when a knock came on the kitchen door, I was at Mama's side by the time she opened it.

On the stoop stood a shortish man in a black suit, shiny from pressing with heated flatirons. He carried a large box covered over with a piece of tattered muslin. My heart began tripping. What was in that box?

The only dark men I'd ever seen wearing suits were preachers. Was he one? I held onto the corner of Mama's apron.

And, sure enough, "How are you, Pastor?" Mama asked.

"I have a present for you. Just some groceries we had down at the church, more'n we need, you see. We giving them to needy families around here."

Mama swallowed. Her high cheekbones and long Indian nose stood out. She started to wring her thin hands.

"I'd better not take those. My husband, Mr. Johnson, he doesn't like to take anything 'less he's worked for it."

The preacher smiled. "Oh, now, lissen, this is no problem at all. Everybody's taking some. It's Depression, ain't it, Miz Johnson? Don' you worry yo'self about it."

"Mr. Johnson won't understand."

"He'll understand." Pastor Evans pushed past Mama into the kitchen and set the groceries on the table.

Mama sighed. "I sure hope you're right, Rev'rend Evans. And I thank you very much. It's awfully nice of you."

"Now just don' you fret about it, Miz Johnson. It's the Lord's work; He wants you to have them groceries."

Pastor Evans left. We could hear his Model T coughing its way back to the country road.

I lifted a corner of the muslin covering. A fat red apple! Dried beans in a Mason jar! Would we have them cooked up with some salt pork?

Mama was rolling out dough for biscuits. I knew supper was to be biscuits and molasses, along with some fat bacon. Now I imagined it might be quite a bit more.

Mama gently slapped my hand away. "We aren't touching these groceries until Mr. Johnson gets home."

My heart sank. Not that we didn't get enough to eat. Even though jobs were scarce and pay was peanuts, Dad always managed to find some kind of job to feed his family. I was skinny, but not from lack of food. I was just skinny, no matter how much I ate, and we had plenty from the farm where Dad was sharecropping.

But we didn't always have enough cash money to buy peanut butter, jam, cookies, fresh fruit, or certain spices Mama talked about.

I tried to get interested in what the cow was doing over in the back pasture, and whether the hens had laid any eggs, the occasional automobile putt-putting down the road, the horses and wagons that clip-clopped by.

When Dad finally came home, my spirits rose. Dad was so tall I could see him coming from half a mile away. He seemed to tower above the trees, striding along that country road. Then he was sweeping through the gate. His enormous hand glided over my head. "Evening, Jimmy."

He strode through the living room into the kitchen. "Hi, hon." Dad gave Mama a brief nod. His eyes jumped to the box on the table.

"What's that, hon?" Dad pointed.

Mama gave a nervous laugh. "Oh, you know that nice minister came by here. You know, the one who lives not too far down the road? In the little house by the big oak tree?"

"Yes?"

"Isn't it wonderful! He brought all these groceries up here and gave them to us. He says they have too much at the church, and he's given groceries to everyone else. Everyone takes them now. He thought we ought to have some, too."

Dad's broad, black, handsome face frowned. His expression eased as he gave Mama a look of love and compassion. He picked up the box and marched out.

"Dad, Dad!" I yelled. "Where are you going?"

"You be quiet, son," he said over his shoulder, almost running down our dirt drive.

Whenever Dad said to be quiet, I was quiet. But he hadn't said, "Don't follow me." I had to run to keep up, but I was accustomed to that. We "walked" eight miles to church every Sunday.

When we arrived at the preacher's house, Dad, holding the box under one huge arm, went up the steps and balled his gigantic hand into a fist. He knocked so loudly, I thought the wood would splinter.

Pastor Evans opened the door. "Ahhhh, you must be Mr. Johnson."

"That's right, sir," Dad said. "Did you give this food to my family?" His voice was deep, firm, but polite.

The minister smiled, his dark eyes with yellowed whites looking a little bewildered. "I certainly did. We have plenty down at the church; we just wanted to give it to a needy family. You have lots of children; God has blessed . . ."

My dad hefted the box into the preacher's arms. "Preacher, don't you ever try to play God with me. The Lord says every man should live off the sweat of his brow. As long as I have my health, I'll take care of my family. Now, you hear that?"

The preacher stepped back. "Now, wait a minute, Mr. Johnson. You got to recognize the fact, it's Depression. I been meaning to talk to you about your religious beliefs. We is supposed to help each other."

"Preacher," my dad said, "I'm going to tell *you* something. I know about the Holy Spirit, the Father, and the Son. I got those three things straight in my mind, and don't you go around trying to mess them up."

Dad stormed off, full of anger.

I was so astonished I forgot all about the extra food and fancy desserts we might have had.

And supper wasn't really bad at all.

CHAPTER

2

Long ago, off Senegal, Africa, before my father or grandfather were born, our Great Father, at more than seven feet, was tall enough to stand above the stinking muck at his feet.

But he was not tall enough to reach the top of the black hold in which he was crammed with hundreds of groaning and dying people. He was a giant with giant's muscles, but he was not strong enough to break the irons attaching him to a corpse on one side and a dying youth on the other.

Great Father's spirit sneered at the groans, retching, and cries all around him, and bellowed out again an ancient song in which could be heard drumbeats, the rhythm of jungle dances, and rituals. Great Father was the instrument to arouse his brothers once again in their time-without-end captivity—rocking and pitching and creaking over a river so wide no man could see the banks or know the depths.

For them, the white man's magic was powerful. First, ones in the white robes and strange headcloths had attacked Great Father's vil-

lage. They came with magic weapons and chains. Many of Great Father's brothers died on the long march along rain-swollen, steaming rivers, through thorny vines, and over mountains of rock.

At that point, where the river widened to an endless width of wind-churned water, clusters of strange houses lined the waters. There, white-robed men talked with other white faces, in even stranger body coverings. Green paper and gold passed from hand to hand. Great Father and others were led up onto a house-of-all-houses that rode upon the waters—there to be thrust down into the underworld.

Yes, the white man's magic was powerful, but Great Father's magic had had force in the past; he had had command of spirit and darkness. His magic had brought him workers from all tribes except the Little Ones, who were too crafty and elusive to be caught.

You see, magic had made Great Father and his people masters, and—he was convinced—if he kept reminding his countrymen, what was left of them, of the Spirit Warriors in the Unseen World, they could be masters over those who now mastered them.

Therefore he burst again into a song as old as five generations of elephants. Sometimes his voice rose to a piercing screech like the sharpness of elephant tusks. And sometimes he sounded as the elephants themselves, trumpeting through the trees, or as other animals wild, hungry, and afraid, or as carrion birds darkening the skies.

Then, as it had happened before, he began to wake the spirits in what was left of the others in their miserable cavern between this world and the Dead World. Many of the dying joined him, chanting and singing; and, as before, the white masters heard it and descended along the halfway galleries around the hold.

Their lashes stung out. One by one their lashes silenced the followers of the Great Spirits. And with the song dying as well as the singers, the shouts of the white master and the crack of the whips echoed. But not over the powerful deep tones of the Great Father, embattled, indomitable.

The lashes could not silence Great Father; only the heaviness of his heart silenced him, and agony made him draw within himself as whips and curses rained down, and the blood on his shoulders dried and stank.

Great Father was the first "American" on my family tree, my great-grandfather. He and his descendants, down to Dad and me, were of the Watusi tribe of Central Africa. This tall giant, who had been master of his lush green homeland, had been trapped and caged and hauled to a new and foreign jungle, to slavery.

My father, Richard Jackson Johnson, lived to be 104 and was too positive a thinker, too great a Christian, too forward-looking and loving to feel racial hatred because of long-ago history. He didn't even like to tell the legends handed down, but preferred to quote the Bible to show the cruelties Satan works through man, the continuing spiritual warfare between darkness and light.

During my growing years, Dad patiently stressed day after day the good that is within men and women. He said often, "If you look for the worst in a person, you will find it. If you look for the best in a person, you will find that, too."

Because of his reluctance to dwell on the evils of the past, most of what Dad told us of our family tree began with him, just after the days of slavery in America. Dad's father had been born in Mississippi, the valuable property of a plantation owner. But this grandfather of mine was to remain almost as much of a mystery to me as Great Father.

Dad also was born in Mississippi, about 1865, when the Civil War ended. But Dad was born free. And all his life he insisted upon emphasizing the positive, the joy of being freed from chains.

In those early days in Mississippi, white people were afraid of education for the newly liberated slaves. Anyone caught teaching a Negro to read, write, or understand arithmetic felt the white public's wrath. But as a boy, Dad had a white friend who wasn't afraid of violating the taboo. The boy taught Dad to read, and the "reader" he used was the Bible.

Once, when they were caught at it, their reading matter saved them from punishment. The rationale was, "Well, seeing as how it's the Bible, I suppose it's all right, 'cuz it'll make him a good boy. I reckon y'all kin read that."

It was a different matter when Dad had advanced to the point of applying "higher" mathematics to his "business dealings" at the little country store. In reading the Holy Book, he'd picked up quite a lot about numbers.

The proprietor of the store was well known for cheating Negro customers who couldn't read or add. When Dad started questioning the tally on groceries he was sent to buy, the storekeeper barked, "Who taught you all this stuff?"

When Dad wouldn't answer, the storekeeper yelled, "Don't y'all ever come in this store again, hear? Not even in the sections for Negroes."

Which made Dad want to learn all the more.

When he was seventeen years old, Dad walked away from the Mississippi farm where his parents lived. It was a long walk from Mississippi to the Blackfoot Indian Reservation in Oklahoma, where he found work as a logger.

He worked among the Indians for twenty years before he married my mother, Veola. During those years, he "walked where he wanted," respected, almost worshiped, because of his giant stature (six feet, nine inches) and iron strength. Watusi were a rare sight on an Indian reservation.

As big as he was—275 pounds of muscle—he was tested in Indian wrestling by the braves he met on arrival. Opponents, elbows together on the ground, clasped hands and sought to force the hand and arm of the other to the ground—a quiet, nonviolent competition. They also lay near each other on the ground, head to feet, and twined legs in a similar contest of muscle.

Dad won most of these bouts. And he so won the chief's admiration for hard work that Dad was given a tepee near him, a symbolic honor. The chief of the Blackfoot tribe cottoned to hard workers, and Dad was just about the hardest worker in Oklahoma.

Dad was a champion logroller. In those days, two men faced each other with a huge log between them resting on two poles. The contestants bent and gripped one of the poles in each hand and lifted. The object was to see who could, by means of these poles, lift the log higher and roll the log toward the opponent.

As the balance became tougher for the weaker contestant, and the monstrous (400 pound) log began to roll toward him, he had to yell "uncle" loud and clear if he didn't want the log crashing into his chest.

Often, the victor had to start easing a log down when he saw his opponent buckling. If the man's knees gave, he was dead. Beating your opponent was one thing; killing him was another.

Dad almost always won. Years of catching logs with his hands and pushing them over had developed his muscles so that few men could rival him in any test of strength.

My father would take chances no one else would. During his early years among the Indians, before he knew about buffalo, he thought buffalo could be tackled like a steer and, after bringing one down, he could rest assured that the herd would swerve to one side to avoid trampling their downed champion. Dad succeeded in tackling a buffalo by the horns and flipping him over to the ground. But the charging herd just kept coming. They stomped over their fallen comrade, killing him. Dad was saved only because he was on the opposite side from the oncoming herd. He received painful hoof cuts on his legs that left lifelong scars.

In those days in Oklahoma, hard workers didn't labor so much for money as for livestock and goods, the accumulation of which determined status and bargaining power in the community.

When Dad met young Veola, a rare combination of Blackfoot and Cherokee, he set out in earnest to consolidate his gains. Her father held out for a stiff price, and by the time the negotiations were firmed up and the agreement "signed," probably in blood, Veola cost my dad just about everything he had—a horse, two calves, and some blankets.

They had an Indian wedding ceremony, dancing in the night around a roaring fire, feasting, and singing. The knot had been tied by the chief himself in an ancient chanting ceremony.

By the time Dad married, he was thirty-seven, and my mother was an Indian maiden of fifteen. The twenty-odd years separating them did nothing to diminish their love, but she never could quite call Dad anything but "Mr. Johnson." She was passionately devoted to him. She thought about him first (and, later, him and the children). Never herself. If food was short, she would insist that Dad eat, pretending she had something put aside for herself.

With her long black hair, copper complexion, and handsome, long, high nose, Mother was very attractive. She was only five feet, three; her husband towered over her. Dad taught her how to cook, sew, read, and write.

My father worked for a while longer in Oklahoma, then went to Missouri, where he and Veola were married a second time, in a civil ceremony. Leaving Missouri for southern Illinois, they moved next down into Arkansas.

Railroads were expanding everywhere; strong men who could cut down the forests for railroad ties were in demand.

In three years, two children were born, fulfilling the Bible's exhortation and society's expectations.

Dad gave up logging finally for sharecropping on a farm, and, at the age of forty, he had an opportunity to go to school.

He'd kept up learning on his own, and now in a dilapidated, ungraded, one-room country school with a rusty wood stove in the middle, he became a pupil. He attended school during school hours and took care of the farm before and after.

The authorities didn't suspect Dad was forty. Because many students at the school were grown men in their midtwenties, his size did not give him away.

What tripped him up was his tremendous ability in spelling. On the day of a spelling bee, as the words became more difficult, going from "entirely" to "Mississippi" to "bravado" and "innuendo," students one by one sat down. Eventually only one remained standing —Dad, as usual.

"How old are you, anyway?" the clerk of the school district finally asked.

"Just forty," Dad replied. "I told the teacher once."

The teacher looked at him. "Yes, he told me he was forty. I thought he was joking."

The clerk eyed Dad. "Young man—er, Mr. Johnson—it is unfair for you to always end up head of the class in spelling. It's giving the young ones an inferiority complex."

"But that's why I'm here, to learn," Dad protested.

"Nevertheless, you can no longer be allowed to spell with the class."

Dad refused to accept the decision. "That's not fair to me." He banged his mighty fist on the desk.

"One other question, Mr. Johnson," the clerk said. "Are you married?"

Dad had been walking several miles to school. Nobody, he thought, knew anything about his personal life.

He hadn't intended to deceive. Since nobody had said anything, he thought the fact that he was married was accepted and overlooked. From the clerk's tone, Dad knew he had been mistaken. He also knew the rule: Married people were not allowed in school.

Meek as any schoolboy, Dad hung his head.

The clerk was triumphant. "Of course, I suppose we could make an exception, since you have no children."

"I'm sorry. I do have children. Two. And we're going to have another one soon."

"You will not be allowed in school any longer, Mr. Johnson."

All right, then. He would have to get educated on his own.

For the next twenty years, while Mother raised children, Dad logged and farmed and learned. They kept moving, returning to Arkansas, then back to Missouri, and again to Illinois.

During the roaring twenties, Dad became a sharecropper on a farm near Madison, Illinois, and Mama prepared to have her ninth child. Dad was sixty-four, and Mama, forty-two.

From my point of view, it was a major event.

CHAPTER

3

Mama used to like to tell me the story of my birth mainly because I was the last child. "There was something different about my baby," she would say. "Right from the start, Jimmy was a big boy, weighed over thirteen pounds."

I had crowded out a twin brother, who had weighed only one pound. Dad had looked forward to having more sons, and when he was told he was going to get two at once, he was more than elated.

Mother said she could remember the midwife telling Dad, "I not so sure 'bout th' littler one, Mistah Johnson. Oh my, the biggest one am strong and healthy, but I don't reckon there's much hope for t'other."

The small baby's death made them both very sad. They had done their share of raising children for twenty-eight years, most of them girls. Besides Dad and Mama and me, there was Annie, Nella, Dempsey, Roberta, Ida, Hattie, Classie, and Amos. And whenever a lesson was to be taught, Dad was always there to be sure we understood. He knew I didn't understand why he had taken the groceries back to the preacher, but he would repeat, "You'll understand these things when you grow up, Jimmy."

Jobs were scarce in the Depression, but Dad always had one. "I have never been out of work and never will be," he'd say, "because when that boss gives me a dollar, I give him a dollar and a half's worth of work."

On a new job, he'd be the first man there. Because Dad could read and write, he'd put down the time the other men arrived, take out the tools, pick certain men for certain jobs, and have them all working before the boss arrived.

Dad would say to the boss, "Since you weren't here yet, I took the liberty of opening the tool box. When I saw we were wasting time, I assigned those two big guys to cut trees, started those two in the underbrush, and those two in the ditch."

On most jobs Dad usually became straw boss. When men were laid off, he was always the last man to go, and every time he finished one job, he'd be recommended for another.

"Then I'd be the last one to leave, too," Dad would tell me. "I'd collect the tools and clean them and put them away. I was the last one. I'd lock up and hand the keys to the boss.

"Now, you don't tell me they aren't going to keep a fellow like me on. I believe I should give a boss every ounce of work he deserves, because when payday comes, I don't want him to cheat me out of one penny. That's why I give him a dollar and a half's worth of work."

Dad and Mom had taught me to read and write, and I always looked forward to putting my learning into practice—especially on Sundays, when I would try to follow Bible verses the preacher read.

On Sundays, I not only learned new things about the Bible, but I could play with my friends. It was our only outing, and we spent the whole day at church.

All week long, the women would plan picnic baskets for Sunday go-to-meeting. The food had to last all day, and these proud cooks were eager to exchange recipes and try out each other's favorites.

There would be extra-thick slices of bread with fresh home-churned butter, jams canned from fruit in the orchards, yams, and whatever fruit was in season. All the families would bring enough food for themselves and more, and it always looked like so much more when all put together and shared.

In a kitchen in the church basement, all the baskets would be lined up on tables. My friends and I would sneak in to look under the bright dishtowels covering the baskets, staring at cakes and fried chicken and baked ham. We never touched anything. That would have meant serious trouble.

Dad had looked at many of the cars popular then, the Model T's, Model A's, the Chevvies, roadsters with rumble seats, and others. But he didn't cotton to any.

"Animals are man's best friends, son," he'd say.

He decided that when we got a little more money ahead, he'd get us a cart and hitch up the horses; we'd no longer walk the eight miles to and from church.

Our family was one of the larger ones in the congregation. When the minister called on us, we felt we must be ready to say something. One morning Rev. Evans had a particularly long service, and after about an hour of testimony by the adults, he decided to hear from the young people. He pointed a rigid finger at me. "Jimmy, tell us what the good Lord has done for you this week."

I gulped, then blurted, "Ahhh, er, uhhh, well, sir, I guess I'll have to thank the Lord for my hen."

For some reason, the congregation began to laugh.

"On your feet, son!" Dad whispered.

"I mean, my hen was a chicken once and she didn't have both her legs." More laughter.

"You see, I found this little chicken, only it wasn't a normal chicken."

The minister shook his finger at the congregation. "Jimmy, you just keep on telling your story, praise the Lord!"

"Well, er, uh, I picked up some matchsticks and made a splint for the little chicken's leg. I tied them on with a string," I explained. "And finally, my little chicken started hobbling on her leg. The Lord let her walk."

Now the congregation interrupted in a different way. "Praise the Lord!" "Hallelujah!" "Ohhhhh, Jesus," people moaned.

"Anyway, I know I didn't do it. And that's what I'm thankful for —my hen."

I sat down fast.

A woman in front of me turned around. "That's faith. I never in my life heard of putting a splint on a chicken's leg in all my born days. And he is right! The Lord went and done it, hallelujah!"

I got a real pat on the back from my dad that day.

Even as a youngster, I could see how important the church was to the black person. He would be put down all week, told he couldn't go into this restaurant, or buy that piece of goods, cheated out of some of his pay, and cheated at the general store. He was told where he could sleep, eat, and walk. But on Sunday, in our little community church, he was important, a VIP, in God's eyes.

So often we were reminded by our pastor of Jesus' many consolations to the poor, the weak, the downtrodden, and the hopeless. What music it was to hear Rev. Evans read from Matthew 19:23, "Verily, I say unto ye, that a rich man shall hardly enter into the kingdom of heaven." Also, in Matthew 20:16, "So the last shall be first, and the first last: For many shall be called but few chosen."

Rev. Evans also was fond of quoting Philippians 4:13: "I can do all things through Christ . . ."

During testimony time, the minister didn't miss a chance to give each brother his say. Then he made sure that man was grateful for what he had before he left the church. "Oh, thank You, Jesus!" would be the cry. "Thank You for jest a crust of bread, God."

Back in those days on Sunday, our church had standing room only, and we could feel the Holy Spirit coming right down into us as we praised God with tears of joy in our eyes. When we left church after the long day, the Spirit was with us all the way home, long enough to last until Wednesday night prayer meeting, when we really let loose for the Lord!

Pastor Evans knew how to bring his congregation to a certain emotional response. All of his sermons would be accompanied by hand-clapping, pulpit-pounding, and panting.

By the time singing was over, Rev. Evans would have worked himself to the rear of the church, where he would fling open the doors. No one dared turn around. No matter how eager to go, no one wanted to be the first to leave.

When he opened those doors, the preacher had two ideas in mind: to give everyone a little spell of fresh air, and to give a change of pace for his next message.

Almost blocking the doors, he'd say, "All those who are truly believers of God, who have been baptized, and who are members of this church, and who have the Holy Spirit, who truly believe in Jesus Christ, sit down."

Just as he knew, a lot of people were left standing.

"Now, I just think this is the day we are going to let everybody sit down!" He'd go down the line. "Do you believe He died on the cross to take away your sins?"

"Yes."

"Your sins are now forgiven. Do you believe?"

After he'd traveled around the room, he'd say, "If you really believe Jesus Christ died on the cross for you, to save you, give me your hand. Congratulations, praise the Lord!"

When this call to come to God was given, many responded. Rev. Evans was pretty hard to turn down. And new converts meant a trip to the river to be baptized.

The baptismal service was almost like a well-rehearsed play, complete with costumes. Those being baptized wore long white robes. The rest of the congregation was dressed in "Sunday best." A visiting minister would make the occasion special.

I liked it when we sang, and I could look up the hill and see everyone winding slowly along the path in a single line. When we sang, "Shall We Gather at the River," I sometimes had to slip my hand into Mama's and squeeze a little. She always squeezed back.

As soon as the baptismal service was over, all the children helped get out the picnic baskets and set them on makeshift tables under the trees.

Had it not been for black ministers in Negro life, the frustrations of the blacks would have been unbearable sometimes. People have to have someone to listen to them, to encourage them.

At church, the black minister would assure the black man, "You are a good man. You are a person. God loves you."

When the colored man went to church, he had a feeling of worth, he had the promise that God does not discriminate.

CHAPTER

4

I had my first encounter with discrimination when I was eight. I was telling the Bible story of Daniel and the lions to my special chum.

"Come on over to my house," he said. "I've got a colored picture book of that story. We could play Daniel and the lions with my set of animals."

He started describing his toys, and by the time we neared his house, among the bigger and better homes a quarter of a mile from mine, I was excited.

When we opened the front door, his mother greeted us with, "Where did you get that little boy?"

"I went over to his house this morning," my chum replied. "We're going to play Daniel and the lions with my new set of animals."

The mother, a very tiny woman, put her hands in the pockets of the starchy white apron she was wearing, looked me up and down, and said, "Well, little boy, you can't come through the front door. You may go around back and into the kitchen and wait there."

"Why?" my friend asked. "His shoes aren't dirty."

She turned to her son. Crisply she said, "That's not the point. He's colored."

"What color?"

"Never mind that, son. He knows his place."

But instead of going around to the back door, I started for home, my legs pumping, swallowing tears. My pal ran after me, crying, "Are you mad at me? Please say you're not mad at me. Gee, you're my best friend."

"No." I stopped. "But your mother doesn't like me."

"Oh, she does, she does. You just probably had a little dirt on your shoes."

I finally said, "It doesn't matter, anyway. I—I forgot: I was supposed to help my mother with something."

When I got home, I told Dad, "Dad, I guess she's not an American. She won't even let me come to the front door."

Dad put his hand on my shoulder. "You let that hurt you? Why? You have a front door you can come in, don't you?"

"Yeah."

"Just remember she's the one hurting inside, not you! Because she doesn't know what a fine boy you are, she didn't get a chance to know you."

I thought that over. Going to my friend's house had been almost like going to the lions' den. I punched my fist into my palm. The next time something like that happened, I would try to have more courage. Like Daniel.

One day I had a toy truck with me when I ran into the neighborhood bully.

I tried to dodge, but he jumped at me and grabbed my toy. I tried to hit him. He turned and whistled for his friends lurking around a corner. Three of them came running from out of nowhere. One punched me in the stomach, and two pinned my arms behind my back.

Sobbing, I tried to work loose, but they pulled my arms tighter. When they did let go, I went flying to the sidewalk. I picked myself up and started running.

The faster I ran, the harder I cried.

Dad was home, and I threw my arms around his leg. "They beat me up!" I whimpered. "They took my truck."

"Oh, they did, did they?" Dad put his hands on his hips. "Well, well. Let's just go and teach them a lesson they won't forget."

When we got down to the corner, the four boys were playing with my truck. "There they are, there they are, Dad! Let's get them!"

One of the boys saw Dad and started to run.

"Come back here," Dad commanded quietly.

The kid stopped.

"Jimmy and I just came down here to teach you a lesson. A real lesson about beating up people."

Fearfully, but doubling up their fists, they edged closer. The big kid, who had looked so menacing to me before, now looked sort of silly. I felt like a big kid myself now, standing there with my Dad, thinking he was going to knock them around.

"We're going to teach you a lesson you won't forget," Dad drawled, as I clenched my fists. "Jimmy and I are going to forgive you and show you we still love you. You hear that? We forgive you and love you. Let's go, son!"

I looked up at my dad. I was supposed to love these good-for-nothing bullies who beat me up? I pulled on Dad's arm. "What do you mean, love them?" I felt like crying all over again.

I was so disgusted and hurt, I turned and ran home. He'd let me down; my father had backed out of trouble, an easy fight. He didn't have any guts. I was miserable.

Unless he said something to me first, I didn't speak to Dad the rest of the day. I couldn't bear to look at him. All my admiration for him, for his wisdom, his giant's strength, was gone.

About seven o'clock that night, someone knocked on the door. Dad answered it. "Jimmy, here are some boys to see you."

I ran to the door, then backed away. "These are the guys who beat me up; I don't want to play with them!"

Dad grinned. "They brought your truck back."

I was dumfounded. Finally I asked, "Well, what did you bring it back for?"

The leader of the "gang" shifted from one foot to the other, holding out the truck. "Gee, I dunno. Can you play now?"

"Huh? Play? Uh, I guess so." I took the truck and followed them into the yard. I was all mixed up, but something started registering.

Vaguely, I thought of Daniel in the lions' den. Lions, I thought, maybe just need a little petting.

It took me some time to realize that my father had been trying to teach me forgiveness—and the power of love. Life was to bring me many opportunities to put that lesson into practice.

When I was ten or eleven, I was in our little "general store," watching some white boys try on fancy-looking baseball caps. I wanted one too, and sauntered over to the counter, looking for a blue cap, not noticing that they were stacked according to size. As I was about to try on a cap, a hand reached out, grabbed my arm, and jerked the cap from my hand.

The storekeeper said, "Don't put that cap on unless you're going to buy it." He gave me a mean look. "Are you going to buy it?"

"I don't know whether it fits or not."

"You'll just have to guess. You put it on, we can't sell it."

"Why not?"

"No white customer wants it after you put it on."

I hung my head and put my hands in my pockets, feeling coins. I didn't want the cap. I forced myself to stroll out of the store, my chest tight.

Dad was out in the yard planting, and I ran right past him. He leaned on his shovel and called, "What's the matter, Jimmy?"

After I tumbled out the story, Dad didn't say anything for a moment, then, "What kind of cap was it?"

"Blue and white."

"You feel awfully sorry for that man, don't you?"

"I can't feel sorry for him!"

"Well, son, he's not going to make very many sales, and he might even have a family, and his family is not going to learn to enjoy life like we do. He's hurting himself."

I tried to feel sorry for that man.

Dad put the shovel away. "Come on, son, let's go down to the store. I'll tell your mother where we're going. It must be getting close to supper."

We went back to the store, me with a funny feeling in my stomach. I had faith in Dad, but I thought it would take a miracle to straighten this one out. "You go over to where the caps are, son, and I'll find a clerk."

I went straight to the caps, this time careful not to touch one. Dad and a clerk came over. "Which one do you want, son?"

I pointed. The clerk looked, then picked up another blue one just like it. "This one?"

"Yes, sir."

"Go ahead and try it on," Dad suggested.

I looked at the clerk, and he nodded. I tried it on, and it fit perfectly.

Dad smiled. "We'll buy it."

I wore the cap out of the store, feeling ten feet high.

I didn't know until years later that my dad had gone over to the clerk and given him my right hat size, so the first cap I'd tried on was the "right" one. Dad thought the worst thing anyone could do was hate. He'd been afraid this incident might cause hatred hard to erase.

A year later, we moved to Chicago. The worst days of the Depression seemed over.

I got a job selling newspapers after school in the thick of traffic on a busy corner, hawking the Chicago *Defender* and the *Gazette*. I was always quick to spot a hand out a car window, take the nickel, and thrust in a newspaper still smelling of printer's ink.

"HITLER STORM TROOPERS ENTER AUSTRIA! Read all a-bout it—Chicago *Defender!*" I would scream at the top of my lungs. "Extry! Extry! VIENNA FALLS TO NAZI TROOPS. Re-ad all a-bout it!" I stayed hoarse from constant yelling to make myself heard over the crackling of radios in the shops turned up full blast to attract customers, perhaps broadcasting, "Hap-py days are he-re a-gain, we'll sing and dance and play a-gain!"

Or, as I hollered out, the resonant voice of America's hero President, Franklin Delano Roosevelt, might flow warmly from nearby radio stores, hot-dog joints, and pool halls.

Americans were assured that the signs of progress were real, prosperity was right around the corner.

I was too young to see the contradictions, the soup kitchens, the bread lines, and far too naïve to see the rush from the empty frying pan of poverty into the hellfire and damnation of war.

But I was not alone. Not even the oldest on those crowded streets seemed to recognize the direction history was marching in. Happy days were here again, and everybody was jitterbugging.

My news beat was in front of the old Savoy Hotel, where there was a roller-skating rink, and where the big bands came. Kids played around the back stairs waiting for the musicians to come out. They'd throw us dimes, nickels, even quarters, and shake our hands.

One kid who had the job of polishing the drums, wiping off perspiration on the instruments, and putting the canvas over them for Lionel Hampton, started showing up late. I decided to go after his job. I was small and skinny, but I tried anyway. I asked Hampton, "Could you just let me polish your drums? I won't charge you anything."

Hampton grinned down at me. "Well, the other kid isn't doing it proper; sure, you can do it. But I'll be glad to pay you."

"Oh, you don't have to," I said.

He shook his head. "Either I pay you or you don't do it. Okay?"

When Lionel Hampton was in town, perhaps for a week-long engagement or a special one-nighter, I would rush to the Savoy after school, get out his drums, and polish them until they shone like gold.

I really loved Hampton. He let me bang on the drums, and for a while, I thought I would be a musician. Hampton, Calloway, Lunceford, Ellington, and Count Basie came to Chicago regularly to play, and their music helped celebrate the recovery from the Great Depression. They were the visible signs of returning prosperity and of the "new spirit."

Hitler was playing music, too. "Strength through joy" was persuading youth to the service of the Fatherland, while in America too few of us had any serious purpose, any goal to strive for, to make our country better.

Even at twelve years of age, I wanted to earn my own way. It was something Dad had instilled in me. His anger at the preacher who had tried to give us the free groceries had made an indelible impression on me. I'd never accept handouts either. I'd work hard and make my own way. I wouldn't ask favors; I'd earn everything I got.

Since my newspaper job didn't pay much, I was faced with a dilemma: I had a chance for a job that would pay more but give me less freedom to hang around the Savoy. I made the sacrifice and took the job, cleaning out furnaces in three big apartment buildings. I had to get up at three in the morning and walk several blocks through snow, ice, and darkness to the first building on my route. I would clean out the ashes, start the fire, scoop coal, and bank it. I'd do this for each building, then run home for a quick bath and rush off to school.

After school, I'd go back and bank the furnaces with more coal, and that would be it until the next morning.

I was paid twenty-five cents a day for each building I cleaned—big money for a twelve-year-old in those days. I used my salary to buy shoes and clothes. Sometimes I chipped in to the family pot.

My intentions were good, my motives lofty, but I had failed to take the gangs into account. Nobody had warned me how they could make mincemeat of the best of intentions. The part of Chicago in which we lived was infested with juvenile gangs. For a while after we arrived, I managed to stay clear of them. But some classmates at my school were in the gangs, and as I became known around school, they started watching out for me on the streets.

Inevitably, I was "invited" to join one of the gangs, the Saints—or else. They were "Saints" who ruled with their fists. The leaders extorted money from the rank and file and pressured members to steal and beat up people. Stealing was mostly limited to hubcaps, items from the five-and-dime, food from stores, and pennies and dimes from nonmember kids who strayed into the Saints' "territory." Some of the Saints tried pickpocketing when it was safe.

Members stayed away from serous crime and seemed to have a built-in radar that kept them out of serious trouble with the police. Their activities expressed aggressions built upon deprivation and persecution. In the South Side of Chicago, it was always Depression. These kids were black, most of them, and they didn't stand a chance of a better life—or thought they didn't.

These kids sensed a futility, instinctively realized they were being kept down, and their inner, hidden, unconscious hostility expressed itself in violence. They would graduate, as they went through the grades in this blacktop jungle, to stealing cars, armed robbery, and murder.

I had not experienced threats and intimidation. I wasn't accus-

tomed to fighting—me, so full of ideas of love and peace, forgiveness, self-sufficiency, and reverence. In the face of leering,
yellow-toothed hoodlums swaggering up, punching, poking, spew-
ing verbal garbage in my face, such concepts began to sound hol-
low.

"Hey, punk, you gonna join us? Sure ya gonna, AIN'T ya?" A
hand reaching into my pocket.

When I'd try to pull away from a scar-faced muscle machine
draped in long jacket and striped pants, others sidled up. "What's a
matter, Julio? Won't Mama's baby pay up its initiation fee?" Arms
grabbed from behind, a hand against the base of my neck.

I was shaking. All the fine words my father had said all the years
were drowned in fear.

Rough hands pulled my pockets out, scattering my possessions on
the sidewalk as hands sifted for money.

"Is that all, thirty-two cents?" Someone shook me. "That's just
peanuts, kid. Where do yer work, anyway?"

My chattering teeth wouldn't let me speak, until I was jabbed
hard. "Answer when yer spoken to, punk."

Stuttering, I told them about my job.

"That's highway robbery, yer stupid sucker. Shake the kid down
for at least forty cents a building. See?"

"Whadda yer think?"

"Ahhh, he can't pay up proper." A well-rehearsed, phony routine.
"But maybe he could be good for something."

"Yah, yah! When the cops are on our tail, he can be a decoy."

"Okay, yer're in. All yer got to do now is be initiated."

"And pay up half yer wages every week, see? Don't yer forget
that, hear?"

"Half?" A jab, a shake, someone sliced me across the face with
the flat of a hand.

"Yer arguing? We're letting yer off easy, boy. Better keep yer trap
shut or the price goes up, see? And yer better pay up on time or the
enforcer'll get after yer, see?"

I tried to keep from crying, from heaving my guts in the street.

"An' don't y'all go thinkin' about stoolin', boy. Yer'll get a knee
right where it hurts, see? Open yer trap, an' yer'll be doubled up.
Permanent, see? Get it?"

My initiation: I had to fight each one in turn, about twelve of them. I lost count as I kept picking myself up off the pavement and, toward the end, didn't try to stay on my feet. Easier to let myself fall from the blows, because once I hit the pavement, it was the next one's turn at me.

Despite their warning, after I was finally allowed to stumble home, I vowed I'd tell my dad.

By the time he got home late from work and asked me why I was all bruised and bandaged, I was ready to tell him the same story I'd told Mama. I fell down a hill and rolled and rolled and rolled.

After all, Dad worked so hard. Why should I give him another problem? It didn't occur to me that failing to confide in him was the biggest mistake of my life.

Anyway, I was scared.

And bitter.

Where had all my lofty thoughts gotten me? They were fine in Madison, Illinois, even if you did have to watch out for the white folk and knuckle under to them. In a small place, if you followed the rules, you had a chance.

In Chicago, the cards were stacked against you. Even if you followed rules, you weren't safe. One gang's rules were another's poison. And if you followed the gang's rules, you got in trouble with the cops. If you followed the cops' rules, you might as well make out your will.

I found ways to get around some of the rules. When the gang demanded weekly "protection money," I'd tell them my boss hadn't paid me yet, I hadn't worked the buildings for a couple of days because I was sick, or they'd gotten someone else. I outfoxed them as far as their inspection process was concerned by asking my boss to mail the money in care of my dad. Still, to keep in the gang's good graces, I forked over something every week. I had to make up for my inadequate dues by being the gang flunky.

At first, I tried to fake it. One of their favorite tricks was to sic me on some white guy, even an older man, who had invaded our territory.

If I saw a white man coming, I ran ahead of the group as I was supposed to do, but instead of luring him into the gang, which lurked around a corner, I'd say, "Lissen, pal, you better get out. Right now."

The trouble was, the man usually took it the wrong way. A little punk ordering him to beat it was only a challenge. "Get out, my foot. Who do you think you are? This is a free country."

"South Side is not free. You'd better move!"

"Lissen, nigger brat, don't tell me to move out!"

Not far away, the gang heard a lot of this. They thought I was playing it straight, not realizing any more than the white guy that I was trying to save the poor sucker from a beating.

Usually, at about this stage, the white guy had had time to think about it and to work himself up into a sweat. He'd reach out for me, and I'd have no choice but to run.

He'd chase me right into the trap!

With those snarling, vicious thugs around him, fists flying out, feet kicking, he didn't have a chance. After each gang member had punched him a few times in the face and stomach, thrown him in the gutter, and taken turns at kicking him in the face or back, they'd tire of their little game, or someone would have yelled for the police.

For that we had our strategy all worked out, knew all the escape routes and hiding places, knew how to scatter in all directions. Usually we got away scot-free.

When I would lead a victim into a trap this way, I earned points. "He's comin' along! He's gettin' great!" And I would continue setting up people for beatings on a daily basis.

The gang's acceptance of me and my victims' antagonism and stupidity combined to condition me. I no longer made any real effort to try to warn my victims. They wouldn't listen anyway, and the sooner I let the gang push me out of an alley, and the sooner I trotted up to the guy strolling down the avenue and said my little piece, the sooner it would be over.

They would have gotten him anyway, wouldn't they?

Fear, frustration, and futility gnawed at me day after day; pretty soon, it was a way of life. I was a dusky zombie jumping to the off-beat rhythm of gang life, living two different lives: one at home, another on the streets.

The gang added some refinements to my approach to victims. Sometimes the white guy really would take a detour, or he'd catch on.

"The only way to make sure he follows yer when yer run," one of the leaders said, "is, from now on, punch him hard in the belly. I don't care how big he is. You smack his gut hard an' run, an' we'll pop out and take care of him, see?"

I was too sucked into it now to argue. I felt miserable day and night, but I followed directions. If I didn't, they'd tear me apart. I'd get the white guy's beating.

Once a white fellow six feet tall and dressed in a business suit came sauntering along. "Thinks he's big stuff. You get him for us." I was pushed into the street.

When I was almost even with the man, I moved and stood in front of him.

"Get out of my—"

I didn't give him a chance to finish. My fist shot out, buried itself in his soft stomach. He went "Oooooofffff!" and bent almost double. When he'd caught his breath, I was a dozen feet ahead of him, waiting for him to chase me.

He did.

When he entered the alley after me, he ran into six other fists extended like lances. He made a bigger "Oooooooffffff!" and jackknifed. Then the hard-toed shoes shot out, in his ribs, head, stomach.

I was almost as sick as he was.

These were the days I was dying. I could feel myself dying. I no longer had a will of my own.

After a while this gang way of life became so routine, I hardly thought about it anymore. *When you feel like having an apple, just help yourself.* We had our method worked out. One guy would go over to the fruitstand and "accidentally" knock something over to distract the proprietor. Meanwhile, one of the boys would grab apples.

The day it was my turn, Charlie distracted the proprietor, putting on an innocent act, helping him pick up packages of dates "accidentally" spilled.

I grabbed apples, and started stuffing my pockets. As I turned to melt into the foot traffic, a blue suit turned up in front of me. At my nose was a long, long, long billy club.

I looked at the cop with an artificial grin on my face. "Aren't they pretty?" I said, as I put them back very easily.

"Yes, little boy. And these things called handcuffs are very pretty, too."

I felt faint. My conscience sprang alive in me, and I was sick with remorse at what I had done. All my training, my life before gone, and Dad and Mama dying when they found out. That was the worst; their grief, sorrow, misery, knowing that all their words and love had led to this.

"You're not gonna need them!" I'd change my ways no matter what the gang did to me. But the cop wouldn't have believed me if I'd been able to stammer the words out.

"Oh yes, I'm gonna lock you up."

That was the worst moment of my life. At fourteen, I would be arrested, booked, and sent to a home for delinquent boys.

"Dear Lord," I prayed. "Let me die here and now." I began to cry until I thought my heart was going to come out of my mouth and splatter on the sidewalk.

Then I heard a voice.

"Officer, officer. My name is Mr. Williams."

The man who was standing there I'd seen several times in the neighborhood. He too had a uniform. I thought perhaps it was Salvation Army.

"Officer, I'm the scoutmaster for this area. I've watched this boy fooling around with the gang. He never seemed quite to fit." He hesitated, looking down at me. I hung to a thread of hope that snapped when the officer opened the handcuffs.

"You're crazy," the officer said. "This kid's nothing but a little thug, just like the rest of them."

The scoutmaster shook his head. "No, no, you're wrong. This is an unusual kid. Look . . ." He went on talking rapidly, trying to keep the cuffs off. "If you'll let me take him and get him into scouting, he'll be in my custody every Tuesday, Wednesday, and Thursday."

The policeman stared at him.

I blurted out, "Scouting? What's that? You mean, Indian scouting?"

"I'll teach you what it is. We meet in the basement of the Collins Building—a real good bunch of guys. How about it, son?" He put his arm on my shoulder.

Up until then, I had looked from police officer to scoutmaster and distrusted both. How ironic it was: a tall Negro cop, and a short, fat, white man. The cop was all for booking me. The white man, my "enemy," was fighting for me—he even had his arm around my shoulder. He didn't mind touching a Negro boy.

"Please," I begged. "I'll do as he says. I promise." My eyes stung.

The officer shrugged, then gave Mr. Williams a hard look. "Okay, mister. But I'll hold you personally responsible if he gets into trouble. You could get in trouble yourself."

Mr. Williams smiled. "Don't worry. I have all the confidence in the world in Jimmy." With a friendly arm still around my shoulder, he led me away.

My heart thudded. How'd he know who I was?

When he took me into a little basement office, my eyes just popped. "Hey, that's an Indian relic. I know about that. My mother is part Cherokee!"

He started talking about scouting, and I told him about my mother and father.

"Would you like to come back?"

"Yeah."

"But you'll have to stay out of the gang. If they bother you, you come to me. I'll get them off you."

"What's going to happen when you're not around?"

"Don't worry about it. You just start coming."

That marked the end of my life of crime and the beginning of my career in the Boy Scouts of America. It was also the beginning of the end for a number of neighborhood gangs in the area.

My personal problems were not eliminated overnight. A few weeks later, one of my former cohorts accosted me as I was walking, in my brand-new uniform, toward the basement scout meeting.

"What are you doing in that monkey suit?"

"Hey, this is no monkey suit. This is Boy Scouts."

"Sissy outfit." He pointed a stiff finger.

"No, it isn't, it's great, you ought to join."

More of the gang members came snaking up. One guy ripped off my scarf, another put his fingers inside my shirt to rip it. Buttons popped off. I felt a half nelson curling around my neck.

Then someone started to grab the American flag sewed on my uniform pocket, and I saw red, white, and blue. I lashed out, my forward lurch breaking the half nelson hold. One guy fell over backward. But I was outnumbered. They surrounded me, jeering and catcalling.

Then over the shouts and obscene laughter, I heard the screech of a car braking and a loud, "Hey, you!"

Suddenly my tormentors were gone like deer.

My lip and nose were bleeding; my neck hurt, but I still had my American flag. I went on to the scout meeting.

Our scout unit declared "war" on the neighborhood gangs, a war of love and gentle, gentle persuasion. We confronted them in many ways, by getting individuals to one side and helping them over-come their fear of their leaders; by helping those in trouble; by giv-ing them a chance to channel aggressive impulses and youthful energies into sports activities like boxing, emphasizing sports-manship and fair play. Besides, the winner got ten dollars, and the loser, five. I became a boxer myself.

The scout "war" against gangs resulted in one thousand gang members becoming scouts in Chicago during the next five years.

My dad was very pleased about my scouting activities. Scouting emphasized the four efforts to which Dad had dedicated his life: serving God, helping mankind, positive thinking, and patriotism.

He didn't think the knot-tying and camping aspects were so significant. He would say, "But what did you do today to help peo-ple, to help mankind?"

Dad's teaching and my rescue by Mr. Williams were strong influences behind the slogan used today on national scouting litera-ture: "You can't go wrong helping a boy go right."

Scouting got me just in time, reviving in my life all that Dad had taught me. I knew love and positive thinking were the values to strive for; also, serving God was a part of scouting, and I wasn't ashamed to tell people about Him.

Scouting taught me, too, that America was for everybody, not just the majority.

Our patriotism was boiling over at this time. Japan had just at-tacked Pearl Harbor, and the country was mad for revenge. One of the greatest thrills of my life came the day I was privileged to carry the American flag in a parade. Weighing only 120 pounds, I strug-gled with that heavy flag while the Windy City's winds howled down Michigan Avenue. I looked so pitiful, I guess, that a white man on the sidelines ran over and said, "Son! For Pete's sake, let me help you with that flag."

"No, sir," I puffed. "This is my country, too."

That night, I couldn't sleep. I kept carrying that flag, all night long, and there began to build in me an intense pride in my coun-try. I wanted to serve it—somehow. Maybe in the government. Someday. In the meantime, I was looking for a better job.

CHAPTER

5

Naked light bulbs hung down from high rafters, scores of bulbs strung along the whole spine of the roof and the ribs on either side, yet there were not enough to fill the hangarlike building with any real illumination.

The whirl, drone, and clatter of the machines were constant; different kinds of machines, doing different kinds of things, all ending up in one finished product: corrugated cardboard boxes.

The weary-faced machine operators worked mechanically, cheerlessly, subdued by the dimness, the lateness of the hour, the sheer boredom of simple, repetitious tasks, and by the constant, unvarying noise.

When I first went to apply for my job at a Chicago box manufacturer, the man asked, "What can you do?"

"Anything you tell me to do."

"If you have that attitude, fine. First thing we want you to do is sweep away the small pieces of cardboard that fall from the machines. Keep all the machines clean."

My first full-time job. I remembered what Dad said: "Whenever your boss gives you a dollar to do a job, give him a dollar and a half's worth of work."

The first day I went to work, all I wanted was to do everything right. "Your job is very simple," the supervisor, Mr. Mooney, said. "It'll probably take you all night to sweep and clean up the cardboard around the machines. And if you don't get it all done, we'll understand, because the last boy couldn't keep up with the machines, either."

"Fine."

Before my first night on the job was over, I had devised a way to keep the area around the machines clean in a quarter the usual time. I simply installed a sixty-eight-gallon basket beside each machine to collect the scraps. I wheeled a dolly with a large bin on it down the aisle and emptied the accumulated trash.

This "invention" gave me time to learn other things. While I was watching a young fellow operate the box-taping machine, Mr. Mooney came along. "Johnson, you're going to be fired the first night. The area around this machine is clean, but I'm sure the rest are filthy. And you're standing here, watching Perez. You're not getting paid to watch."

"Sir, all the machines are clean."

"Don't give me that, Johnson. Come with me!"

We walked around to the other five machines. At each machine he stopped, bent, looked under things, and all around. I'd also placed cleaning rags at various stations to keep the grease wiped off the machines. They were all cleaner than the one I had been standing by.

"Who helped you?" he asked.

"No one."

"What did you do with the trash?"

"I put it outside in the dumper."

"It must have taken you twenty-five trips to take it out there."

"You see that little dolly over there? I got some extra baskets, and what I did was put one on, and when I picked up the old basket, I put a new one down right where the pieces would fall into it. None of them even fell on the floor."

He scratched his head, his bald spot starting to get red. "I'll be darned! Why didn't anyone else think of that?"

"Now, I want to learn how to operate Perez's machine."

"Operate that machine! It took Perez almost a year to learn how to operate that machine."

"I'd like to learn. And if the place ever isn't clean, I'll stop helping him and clean up."

"Just so you keep the place clean." Mr. Mooney walked off, muttering.

At the machine, Perez showed me how to thread the tape into his machine. "You put the tape in, and you have to thread it like a projector. You wrap it around these little things, then you set the lift for how many inches you want; then you have to set the bottom head so it rolls through the water so it'll get just enough moisture. If you get too much moisture, it won't stick. Then you have to heat the water to the right temperature. It's complicated," he concluded.

"Okay. Can I try?" I threaded the tape. "Could I run a few boxes through?"

"Okay."

I ran a few cycles, then went back and picked up trash from the other machines. In the meantime, Perez threaded the machine again, then turned it over to me. The other guys who saw what was going on began to brag on me. "Hey, this is the smartest kid we've seen around here."

"Yeah, but I bet he can't tie these damn strings over here."

"Hey, kid. Can you tie a figure eight?" questioned another man.

"I'm a boy scout. I can tie a figure eight and a few other knots, too."

"Try this figure eight."

I went over and tied it.

"That's right." He turned to the other fellows. "He can do it."

They turned that job over to me for a while. Then I left to collect trash again.

There were two white ladies at the company. They were sisters, both in their early sixties, and had never married. They'd watched me all that night. When we had a break for lunch, I went around cleaning up. One of the sisters put her arm around my shoulder. "Jimmy, Gertrude and I want you to come over and have a sandwich with us."

"I'll eat when I get home."

She peered at me. "In other words, you didn't bring a lunch."

I nodded.

"Well now, listen, Jimmy. Gertrude and I have plenty. We always bring extra sandwiches in case anybody forgets."

I was hungry. I walked with Mabel to a corner of the huge "factory" where the two women had set up a table. A nice clean tablecloth with lacy edges hung over upended boxes. Places were set.

There were even cloth napkins! Mabel set a third place and motioned me to pull up a wooden box.

"So this is your first real job?" Gertrude said, handing me a tuna fish sandwich and a quart of milk. "How old are you?"

"Sixteen, ma'am."

The two old ladies looked at each other. Gertrude said, "He said 'ma'am,' Mabel. Did you hear that?"

Mabel nodded. "I had to stop a minute and think what it meant!" She looked at me. "You're a very nice young man. Would you like an apple?"

I decided to repay their kindness with some conversation. "This apple reminds me of the time I almost got arrested," I said.

The ladies blinked. A look of disappointment flashed across Mabel's face. "Arrested?"

I told them about the petty thieving, beating up adults, and playing cat-and-mouse with the police. And how I had prayed to die when I was caught stealing. But God hadn't let me die. He had sent the scoutmaster instead. After that, the ladies asked me to have lunch with them every night.

"Oh no, I couldn't do that," I protested, "unless you would let me pay for it or do something for you. My dad wouldn't like it."

"Why not?"

"He never likes us to take anything we can't pay for."

"You come over to my machine and keep it clean for me," Gertrude said. "That'll pay for it."

"I'll do that, ma'am."

"I haven't had anybody say 'ma'am' to me in so long, it's music to my ears. Where did you learn that?"

"My dad and mom. They always told us to be very polite to people, especially strangers. Dad says all you have to offer strangers is kindness."

When the quitting whistle blew at 2 A.M., the workers scrambled out. I stayed behind to set up the machines for the next shift. The supervisor started turning off the lights.

"Just a minute."

"What are you doing back there?"

"I haven't finished setting up these machines. The people on the next shift should be able to go right to work." I remembered that Dad always urged, "Give them a dollar and a half's worth of work for each dollar you get." It seemed like a good idea.

On the lonely way home, the almost-empty streetcar clanged and rumbled while I dozed and dreamed. But when I got off at the end of the line and started walking cold, deserted streets, I snapped wide awake in a hurry. Those four blocks to our place seemed like four miles.

Mama was always waiting for me with hot cocoa ready, and a few words to make me know she loved me.

It was satisfying to know that for those ten hours of "educational" work, I had earned four dollars!

I woke up at 5 A.M., forced myself to do my usual quota of pushups before school—25 at a time, until I had done 125—and went for my 3-mile run. The exercise was a daily task I set for myself to improve my track record.

After the run, I had a quick shower, dressed, downed a hot breakfast Mama fixed, and was off to school.

I was determined that my track record wouldn't fall, even with my new job. My coach had spurred me on to this extra training. When I had come in second, he had screamed, "Why do you let a white boy come in first?"

If you were black and had long legs, you had to be a champion. "I'm completely disgusted," he would yell. "You have all the advantages. Your muscle tone is great, you're skinny, you're tall, and you're a Negro. All of you guys can run, but you, Johnson—you've got to win!"

Dad asked me one day how I was doing in track. "Well, Dad, I've outrun all the boys except one."

"So, stop racing against the other boy. Race against yourself."

"How can I do that?"

"Very simple. Today, you run good. Tomorrow, you try to run better. You don't worry about the other man, just yourself."

I thought about that, and it wasn't long before I began to improve in my running. Dad's advice helped me when we went for the championship track meet in the fall of 1942.

At the starting line, I looked around at a huge crowd. I couldn't pick out anyone I knew. I thought about how well all the other kids could run. Then I began to think, "No, no. I'm not racing against them anymore. I'm racing against myself."

I felt as though I were someone else.

"On your mark, get set, ready . . . go!"

All I heard was the signal to go. No one caught up with me that day. I was beating my own record. I didn't even know what anyone else's time was, just my own. I could hardly wait to tell Dad. It seemed that everything he ever taught me got results when I put it into practice.

A few days later, when I was cleaning up at the box factory, one of the men had to leave. He shut down his machine, and the supervisor was wild. "Look, we've got to have this machine going, or we'll get behind in the Shipping Department."

I went up to him. "I can run the machine, sir."

"Look, son. We're busy. This job is for a man."

"But sir, if you'll just let me show you, I can operate that machine."

"Okay, okay. Go over there and start the machine, and if you break it, you're fired!"

Before I pushed a button, I checked everything about ten times, and prayed. "Lord, if you'll just help me now, I won't ask you for another thing tonight."

The first box came out perfectly.

I was just as surprised as the supervisor and the rest of the workers when I maintained the average at that machine and scored several extra runs besides. We met our quota, flabbergasting Mr. Mooney. He asked me into his office and shoved a cup of coffee at me. The office people came around and shook my hand. I felt ten feet tall. But inside, I knew my "success" hadn't been my doing. I had asked the Lord to help me, and He had! It was exciting. I'd never asked Him to help me run a machine before.

When I got home that night, I just had to go in and wake up Dad. "You know, when I ran that machine, I just said to the Lord, 'Help me do it right, Lord!'"

"That's great, son."

"Well, I don't know whether the Lord did it, but it turned out fine."

"Son, when I ask the Lord to help me, and something happens that's good, I know He did it. And I always say, 'Thank you, Lord.' If you don't believe He'll help you, then don't ask Him."

It was getting through to me that the Lord was the one who deserved all the credit whenever I did something right. I remembered the time when I was about ten and Dad asked me one day how my grades were because he never saw me doing any extra homework.

"Er, well, they're okay, Dad." I knew he must have checked. I didn't dare lie to him.

"Are you getting all A's?"

"Uh, oh, no, Dad. . . ."

"Why not? Is anyone else getting all A's?"

"Oh sure, Dad," I answered. "A couple of the white boys are getting A's."

"And you're not getting all A's, and you have the advantage over those white boys."

"I have the advantage?"

"Of course you do! I've never said too much before because I don't want you going bragging about your advantage. That's not nice. But you see that dark skin you have that wraps around your head? That keeps the light out, keeps your brain cool."

I nodded without really understanding.

"Now, take the poor white boy. He has that light skin, and the sun shining through it heats up his brain, and he can't study for long. But you, with your cool brain that God gave you, can study for hours and hours, and you'll never get tired, and your brain will never heat up."

That little talk psyched me into studying harder. My grades zoomed up, I was so proud of the fact that God had blessed me with a cool brain that wouldn't heat up.

My white friends wanted to know what had happened, but Dad had warned me not to say anything. Finally, after one of the white boys kept pestering me for the secret, I told him, "Maybe if you get a real dark suntan, that might help."

The next few weeks on the job, I learned to type and fill out invoices in the Shipping Department. "Now, whenever you have any spare time, you'll be able to help in this department, too," Mabel promised.

One night, when Mabel was ill, I asked Mr. Mooney if I could take her place. "Sure, go ahead. If you run into any trouble, just call me."

I didn't know what he meant, but I found out when one of the laborers came into the office.

He stared. "What are you doing back here, boy?"

"Sir, I'm the shipping clerk," I said proudly.

"The hell you are. I'm not going to work for a little snotty-nosed nigger. Get out of here." He rushed over, grabbed my arms, and started shoving me out the door just as the supervisor came around the corner.

Mr. Mooney was a big man, bigger than the one who had just thrown me out. Mr. Mooney shook his head. "I don't want you to see this, Jimmy. You just go back in the office."

As I turned to go, I heard an "Oooooomph!" and scuffling down the hall and out the side door. Out in the yard, stacks of boxes, waiting to be loaded onto trucks, were flying all over the place. I looked out. Mr. Mooney was dragging the worker toward the gate. "If I ever see you back in this place again, I'll kill you."

When Mr. Mooney came inside again, he stood in front of the other laborers. "Now, is there anyone else who doesn't want to work with that little 'snotty-nosed nigger'?"

Nobody said a word. And that night everybody worked their hearts out.

The next night the smallest guy came into the office and said, "Jimmy boy, I got something in my lunchbox you're going to love. You're going to eat with me tonight."

"That's great," I said.

About thirty minutes later, in walked the next guy who said, "Jimmy, I got a nice lunchbox and something I know you're going to love."

I continued to hunt and peck on the typewriter, and just before the lunch whistle blew, in walked the third guy. "Jimmy, come on over. I got a spot picked out over here, and we're going to have lunch together."

"Oh I can't. I already have something."

"No, you come over and just have something with me."

"But wait," I tried to explain.

Then of course Mabel came over, and all three discovered what the others had done, and each had thought he was the only one doing it.

"Wait a minute, fellows. I appreciate it, but I'm going to eat with Mabel and her sister tonight," I told them.

"With that old bag? What's she got? Look, my wife went to a lot of trouble to fry chicken."

The other guy said, "Why, that's what I have, chicken."

And the third guy said, "Hey, that's what I have, too, chicken."

"Why so much chicken?" I asked.

"We thought colored people liked chicken," he replied.

"I do," I confirmed. "I also like tuna fish, roast beef, turkey, and so on."

The box company job helped me in my school activities, which gave me special status with my peers. I even decided to run for class president again. I had run the year before and lost out to a pretty girl. But this time there was no "girlie" competition, and the gang problem had flared up. Dropouts had invaded the school, throwing firecrackers, disturbing classes, and shouting obscenities. When the police were called, they would run into booby traps—wires stretched neck-high across the hallways.

My campaign helpers and I wrote up our suggestions, urging greater police protection. Most of the student body was enthusiastic about our platform. I won easily.

After the election, I followed through with my promises. Our class was able to get some parent participation—volunteers who wore armbands and patrolled the halls. The gangs were scared off for a while.

Winning that election fired me up about politics. I couldn't get enough of talk about the "party," meaning the Republican Party. I joined.

I was the only Negro American in the group, because in 1933 the Democrats had lured most Negroes into the Roosevelt camp with slogans like "Party of the little man" and "The Democrats are for the common man."

My dad had different ideas. He was sure that when the Democratic Party had re-organized in the South, it had done so under the influence of the Ku Klux Klan.

"But," Dad said, "the Republican Party is the party that will allow a man to go as far as his talent will take him. That's what you want. You don't need politicians who do only what you can do better yourself."

After I joined the Republican Party, I attended meetings whenever I could. Several old men there loved to talk to me about bringing back Lincoln's party. I listened, but I wondered just how many others felt that way. I started to sense that I wasn't as welcome as I would have been if I were white.

"Maybe I ought to change parties," I said disconsolately when Dad and I were discussing the prospects for the next presidential election.

"But son, the Republicans are the ones who freed my father. You'd be a slave today if it weren't for that."

"But now they're saying at party headquarters, I should join the Democrats because they have a minority group. Even the Negroes are calling me a 'white man's nigger.' "

"Oh ho!" Dad exclaimed. "Since when did we Johnsons ever worry about what people were saying about us?"

But Dad knew I was discouraged.

Before I had made up my mind whether to switch or not, Dad asked me to go with him to hear New York Governor Tom Dewey, who was running against Franklin Roosevelt for the presidency. Dewey was scheduled to speak at the Lincoln Day dinner at the Conrad Hilton Hotel.

The elegant surroundings of the hotel dazzled me. Everyone was in formal attire. I thought Dad looked especially dignified in his dark suit, white shirt, silk tie, and shoes so well polished no one would have thought they were ten years old.

It suddenly dawned on me that Dad and I were the only Negroes in that enormous assemblage.

Governor Dewey outlined the Republican platform, then began to talk to me. I was the future! He said, "The Republican Party is one that will allow all Americans, regardless of color or creed, to get into politics."

I stared. Did he mean me?

"The Republican Party will be the first to have a Negro senator!" he said. He didn't have to shout the words; the meaning echoed throughout the hall, especially to me.

Dad was smiling broadly. No wonder he was a Republican!

I wanted to do something for this man Dewey. I wanted to do something for my country.

Late that night, I woke up clenching my jaw. I was going to do something. Set some goals. Governor Dewey had been talking to me. "Lord," I said aloud, "talk to me. Tell me what to do. I'm right here and ready to serve you and my country. Just tell me what to do."

When I finally slept, I had the craziest dream or a vision—anyhow, a direction for my life. Someday, maybe far in the future, I would serve my country in a high office. I would run for the U. S. Senate! The idea was so outlandish, so farfetched, I could scarcely admit it to myself, much less talk about it to anyone else at that point. But I would begin preparing myself right away, just in case.

The next morning, I told Dad I wanted to join the Marines. I assumed all I had to do was march down to the Marine recruiting office and sign up. But I was sadly mistaken.

The quota for Negro recruits had been filled. In those days Negroes couldn't fight on the front lines, and there were other restrictions on using a black Marine because of the Armed Services segregation policy during that part of the 1940s.

I went home rejected, dejected, and angry. I told Dad, "I don't want to join the Navy, and I guess that leaves the Army."

Dad gave me one of his long looks. "You mean you're going to give up joining the Marine Corps after just one try? Don't you realize that the turndown should make you all the more determined to get in?"

"How's that, Dad?"

"If it was that easy to get into the Marine Corps, everyone would get into it. Why don't you go back and give it one more try?"

"I don't want to be turned down again."

"This time, put on your best suit of clothes and type out a little card with your name, address, phone number, and how much schooling you've had. Include something about what your interests are. Then when you start talking to the recruiting officer, tell him your name is James E. Johnson; you would like to be in the Marine Corps, and this card has some basic information. . . ."

Dad talked me into it.

When I got dressed, made out the card, and went down, a gunnery sergeant greeted me with, "Whatta you want?"

"Sir, I'd like to go into the Marine Corps. Here is my card, sir."

He looked at the card and said, "I'll be darned. That's pretty nice. What do they call you?"

"They call me Jimmy."

"I think we can find a spot for you. Can you type?"

"Yeah, with two fingers."

"Look, we don't care if you type with two or four fingers. Nobody around here can type with more than two."

Then the real crucial time came. I had to take a test.

Afterward the sergeant looked at the test, then at me, and signaled for the lieutenant in the office to come over. They mumbled.

The lieutenant looked at me. "You ever take this test before?"

"No, sir."

"Would you take it again in my office?"

"Yes, sir, if you want me to." So I took it over again.

They were checking it with the answer key sheet. I heard them whisper, "Hey, he made a better mark this time than before." The lieutenant whispered, "We've never had anyone come this close to making a perfect score."

They kept shaking their heads. "It's hard to believe a colored boy could do this. Are you sure you've never taken this test before?" the sergeant questioned.

"Yes, sir."

I didn't know until years later that my score had been lowered to the "average colored score." I didn't know this until I wanted to become an officer and was told I couldn't because my test score was too low.

The people at the box company gave me a going-away party. Mabel and Gertrude were sad. There were speeches, and people said there was something different about me. I never could figure out what they meant. All I knew was that I was a little skinny black guy who loved the Lord and wanted to do what was right.

My Dad had one blessing for my departure, which he also always said at mealtime. "Well, Lord, we're all here, and we're getting along just fine, and we're sure much obliged. Amen."

I was put in charge of four other fellows for the long train trip from Chicago to North Carolina. It didn't bother me when someone said, "You'll never make it through boot camp; you're too small, too skinny. They'll break you in half."

"That's ridiculous; I'm already an acting corporal," I told myself. I didn't know how they appointed people to jobs in the services, and how transitory an acting title could be.

Within twenty-four hours of hitting boot camp, I would almost have traded places with a prison inmate.

CHAPTER

6

We were standing in the hot North Carolina sun in 1944, while a white Marine with Pfc stripes tried to terrorize us with doom predictions. I took his words with several grains of salt. I was feeling big, real big. Standing in a motley crowd of black recruits in civilian clothes, I was sure I was one of the best dressed. Some big black guys from Mississippi, who formed almost an entire squad, were dressed in clothing that resembled jail-issue overalls with bibs.

I wore a "zoot suit"—fancy-dress shirt with french cuffs; long pants with wide cuffs and a high, tight waist; long jacket with wide lapels; and long, dangling watch chain. And a big-apple hat, sloppy crown with wide brim. The zoot suit was a symbol of rebellion, but the gangs had popularized the costume so that even "straights" like me thought we were a pretty impressive sight.

The Pfc didn't think so. When he got to me, he stopped and stared. "I feel sorry for you when you see Sergeant Young." He stepped back. "Men, we have some fancy-dressed lady-killers in our midst! But I'm going to introduce you to Sergeant Young, someone who'll tell you what a Marine should look like. Sergeant Young will be in charge of all you men. He'll call the shots. You'll recognize that he is Papa, Mama, Sister, Brother, God, and the Devil. Is that clear?"

"Yes, sir," I nodded vigorously. I wanted to go along with it. My momentary fears had gone. On the bus after we'd been unloaded from the train, the group of blacks from Mississippi, had told the rest of us—from Chicago, New York, and Louisiana—wild stories of torture and mayhem.

"Yo're gonna run åt leas' ten miles every day, and only git two hours' sleep at night. Yo're gonna do a hundred pushups every day, and they're gonna keep y'awl out in the sun till y'awl bleached white like a white man, cuz they doesn't like we black Marines." And if we left the base for any reason, "Them white mens in the little towns just love lynching black dogfaces, with a slow noose."

I realized they were just trying to scare us, were probably jealous because we from the northern states were better dressed and better groomed than Mississippi jailbird farm boys.

"I'm leaving you now. I can't stand to be around and see Sergeant Young when he's working," the Pfc said.

We all started to hear pounding noises from a nearby hut as the Pfc concluded, "Some people say he's a wild man, but he keeps saying he's peaceful."

He took off running as the door to the hut broke into splinters, and Sergeant Young came through it bound by a straitjacket and literally foaming at the mouth. (I learned later it was shaving cream.)

He was a big black sergeant. Ripping off the straitjacket, he yelled out, "I'm gonna kill you!"

We flew in all directions. It took some time to round us up for another appearance before Sergeant Young. Still I was bursting with pride at being a Marine. Soon I'd be wearing that classy red-trimmed blue uniform or even those lowly green fatigues. The United States Marines! Boy, oh boy, I'd made it. I knew at least one third of us would be weeded out, but I was ready for whatever boot camp could dish out.

Sergeant Young walked down the line of men, looking at each one carefully, jabbing his swagger stick into the stomachs of most of us.

"What do I have here?" he questioned, his eye on my big-apple hat. "Where did you get that hat?"

Believing that his appraisal of my dress had changed his tune, I proudly said, "I bought it."

"Well, now, ain't it pretty?" Sergeant Young said.

"Oh yes, sir," I answered, beaming.

"Take it off, throw it on the ground, and stomp it."

I had paid fifteen dollars for that hat, at an hourly wage of forty cents. I took the hat off very gently and put it on the ground.

"Now stomp it!"

I put my foot on it lightly and took it off.

He turned to a new recruit who had had his hair shaved off. Sergeant Young stuttered when he got excited. "BBBBoy, get mmmmmme mmmmmy brick."

"Yes, sir."

The recruit came back in half a minute with about the longest brick I had ever seen.

"BBBBoy, come here. Pick the hat up, and stand over bbby the hut." Sergeant Young walked over and broke the brick over a saw horse. "Now, stomp that hat, bbbboy." I put one foot on the hat and gently crushed it again. He drew back and started to throw the brick.

I ducked, and the brick missed my head and went straight through the hut's wall. I started jumping up and down on that hat like crazy, saying, "Yes, sir, yes, sir, yes, sir."

"Now, boy," he said, "gggget me mmmmmmy bucket."

He took the bucket and put it over my head. Now I was jumping up and down on my hat, saying, "Yes, sir, yes, sir," with a bucket covering my face.

"I want you to sound off, bbbboy."

"Yes, sir, yes, sir," I shouted frantically inside the bucket, my ears pounding.

"I didn't hear it." The stick jabbed my stomach. Oooomph! The sergeant pushed the stick up under the bucket and poked me, snapping my head back. Then he said to the recruit, "Boy, get mmmmc one of your drumsticks. You used to be a drummmmer, didn't you? How about playing me a tune? On that bucket."

If you have never had someone pounding on a bucket with the bucket on your head, let me tell you, there is no ringing like it.

"JJJJJJJohnson, yyyou got a little graveyard duty." He lifted the bucket off.

"Yes, sir?"

"You are going to bury something. You are going to say a little prayer. Here's a shovel." We went out.

"What am I going to bury?" I asked meekly.

"That damn hat."

"But sir, I'm going to send it back."

He shook his head. "Ttttthat hat is dead! And you're ggggoing to bury it. You stomped the hell out of it, and now we're going to give it a good funeral."

So I got my hat. The whole platoon was looking at me like goons. He marched me over to the spot, followed by the platoon.

"YYYYou got any last remarks to make over the hat?"

"No, sir."

Then I started digging a shallow hole for the hat so I could come back later and get it. I gently put the hat into the hole and covered it with six inches of dirt. "All done, sir."

"Don't you know how deep a grave should be?"

"Ah, four or six feet."

"Well, that's what I want, bbboy."

"Six feet, sir?"

"Dig it six feet, boy."

"Six feet, sir? It doesn't have to be that deep just for a hat."

"You want it to come out and bite you?" The recruits roared with mirth.

When I finally got the hole dug to his satisfaction, he asked, "What kind of a song do you want? You know any songs?" Not waiting for my answer, he went on, "How about 'The Old Rugged Cross'?"

"Yes, sir." And he put the hat in my hands, and I had to stand there in front of everyone and sing, "The Old Rugged Cross."

"Louder."

All the guys started laughing. The sergeant went over to them and said, "TTTTThis is a serious business. Don't you have any respect for the dead?" Then he turned to me, "Go on, you're doing fine."

When the song was finished, he had me repeat what they say at a real funeral: "Ashes to ashes, dust to dust." Finally I filled in the dirt. "Is that all, sir?"

"Where is the cross? You just sang 'The Old Rugged Cross'!"

"But sir. I don't have one."

"I guess we'll have to go gggget one." Sergeant Young marched me all the way back to the hut and made me take a crate apart and make a cross. Then we went back to the "grave" and put up the cross. Then he asked, "You really liked that hat, didn't you?"

"Yes, sir, I sure did."

"Wwwwwould you like tttto have a last look at it?"

I was utterly exhausted by this time. I could not have cared less about that hat. "A last look, sir?"

"Yes, you loved that hat, didn't you? Well, nobody is going to say that Sergeant L. K. Young does not take care of his mmmen. We want you to be happy here. This is your new home. Start digging."

It was harder going back down those six feet in that hole to get the hat than it was burying it in the first place. Of course, after I dug it up, I had to bury it again.

That night I cried. I wrote a letter to my sister. "Please, please, get me out of here. They are going to kill me. Sergeant Young told me tomorrow is my doomsday, but I won't last until tomorrow!"

The next day we went to the barber shop, marching all the way. I thought those barbers looked pretty cruel. My hair was very long, and I had some goop on it to make it straighter. As soon as it was my turn for the chair, Sergeant Young spotted me.

"Let me cut it!" he called out. He took up the scissors. "BBBBBoy, hhhhhow would you like your hair cut?"

"Well, sir, take a little bit right off the sides and taper it down in the back and just a little bit off the top."

Sergeant Young repeated my words. Then he turned to the barber. "DDDid you hear him?"

I felt those clippers land right on the top of my head and zing through my hair. "Wait a minute," I cried, "I thought you were going to take a little off the sides."

"Yeah, and I'm going ttto take a little off the tttop, first."

He skinned me.

Then we marched to where clothing was issued. When we got there, all of us had to take off our civvies and put them in a bag to be shipped home. I put on my dungarees and was finishing up with my shoes when I felt a tap on the shoulder.

"Johnson, do you have all of your civilian clothes in that bag?"

"Yes, sir."

"All of them?"

"Yes, sir."

"But I distinctly remember a hat. Wasn't there a hat that went with this outfit?"

"Yes, sir, but I buried it."

"You buried it?" Sergeant Young turned to the other men. "And we have to be responsible for it. What do you think people are going to say when you write and tell them you buried your hat? Don't you think they're going to want to see that hat?"

"I guess so, sir."

"Boy, go get me a shovel."

"Oh, I don't want that hat."

"We're not going to let this hat contaminate the earth. It's going back, back where it came from."

So we went back, and I unburied the hat. I put the dilapidated hat in the bag to be shipped home.

As I lay in my bunk finally, aching, miserable, I tried to understand. I knew we were at war, but I had thought we were at war with the Axis powers, not with ourselves.

Sergeant Young had many more goodies for me, and we did run for miles at a time, with packs on our backs and nine-pound rifles in our hands. It was horrible, and I wasn't mature enough to see why, any more than I had been able as a kid to understand Dad when he'd told the bullies who beat me, "We love you."

When we came to the halfway mark in our training, matters grew worse. We were introduced to an even more despicable monster, Sergeant Major Huff.

"Now I'm telling you," Sergeant Young said, "the last time Sergeant Major Huff was on the field, fifteen men died. If any of you men haven't made out your will, now is the time to do it. If you plan to call your parents, now is the time. I will not be responsible except to notify your next of kin."

Sergeant Major Huff was far more creative and ingenious with his torments than Sergeant Young could have hoped to be. I found that out upon my introduction to him.

We were standing at attention when I first heard the sergeant major speak to us from the side. He had a very high-pitched voice, like a woman's. With a voice like that he couldn't be as bad as they said. I turned my head for a quick look.

He slapped my ears so hard with his big hands that I nearly collapsed. "Okay, boy, I want you to take off and give me five."

"Five what?"

"Five miles!"

"Five miles, sir?"

"Yes, five miles, boy!"

I took off. I figured I would be alone and could walk some of the way. When I got around the hut on the trail through the wood, I started to walk. Then I heard pounding on the trail. The sergeant major rode up on a horse.

He rode the horse while I ran for five miles.

When I returned, he had me sit with my feet six inches off the ground and a rifle across my toes for thirty minutes. He put a blow-torch under my legs just behind my feet to keep me from dropping the legs.

Then I had to run another mile.

I learned not to look around.

I was almost broken in half, as had been predicted. Almost. I made it to within the last two weeks of boot training.

And then a miracle happened.

Suddenly we started looking at ourselves as nearly fully trained Marines, comparing ourselves with the rambling, awkward, arms-akimbo softies we had been just a couple of "short" months before.

We were a crack outfit! We were tough! We were skilled, unified, efficient. Fast, alert, and dangerous.

Just days before, we'd vowed that as soon as we got a rifle in our hands, we'd start shooting our oppressors and humiliators.

Now, suddenly, we realized they were "gods." They had turned us into Marines, turned us into men who could defend our country, fight for our democratic principles, protect our families from aggression.

On the firing range, those "monsters" now were our "buddies." Our drill instructors, even Sergeant Major Huff, treated us like human beings. He showed us how to put the weapon to our shoulders and how to squeeze the trigger. Every time one of us made a bull's-eye, he was the guy who came over and patted us on the back and told us what great guys we were. When one of us thought we deserved a higher score, he was the one who argued with the scorer and made him give us a higher mark.

We ended up loving the guy. He was our father, after all.

We were the best rifle shots. We had the best track team, and were considered the sharpest outfit on the base. And Sergeant Major Huff and Sergeant Young and our other noncoms had created us.

I came away from the firing range an expert with the M-1 rifle and the .45 automatic, with a badge to prove it.

Suddenly a lot of things began to make sense to me, the contradictions my dad seemed to have been guilty of—his anger at the preacher who wanted to give him a handout, and his forgiving love toward the boys who had beaten me up. I saw that they weren't contradictory at all. They were both part of his love for me, wanting me to grow up to the full potential God had invested in me. He knew I would never come to that if I let myself depend on something-for-nothing handouts, or if I held grudges against people who did me wrong. I could see that even the apparent "cruelties" of our officers had been a kind of love toward us, actions working ultimately for our good. It was a love that wasn't sentimental, but tough, exactly what we needed. It was something to live up to.

I had a lump in my throat standing on parade during graduation, in my dress uniform, with thousands of others, all looking sharp, healthy, and straight. The cadre had erected a platform and decorated it with red, white, and blue bunting. Flags—a huge, silk American flag, the standards of the Marine Corps and of the various units—all fluttered in the breeze.

When the band broke out with "The Star-Spangled Banner," I felt a surge of pure ecstasy, triggering tears.

After the national anthem, the Marine Corps hymn, "Semper Fidelis," burst out, and I was so proud to "claim the title of United States Marines."

Various officers and dignitaries spoke, and each inspiring word of praise and encouragement made us feel bigger and brighter and tougher and prouder.

After graduation, we were to be given two-week liberty. Most of us were scheduled to go overseas, and the chance to go home was particularly appreciated. All during training, we hadn't been allowed off the base; now we had a chance to parade our new selves.

I was disappointed after getting on the train to learn that the troops would not be allowed to get off, except to change trains, until we reached our destinations. The unit preceding us, the 51st Marines, had become so incensed at the prejudice in some of the southern towns in which the train stopped that at one point they'd taken rifles and shot up a station. They hadn't killed or injured anyone, only shown their anger and frustration.

The police had been called when some of the troops had ignored the "WHITE MALE" and "COLORED" signs on the town's public toilets. After going through rigorous training and expecting to go overseas to fight, and perhaps die for their country, they couldn't take this insult. They had reacted violently enough for the railroad and Marine authorities to impose the ban.

I must admit that I was feeling my oats, too, and welcomed occasions to prove how tough I was, because the drill instructors had convinced us we could whip ten sailors at once. When we finally hit Chicago, I allowed my buddy, Ed, to talk me into picking a fight with some sailors.

We couldn't find ten sailors, but we did find three in an isolated part of a park. "There aren't enough for both of us," Ed said. So I went up to a guy who was slumped down on a bench. I kept provoking him until he started getting angry. His buddies were sprawled on the lawn surrounding the bench.

"Oh yeah?" I answered to one of his remarks. "Don't you recognize this uniform?" I kept wondering why his buddies were laughing.

"Sure do. It's a seagoing bellhop's uniform."

That got me. I was a squared-away Marine. I pushed him off the bench, then discovered why his buddies had been laughing their heads off. My victim was the biggest guy I had ever seen in my life, even bigger than Dad, and I knew, then, that this was not my fight. Still, I couldn't back down.

I took a swing at him and hit him in the stomach. It was like hitting a brick wall.

Ed realized what we had done and rushed over to help. The sailor butted our heads together.

I still hadn't learned anything; after that, it was I who suggested we find someone our own size. Again appearances were deceiving. Ed got beat up. The sailor we'd picked turned out to be the middleweight champion of the Navy. We decided to quit trying to prove we were tough Marines.

I went home with bruises and a puffed face. But homecoming was wonderful. Everyone was as proud as I was that I had survived the nine weeks of boot camp.

One evening, a few days before my liberty was over, my family gave a party for me. After eating until I couldn't eat any more, I went to the living room to have coffee with the crowd.

Dad started talking. "Son, what are your plans about this man's Marine Corps? Going to just stay in until the war's over, or think you'll make a career out of it? And what're you going to do after you get out?"

I didn't hesitate. I'd been thinking for a long time of my goals in life, ever since listening to Tom Dewey.

And I was ready to tell my family about the dream I'd had that night. At the time, I hadn't realized it was an answer to prayer, but now I knew it was. Hadn't I gone to bed that night asking God to tell me what to do? And hadn't I awakened the next morning with a certainty that, impossible as it seemed, I would run for the Senate someday?

Dad had told me, way back when I was working at the box factory, that I shouldn't ask God for anything I didn't expect Him to deliver. God had certainly "delivered" that time, all right. And I knew that what He had delivered, circumstances couldn't take away. I took a deep breath and opened my mouth to answer Dad's question.

"I'm going to run for the U. S. Senate," I announced.

My sister Ida almost spilled her coffee. After an instant of silence, the laughter didn't stop for five minutes.

Ida said, "Oh Jimmy, why don't you be realistic? Get out of the Marine Corps when the war is over, get back in school, and get more education. Be a teacher. A lot of Negroes have made a good living at that. You have no business saying you're going to be a U.S. senator!"

She was right about it not being my business. It was clearly God's business. He was the only one who could make it come to pass.

"Why can't I be a U.S. senator?" I asked.

"Don't you see, Jimmy?" she replied. "You have to have people vote for you. And believe me, there just aren't enough Negroes to get you elected. Besides, you have to be rich."

"But my Jimmy is special," Mama spoke up.

Everybody chuckled. They had heard this so much from her, it had become a family joke.

I said, "Abe Lincoln wasn't rich."

"But he was white," Amos, my minister brother, murmured.

Dad finally said, "Son, you can run for U.S. senator. Uh, what is your time schedule?"

"I'll stay in the Marines for twenty years. When I retire, I'll run."

Dad thought for a moment. "You can do it, providing you're willing to sacrifice for what you want and don't give up your goal."

"How's that, Dad?"

"In order to meet that objective, you must be well educated, successful in business, qualified for the job, make a new friend each day, and if you keep God ahead of all these things, you will succeed!"

Dad and I understood each other. With God at the top of the heap, nothing would be impossible.

"How long do you think it will take you to get ready to be a senator?"

"Allowing for twenty years in the Marines to become an officer and then time in civilian life to get acquainted with conditions and people, I figure, oh, probably about thirty years."

There was a low whistle. "Boy, he believes in long-range planning."

"Thirty years," Dad mused. "That means you'll be running in 1974." He sighed. "Well, at my age, I'm not sure I'll be here, not physically. But I believe you can do it. Keep telling people you're going to be a U.S. senator and that's why you keep going to school. And doing a lot of other things. Write it down. Look at what you've written and keep that in front of you all the time. Don't ever let it out of your mind. 'I AM GOING TO BE A U.S. SENATOR. I AM GOING TO RUN FOR OFFICE IN 1974.'"

I clenched my jaw and stood up straighter. His words, his confidence were all the confirmation I needed that God had answered my prayer the night of Dewey's speech.

"If you educate and qualify yourself at all levels—local, state, national, and international—and learn about government, you'll be a statesman and not just a politician. No one can stop you from making the American dream possible."

The American dream—the phrase stirred me deeply. How many times had Dad told me how proud we should be to be Americans, proud of the flag that stands for all of us, not just the majority, not just the whites, or the rich, or the lucky. God would prove that the American dream was still possible. And He would let me be privileged to be one of His instruments.

But first I had to survive the war.

CHAPTER

7

When I returned to North Carolina from my liberty just after boot camp, I was asked if I wanted to learn etiquette at a service school. Even though I wasn't sure what etiquette meant, it intrigued me because I was told I'd be working with officers near the action.

I signed up for the school and discovered I was to become a waiter. Although many of the others felt it was servitude, I decided I wasn't going to let the deception disturb me, but learn everything possible and be the best waiter anywhere.

When I graduated from the six-week school, I was No. 1, and proud of it. First assignment?

"You're going overseas. First to Hawaii."

"Then what was all this etiquette and waitering stuff all about?"

"You have to take the dinner trays from one foxhole to the other. No, you're going to wait on a general," the CO answered.

"Oh, you mean type his letters for him, handle his messages?" I could hardly believe it. A general's secretary!

"No. Wait on him. Serve him his food. Take care of his laundry and dry cleaning. His personal man Friday."

I sagged. I'd have to make the best of it. No matter how bad a situation is, a man can always learn something. And I knew I had a lot to learn.

The general wasn't too demanding. I organized his beach parties under the palm trees. "Overseas" wasn't so bad, after all.

But after three months, I was to be transferred back to North Carolina. *That's about the only place that has colored Marines.*

I was in North Carolina just long enough to get briefed with the 52nd Marines, an all-Negro outfit ordered to Guam in 1945.

Guam had just been secured—except for a few thousand mines and booby traps yet undiscovered.

After a short stay, I was glad to be told, "You're moving again."

I tried to remember what April was like in the States. Then I noticed we were headed west.

The orders were unsealed.

OKINAWA.

I was standing at the rail as we plowed through green-white waters streaked with sunset orange. Beyond that horizon, manfire was blazing, death spitting out of rifles, machine guns, mortars, bazookas, flame throwers. The sky there would be raining metal and flame.

Someone beside me said, "General Buckner got it."

"Got what?" I cried.

"It! It had his name on it. He's there, on Okinawa. Filling in a hole in the ground. The Japs got him."

Fear crawled under my skin. If they'd kill a general, I thought, what would they do to a mere private?

On Okinawa my unit was given the job of carrying ammunition to the front. The original beachhead had expanded across half the island. The Japanese on the other half were fighting like crazy men. They would not give up. *Banzai* charge after *banzai* charge was met with machine-gun fire. Hundreds of Japanese waded right into the mouths of our flame throwers. Still, they came on. By day some hid in the caves, and by night they came out to snipe, then melt again into the earth—leaving behind corpses.

It was a standing joke among the men of the Negro 51st Battalion that the NAACP in the States was criticizing the government for not letting us fight on the front lines.

As a matter of fact, ammo bearers were in more danger than the men on the lines.

A blinding light, a head-splintering roar, echo of a blast.

Between flashes of light, pictures stabbed: a figure in battle fatigues and helmet placing a crate of ammunition on a stack, moving to the shade of a palm tree, sitting, and taking a drink from a canteen.

A sudden sharp, droning sound swooping down, then knifing away, an eternity of silence, and in that awful silence the slow body cannot move fast enough for the flashes of light, the thunderous noise. The figure leaps up, arms flailing, and reels back into more explosions.

The figure rises, reels, tumbles backward into darkness.

I saw myself lying still and bleeding behind a shattered tree, my left arm shattered like the tree.

Then, no more pictures.

Finally, my eyes opened. I was on a cot among other cots lined up on either side of a long building with shellholes for windows. "It's Tom, Johnny," the voice kept saying. "Tom Daly. You're in the hospital. Everyone thought you were dead."

Later, the nurse said, "Your injury isn't so bad. The main worry was losing a lot of blood while you were out there at the ammo dump. Tom took care of you."

I healed in time to leave Okinawa with my unit in July of 1945.

When I got back to the United States, I was assigned to Advanced Food Technicians' School. They couldn't get this orderly business out of their minds.

As time rolled along, I decided to try for some rank. That meant I had to go to classes, then to regular refresher training sessions, then to a job, all at the same time. But I was determined to get some promotions. I was the first at work in the morning and the last to leave. I did everything correctly, and studied until my head seemed so heavy it could have been used for a bowling ball.

We were no longer at war. Hiroshima and Nagasaki had been vaporized. General MacArthur had returned. The Japanese had signed a peace agreement, and now our troops were going overseas, not to fight, but to police the enemies' homelands.

After my food technicians' course was finished, I was assigned to take care of one of the generals at Quantico, Virginia. I organized his parties and receptions. I worked hard to make him shine like gold and impress his superiors. He showed his appreciation. I became a Pfc. In three months he promoted me again—to sergeant. I was finally on my way up—not realizing for an instant that I was about to be booted back down.

The general had a white chauffeur who was a genuine twenty-four-karat boozer. Since the general also liked his martini, he didn't complain about his drinking. The driver seemed to me to be a pretty nice fellow; we got along quite well.

He lived on the other side of the base, but I had a little house behind the general's quarters in officers' row, and once in a while the chauffeur would come over to shoot the breeze. Usually he was slightly drunk, but he was friendly and full of stories.

Because of his occasional visits, I wasn't surprised one day when he came to my place carrying a suitcase.

"Say, do me a favor?" He gestured toward the suitcase. "I can't take this home, and I really don't have much time. I'll explain later. But would you keep it here for me?"

I laughed. "Why not? Glad to." We were buddies, weren't we? "Just put it in my locker. I'm trying to get this lesson finished to send in, and I'm due over at the general's."

"Uh, sure, Johnny. I'll just be on my way, too, since you're busy. Thanks again, pal."

I finished my lesson and went over to the general's house to set the table for a function that evening. A major knocked on the door. "Sorry," I said. "I'm the only one here right now."

"Are you Sergeant J. Johnson?"

"Yes, sir."

"You live in the little house in back?"

"Yes, sir."

"Would you come down to the provost marshal's office with me, please?"

When we got there, I saw that the major had the suitcase, the one the chauffeur had put in my locker.

"Have you ever seen this suitcase before?" the major asked.

"Why, yes, sir," I replied. "It's not mine, though."

The major shook his head and said something into his intercom. The general's driver was escorted in.

I grinned at him. "Hey, they don't seem to believe me. Tell them that's your suitcase."

He shook his head. "It's not mine. It's yours."

I laughed. This guy was a real joker. "Well, a joke's a joke, but—"

"You say it's his?" the major asked the driver.

The driver nodded, his face dead serious.

"Hey, man," I said, no longer laughing. "What are you trying to pull? What do you mean? This is your suitcase!"

He shook his head.

"Well, okay," I said. "If you want to give it to me. If you want me to keep it. But it's still the one you brought by and put in my locker."

It didn't make sense. When the major had first talked to me, I had assumed he wanted me to come to his office on some business of the general's. Then, when I saw the suitcase and realized they had come to my place and taken it, I momentarily thought I was being accused of stealing it. Since I had no intention of trying to claim it and could so easily explain its presence in my locker, I wasn't worried.

But they were trying to prove the suitcase was mine. It baffled me.

The investigating officer asked me again, "Are you going to claim this suitcase?"

"No, sir. It's not mine, but if he wants to give it to me, I'll take it. What's in it, anyway?"

"You know what's in it. Liquor!"

"Now, wait a minute!" I exploded. "I don't even drink. Never have. I can prove it! Lots of people will tell you . . ."

The major wrote something on his report, then looked up. "You were going to sell it?"

"Sell it? Who would I sell it to?"

The major shrugged. "You tell us. To the enlisted men, probably. They're not allowed to have it on base. You could make a nice profit."

"I didn't even know liquor was in it. I don't have time to go around selling that stuff. I'm busy going to school to get an education, besides working for the general."

Still I was not worried. I was sure they were giving me the third degree just to make very sure the suitcase did not, as a matter of fact, belong to me. I was sure the chauffeur would admit the case was his once he'd been caught and was unable to come up with a logical story. Certainly it should be easy enough to prove it wasn't mine.

Shouldn't it?

The next few words tipped me off as to what was going on, and made me feel weak and shaky. The major said, "Are you going to tell me this white boy is lying?"

Now I knew what I was up against. "I'm not saying he's lying, just mistaken."

"Boy," the major growled, "don't you ever say that a white man is mistaken anymore."

Their whiteness flashed at me. I remembered I was a Negro. I'd go for days forgetting it, then something would happen. But nothing this bad had ever happened before.

I kept quiet. I figured I'd let them play their game. The general would set them straight. He knew I didn't drink, that I was too busy to sell liquor on the base against regulations, and that I wouldn't dream of doing such a thing. He was a good guy. He wouldn't let them frame me.

First, they were going to lock me up. Then a colonel objected. "The general might not like us locking up his man without being in on the situation. See if he'll come over."

There, I thought. That would settle it.

When the general got there, it was like Okinawa. Inside, it was as though I'd been hit by a bomb.

The general said, "Sorry you did it, Johnny." He turned to the major. "Don't lock him up. Let him come with me. I'll talk to him."

At his house, he said, "Listen, Sergeant Johnson. I've had that driver with me for twenty years. I've never known him to lie or cheat. Don't you try to get that man's record fouled up with your lies."

"But I'm not lying!" Suddenly, I could hold in the anger and frustration no longer. I banged on his kitchen table. "The suitcase is *not* mine!"

I seldom lost control of myself like this. But what got to me was that I liked the general as well as his driver. Thought they were squared-away people.

For a brief moment, I hardly knew where I was. I stood up and banged again on the table. "It's not mine, it's not mine." I stared at him with clenched fists.

The general got up and backed away. "You'd better not hit me," he said. "I'll put you away forever."

I couldn't stand it any longer, being near him, knowing that he knew I was innocent, but wanting to save his chauffeur's skin. I whirled around, left the kitchen, went down the back steps, and ran to my little house. Inside, I banged my fists against the walls. I'd obeyed every rule, worked my head off, and yes, sirred the officers. I had tried to be a true-blue Marine, correct in every detail. Now they were "rewarding" me.

The general called me back. We had both cooled down, and he wanted to "negotiate." It boiled down to his wanting me to plead guilty. "The suitcase was found in your locker, and we have to punish someone for this. If you agree to plead guilty, we'll skip the jail time and just take a stripe away. I'll give it back in a few weeks. Then everyone will be satisfied."

"Except me. I'm not guilty."

"If you keep saying that, I'll let them put you in the stockade," the general said. "I got to make the record look good, and I can't afford to let people think I let one of my men get away with having liquor on the base."

I went back to my quarters without giving a definite answer. I decided to phone Dad.

"Son," he said, "sometimes you've got to be like the good runner, take one step backward to give yourself a good running start. Remember what I've told you about sacrificing your pride? If you can take this wrong, you'll be a better man for it. Then, one of these days, you'll look back on it and think it was a good experience, that you were able to conquer this wrong, and you'll be a stronger man."

Intellectually, I appreciated his advice. Emotionally, I wasn't ready to follow it 100 per cent. However, I evaded a direct confrontation with the prosecuting officers, and it ended up with my not making any plea. At a summary court-martial, a lieutenant stepped forward to tell the court I pleaded guilty. I didn't deny it.

They took a stripe away, knocking me down to corporal—which wasn't as bad as what was said during the court-martial. The general thought he was doing me a favor in recommending a light sentence.

"He's a good boy. He is very loyal. He always comes out No. 1 in his classes. I really believe he's learned his lesson."

What he said next got under my skin. "I believe he'll study hard and educate himself as far as colored people can go."

He had his own peculiar sense of justice. Within six weeks, he gave my stripe back. But if it hadn't been for this injustice, I would have been a staff sergeant by then.

A few good things came out of the experience. It reminded me of my father's wisdom. It made me determine to be more strongly against alcohol.

The most important contribution this made in my life, however, was that it made me more positive in fighting against discrimination. Until this point, I had always knuckled under or tried to avoid situations in which prejudice could hurt me, physically or otherwise. Yet, my dad's words made me compound my crusade with restraint. I was not going to run amuck, hurling stones. On Okinawa I had already seen the results of violence.

No, I would fight discrimination quietly, politely, considerately. But continually. Because it was not God's wish for any man, whatever the color of his skin.

CHAPTER

8

The cafe was crowded. At the counter, Sam Lawson and I had been waiting to be served for almost an hour. "Look, we ought to open our own place," Sam said. "It takes forever to even get a hamburger in these places. If you're black, you're last."

I was still at Quantico, Virginia, working for the same general. We were in a little town called Triangle, just off the base.

"That girl who just came in. I've seen her before. Isn't she beautiful?" I knew it wasn't polite to stare, but there was something special about that girl.

"Hey, man. You're out of your class if you think you can get to know her. She doesn't like Marines, she doesn't dance. Her nickname is 'Grandma.' Enough said."

I sat there watching her while she sat down with a girl at the other end of the counter. "Listen, Sam. A guy can do anything he really wants to do, and I want to get a date with her."

"Never."

"Okay, Sam, you wait and see. I'll not only get a date, but also I think I'll marry her."

"You've got to be out of your mind."

"Are you going to introduce me?"

Her name was Juanita, and she didn't give me the cold shoulder.

After that, I called her almost every day. I thought she was going to be hard to get to know because I didn't think her parents would like the idea of their daughter going out with a Marine.

One evening about two weeks later, I was standing in the box for "rides," waiting to go back to the base, when Juanita and her whole family drove by.

I dashed over to the car, was introduced to the family, and piled into the back seat. Juanita's mother didn't say anything, though her father seemed happy to have me along. Juanita's brother, who was nine, and her sister, who was eleven, were the most affectionate kids I had ever seen. They made me a little homesick for my own family.

After we drove off, I asked where we were going.

"Every Wednesday we go to prayer meeting, and you're going with us." So matter-of-factly. Was I supposed to have known this?

The idea of going to a prayer meeting shouldn't have bothered me. But I hadn't been to church for a while. As a matter of fact, ever since the liquor incident at the base, I hadn't really paid much attention to God. I'd felt let down. Perhaps God might have told me I ought to be thankful they had just taken my stripe away.

Had I nearly lost an arm, or my life, in Okinawa, to be brought back to the States where it was safe, and then had not even thanked God in return for that life? Suddenly I felt very humble about going to prayer meeting.

Strains from "The Old Rugged Cross" came pouring out of a humble building midway down the block. We had to sit in the back. Row after row of people were already seated and all singing right from the heart. I was glad to hear my favorite song.

I stole a glance at Juanita during the prayer that followed. She was in a white, frilly, long-sleeved blouse with a shiny black skirt. Her long brown hair shone. Praying, she looked absolutely radiant.

None of the other people in the church looked especially wealthy, but they were neatly dressed and looked happy. Here we were, in a part of America where discrimination against the Negro cowed thousands, yet these were proud, intelligent people, happy because they were on God's side.

They prayed for good health and thanked Him for the fact that we were no longer at war, for letting the sun shine, for having someone to love, and for children to care for.

"Thank you, Lord," I said as I buried my face in the pillow that night. "Everything is shipshape here, too."

Life in the Marines began to take on a new significance for me. I worked harder than ever at my regular job, taking care of the general and going to school in my spare time—and dating Juanita.

I had had plenty of time to work late on my job and still get to school. Now, however, I had to make out a new schedule. Dating a girl like Juanita, I knew, was going to take a lot of time—time from my studies. I decided I'd better tell her my goals. If she thought I was nuts, I could weigh anchor.

"Run for the U. S. Senate? In 1974?" Juanita repeated one evening on our way to a movie. "Why, I think that's really something. Most people don't even plan an hour ahead. Which reminds me, what theater are we going to?"

"Why, the Quantico Marine Corps theater on the base, if that's all right with you."

Juanita sighed. "It's segregated like the rest of them outside. It's not so bad going to an all-black movie, but . . ."

"It's not segregated for me," I said.

Juanita was mystified after we paid our admission and were ushered to a seat right in the middle of the theater. "How did we get such good seats? I can actually see the movie."

She glanced around. People kept filing in. The Negroes—Marines and civilians alike—were ushered to a small section along the side. Others sat according to rank. But our whole row remained vacant except for us.

"Why doesn't anyone else sit in our row? How come the other Negroes don't sit here?"

I lowered my voice. "When I first came to this movie, I noticed only Negroes were sitting where I'd planted myself. I wondered what would happen if I sat somewhere else, so I got up and moved."

"Didn't they kick you out?"

"Nope. But they tried to. The MP said, 'You can't sit there.'

" 'Isn't this where Marines are supposed to sit?'

" 'Yah, but only white Marines.'

"I shrugged. 'Who told you that?'

"The MP shrugged in turn. 'I dunno.'

" 'Well,' I said, 'you'd better find out before you try to move me.'

"He left. I sat there the whole time without anyone bothering me. I kept wondering what was going to happen. But nothing ever did. Every time I went to the movie, I did the same thing. And no one ever told me to move again."

Juanita whispered, "Why don't the other Negro Marines do the same thing, then?"

"Because the MPs tell them they'll get in trouble. They say, 'Do you want to be a troublemaker like that sergeant there?' But I'm not trying to make trouble. I'm just standing up for what I know is right."

"Good for you, Jimmy."

"It's been kind of lonely sitting here all these months. Since that liquor business, I decided to be very politely equal wherever I went, no matter what it costs me. Somebody's got to do it if we want America to be really the land of the free." I could see that Juanita agreed with me.

During the time I was getting better acquainted with Juanita, there were only two nice restaurants in town, and Negroes weren't allowed in them.

Sam and I decided to do something about the eating situation. We found a place for rent at a reasonable price. It was just a cubbyhole between some buildings off the main street, suitable for a "quick serve" hot dog and hamburger diner. We squeezed in three tables and built a counter at the side where customers could sit on stools. If we served a good hot dog for ten cents and hamburger with all the trimmings for fifteen cents, we could move them in and out fast enough to make it pay.

We worked hard to get the place looking nice, painting tables, chairs, and the counter. When we first opened, I had just thought of it as a service to the people in Triangle, and a small investment. Soon I began to look at it and everything else more seriously. And I began to see myself getting an education more quickly. Until then, I had just been thinking about myself. Now another person's thoughts and dreams were becoming important to me too.

Around this time, my fifteenth boxing match came up. My boy scout boxing experience had shown me what discipline of the body could do for both mind and muscles, so I had taken up the sport in the Marines. I felt this match would be a cinch. I asked Juanita to sit in my cheering section. In our boxing matches, we had to make sure we had our own supporters, or it would be awfully quiet when the bell sounded. I was considered a middleweight, and had won all fourteen of my fights, with four knockouts. I had been training and was in good shape.

The night of the big fight, the place was filled. I looked out from behind the curtain and felt a surge of emotion at seeing Juanita, right up front. I pranced into the ring.

The referee grabbed the mike. "Ladies and gentlemen, in this corner, we have Bernie Evans, weighing 164½ pounds." Everybody booed.

"And, in this corner, weighing 168¾, from Chicago, Illinois, Jimmy Johnson!" I got a cheer. I felt great. I nodded to Juanita. I planned to wipe out Bernie in the first round. Since he was shorter than I, I had my strategy all planned.

When the bell sounded, I went out with a long left jab and caught him on the nose, then hooked a nice left with a right cross. He moved in and banged two punches to the body, and I pushed him away.

He tried to throw some overhand looping rights to catch me on the glove. I backed away, putting out a left jab, catching him on the chin, and he came banging right in with a left and right to the midsection again. I tied him up. Then the bell sounded.

I knew I had won the first round, but he had stung me more than I had anticipated. I glanced over at Juanita. She smiled. I tried to indicate to her that I'd put him out in the second.

The bell rang.

We both rushed out, anxious to get it over with. Bernie headed for my midsection. I shoveled him off with a left jab, a right cross, then a left uppercut that sent him spinning back into the ropes.

Bernie's temper flared, and he rushed at me. I tried to time it just right, and I jabbed with my left, then went for a right cross. I missed.

I had pushed off on my left leg instead of my right. My leg sent shooting pains up to my chest. I felt as if I had been drawn and quartered. Dizzy with pain, I clutched onto Bernie for a minute, trying to get my balance. It was hard to focus. I could barely see Juanita. She was no longer smiling.

My left leg wouldn't move. I hobbled around while Bernie

slammed me with punches wherever he could find an opening. Stall until the bell, I thought, backing toward my corner.

Suddenly my left leg wouldn't move at all. Juanita's scream was timed with the sound of the bell and my last grunt as Bernie found my midsection. Merciful blackness closed in as Round Two ended. I had lost.

CHAPTER

9

I spent four months in the hospital getting my leg back in shape. The injury had been far more serious than I thought. The doctor said, "You can't expect to pull a ligament the way you did and not have real problems. I'm sorry to say it, but I'll be honest: In my opinion, you'll never walk on that leg except with a cane."

After I had been in the hospital about six weeks, I was beginning to get around more and more without the wheelchair. I was determined to prove the doctor wrong. I worked on my leg every day, exercising eight to ten hours, massaging it, staying in the whirlpool longer than recommended, and generally letting loose with the Johnson spirit that my father had programmed in me.

Juanita came to visit me every day.

"Oh Jimmy," she said on one of her visits, "please give up boxing. There's nothing but more hurt in it for you!" Juanita knew the pain I was in and how much being in good shape and a top Marine meant to me. She had tears in her eyes. How could I refuse?

I wanted to get back to the hot-dog stand, too. Sam had had to leave, and we had turned it over to a friend named Joe, but he wasn't working out. I think he was doing all right for himself, but nothing was left over for me except the bills.

"Let me run it, Jimmy," Juanita pleaded one day. "I know I can at least make ends meet and pay the bills."

"Well, if your folks agree," I finally consented. "I would love to know you're in there every day."

A week later, Juanita came in with the receipts. "Look, Jimmy,' you can make at least thirty-eight dollars a day profit from that place. I've paid all the bills first, and that's what left over, on the average, each day."

"I knew you could do it," I shouted. "I guess I'll just have to marry you so I won't have to pay extra help, and then we'll have it all coming in."

"But I can't marry you," she said seriously.

"Why?"

"Because you smoke, and I'm a hard-shell Baptist."

"I can quit any time."

She looked at me. "Not the way you love cigarettes."

When she left, I put two cartons of my favorite brand in the trash. Of course, after eating the next meal, I was tearing at my bag to find the cigarettes; then I remembered. I had quit! And I did! It was just to please Juanita, but I knew they were bad for me anyway.

By the end of my hospital stay, I was able to jog four miles without more than a barely visible limp. I decided it was time to get out.

Still skeptical, the doctor wrote out my discharge slip. "I didn't think it could be done, Jimmy!" he said. "You have a very special determination."

"That I do, sir," I said, squeezing Juanita's hand.

Within the next few days, during every spare moment, I practiced proposing marriage in front of a mirror. "Miss Butler, I'm in love with you. Let's get married." "Miss Butler, I would like to have your hand in marriage." I settled on the latter, the old Baptist traditional way. Then I decided on a more informal approach. "Have you ever thought of getting married?" I set the scene up carefully.

When the moment finally came, however, it wasn't that easy. I was nervous talking to her parents about everyday things, and it suddenly occurred to me that I'd have to deal with them, too.

They finally left us alone, and all the words I'd practiced got jumbled in my head. I blurted, "I, uh, er, just want to ask you one question, honey. You don't have to answer right away. I want to marry you. Will you marry me?"

"Of course, Jimmy," she exclaimed.

"Whu . . . ?"

"Yes, I'll marry you."

"I mean, well, that's really great. But, well, I didn't expect an answer so quick."

"Jimmy Johnson! I have been waiting for you to ask me for months. I've already thought about it at least a million times."

I was floating. The girl I'd chosen didn't need to play games; she was in love with me and not afraid to show it.

Gaining the approval of Juanita's parents would take a little longer. "They've got to get to know you better first," she said. "Let's wait and ask them later." And she was certainly worth waiting for.

Being in love and seeing Juanita almost every day and working hard for the goals I'd set made the months roll by.

I still hadn't asked Juanita's parents if I could marry her, but one day I got up my nerve to mention our plans to her mother.

The next week, we were working on wedding details, when her father said, "Who's getting married?"

I looked up, startled. "Why, Juanita and I."

Then I saw the look on his face and thought, Man, have I blown this.

"Nobody's asked me."

"Well, sir, can I ask you now?" I felt almost paralyzed. What if he wouldn't give his permission?

Seeing my consternation, he laughed aloud and flung his arm about my shoulder. "Jimmy boy, I really had you shook, didn't I? Of course you have my permission. I'm happy for both of you." I had never felt so good.

Juanita and her mother planned a wedding with two hundred guests, and soon it seemed as though the whole town was joining in. This was to be the first military wedding held in the Star of Bethlehem Baptist Church of Quantico, Virginia. We had chosen twelve of my buddies to be in the ceremony, and there had to be as many bridesmaids for the march down the aisle under the swords. Each Marine would be in his dress blues, blue- and red-trimmed jacket with white trousers.

On the day of the wedding, twelve of us packed into two tiny cars. And by the time we'd made our way down Washington Boulevard, stopping and starting and waiting for traffic, it was one o'clock in the afternoon, an hour before the wedding. Traffic crawled. I glanced over at a park we were passing; noticing the lovely flowers reminded me I hadn't ordered any corsages for Juanita's mother and sisters!

I groaned. "Keep your eyes out for a flower shop, men. I just made a first-class blunder. No corsages for Mom and the girls!"

Someone spotted a florist's shop. We were in Alexandria by now, and I pulled over. Sam Lawson stopped behind me.

The lady florist brought the corsages I wanted. "Thank you very much, ma'am. If I don't hurry out of here, I'll be late for a very important date: my wedding."

I paid her, grabbed up the corsages, and barged through the door and up the steps, three at a time.

When I'd reached the top step, I yelled out to the fellows, "I got 'em!" That was the last thing I remember. I came to rest at the bottom of the steps. My throbbing head was bloody.

The lady florist was screaming for help. "You hit your head on the top of the concrete door frame when you started to go out," she said between screams.

I was trying to pull myself to my feet, but I was weak and dizzy.

One of my buddies jumped out of the car and came tearing into the shop. "Who hit him? I'll get him!"

I tried to say something, but blacked out again. When I came to, vases, flower pots, and flowers were being flung all over the shop. The lady was screaming louder than before, and Joe Quint, a semipro boxing heavyweight champion at the base, had the shop owner up against the wall.

"No, no, fellas," I cried.

Quint looked around. "Well, if it wasn't this guy, who?"

Then they started beating up on a customer just standing there. "No," I tried to shout. But it was too late. They were banging the poor fellow against the wall.

"No, no, he didn't do anything!" I shouted.

"Well, who did?" They looked accusingly at the lady clerk.

I jumped in front of her. "No, no, I've been trying to tell you, nobody did it. I hit my head, on the door beam!"

"So why didn't you tell us?" They were disgusted.

Joe picked up the proprietor and brushed him off. "Look, I'm awfully sorry. We are a little excited today. The guy's getting married. Please don't call the police."

The lady started wiping the blood off me while I apologized and said we'd pay for any damage.

The white proprietor said, "That's right, you will, and don't ever come back in here again."

We were all black. The proprietor and bystanders were white. Here I was trying to stop my buddies from beating up innocent people. The lady kept saying, "I understand," but the owner didn't.

Driving at breakneck speed through traffic, I thought about what had happened. I saw that at least some of this prejudice stuff was aggravated by black people being too sensitive and jumping to conclusions. God knows, we have had good reason to feel hurt and to develop sensitivity; but if Joe hadn't taken matters into his own hands so quickly, without even asking questions, a lot of embarrassment and—as I discovered later—nine hundred dollars' worth of damage would have been avoided. The incident brought solidly home to me how expensive a thing racial prejudice always is—for both sides. I longed for the day when America would be rid of it.

I was forty-five minutes late for my own wedding.

The guys had all helped me clean up, and Joe plastered my hair over the cut on my head, which was aching clear down to my shoulders. Still, it was a grand feeling, having my lovely bride on my arm as we walked down the aisle under swords. The Marine belief is that when a man and woman are tied together by swords, sharp as they are, there is no way to untie them.

We ran to the car, guests pelting us with rice. Our first honeymoon stop was the base hospital, where they put a couple of stitches in the cut on my head.

A white friend of mine had tried to get us a room at a hotel. When everything was all set up, he told them we didn't want to be embarrassed about anything. "Why should they be embarrassed?"

"Because they're Negro."

"Oh, I'm sorry, but we're all filled up."

"You just told me there was a room available."

"I said we're filled up!"

"How about your other hotel, on Sixteenth Street?"

"It's all filled up, too."

We spent our first night at the Dunbar Hotel for Negroes in Washington, D.C., and the next morning we tried to get something to eat at nearby restaurants. Some of them let us come in and sit down, for an hour, without service, and without explanation.

On our sixth try for breakfast, I finally went over to the hostess and said, "Ma'am, we've been here almost two hours, and we haven't been waited on."

"Of course not. That's because I didn't seat you."

We went back and forth for a while, and I said, "All right, we'll stand up and wait until you can seat us."

"Oh, it's too late now. All the girls have seen you, and I'm sure they won't serve you."

Even I could see that the situation was hopeless. But the dream of an unsegregated, truly free America never left me.

After our wedding trip, we returned to Washington, where I was working at the Marine base as a man Friday, this time for a major general, the USMC assistant commandant.

Our first home was in the Northeast section, with a widow, Wanda Fletcher; she was glad to share her house in return for help with repairs and a small rent.

At about this time, Secretary of Defense Louis A. Johnson was trying to get the services to integrate. Much pressure was on schools to integrate, too.

In discussions concerning Johnson's policy, the general disagreed with the major policy. On one occasion the general and his wife had invited me in to chat after I had brought him home.

"You know, you read a lot of books, you study hard. You're a pretty smart boy, but you have to understand one thing," my "host" said. "There will never be integration in the Marine Corps. We cannot train a black boy and a white boy in the same platoon. They do not have the same background and cannot be trained together."

"How many white Marines have the same background?"

"What do you mean?"

"You take some white kids from the hills of Tennessee, some more from the Appalachians, some from Georgia, some from

Chicago, New York, and Washington, D.C. They all have only one thing in common: white skin. But their backgrounds are different."

The general's face got red.

"He has you there, honey," his wife said.

"You be quiet, dear! Johnson, as long as I'm here, integration won't happen in the Marine Corps."

"But General, you won't always be here. Things have to change. Now, let me show you here in this book something I've just been reading . . ."

The general snorted. "Don't you ever throw a book up in my face. I know what's in those books!"

He stormed out of the room, and his wife showed me out. "You know," she said, "I see something good in what you say, in spite of what my husband has said." She smiled and put her hand on my shoulder. "I think you'll go a long way."

One day, shortly after this, I missed the general at work. When I went over to help his wife on several occasions, I still didn't see him. He was "resting," she said.

A few days later, I walked into one of the bedrooms, and discovered the general lying in bed, trembling with a severe illness. He looked like death!

I ran over to the commandant's house and told him something must be done.

"They're Christian Scientists," he said. "I don't like to interfere with their religious beliefs."

"Commandant, military law says you are no longer yourself when you are in the Marine Corps. And you cannot refuse medical treatment if it's there, regardless of what the reason. You have a legitimate right to call an ambulance and send him over to the Navy hospital for treatment. If you don't, he will surely die."

The ambulance arrived in about five minutes, and the drivers put the general on a stretcher. Barely able to breathe, still he protested. "I don't want to go. I'll be all right. All I have to do is a little more Bible reading and believing, and I'll be well again."

But they paid no attention. After two weeks in the hospital, he was well enough to return home.

His wife felt that I had interfered. At the same time, she was shocked at the realization that I had cared enough to take action.

"Of course I care, he's a human being," I told her. "We're supposed to love one another whether or not we agree about everything. And one of these days, I'll show the general he's wrong about Negroes not advancing in government and the military."

I hadn't forgotten the far-away goal God had placed in my heart.

The year whipped by busily and happily for Juanita and me. We would never be just old married people, we said. We treated marriage as a fragile bouquet that needed constant watering and nourishment.

By fall we were expecting our first child. And we began looking for a bigger place in which to live.

We found a little apartment on North N Street in Georgetown. The pleasant couple who shared the top story with us, Mr. and Mrs. Clarence Stone, were living a double identity. Clarence was a cab driver, and his wife, Bella, had a good job with the Potomac Telephone Company.

To work at the telephone company, she had to pretend to be white. She couldn't ride to work in the front seat with her husband, but sat in the back seat like a paying passenger.

"I see you have the same Negro driver all the time. How come?" one of the girls asked her one day.

"He just comes by all the time. He's a good driver and very dependable."

"I never see you pay him."

"Oh, I pay him."

She had to make a big production out of looking in her purse for money, paying him, and waiting for change, but no good-bye kiss.

Thousands of mulattoes were coming to Washington, D.C., during the 1950s and passing themselves off as whites to obtain jobs. If you were colored, you weren't hired.

The mulattoes stayed at a job until someone recognized them; then they would have to take off.

Five days before our first wedding anniversary, we made a trip to Bethesda Naval Hospital, where our first son had been born.

When Kenneth came home, he'd never stopped crying.

Nothing seemed to help. He couldn't keep even milk down.

Juanita read everything she could get her hands on, and called her mother for advice; he still cried and seemed to weaken.

I finally took our baby to the base hospital. The doctor in the emergency room checked him over. "He'll have to be operated on tomorrow morning. Will you sign this paper, please?"

The next morning, Juanita and I went to the hospital and found that Kenneth had already been operated on. "We didn't dare wait for you to come, Sergeant Johnson," the tired doctor said. "He had an obstruction in his intestines that had to be removed so food could pass through. Would you like to see him?"

A nurse wheeled in a glassed-in box. There were tubes and bottles everywhere and, in the middle, our tiny son, with tape on his throat. He looked so pathetic, Juanita and I started to cry.

We spent the next four days in limbo, trying to work, checking in at the hospital, and praying. We prayed together as we hadn't done in a long time.

When we went to bring Kenneth home the following week, it was all we could do to keep from shouting, "Praise the Lord!" right there in the hospital. Now he looked like a normal, healthy baby again. There were times after that when we wondered if he would ever stop eating.

Juanita enjoyed her role as mother, and I plunged back into work and school with a sense of added responsibility. We also had a new insight that God was with us more than we had realized. He had made His presence known during our prayers, and we were determined that this time we wouldn't let Him slip out of our grasp again.

God must have been helping me, too, in my determined battle to gain equality for Negroes on that base, for He gave me the strength and might to follow through on an ordinary incident all the way to the top of the Department of Defense, and win my point. I had decided to take in a movie I thought might help me in one of my classes. Juanita didn't feel like leaving the baby with anyone, so I went alone.

At the small movie house on the base, I went in and sat where a sign indicated staff NCOs. After a while, a young private with an MP armband came up. "Sergeant, you have your seat back there."

"Oh I'm sorry, I thought this was for staff NCOs." I got up and started walking back with him. "Where are the staff NCOs supposed to sit?"

"The staff NCOs sit where you were sitting."

"Well, that's where I was sitting."

"That is for white staff NCOs."

"It didn't say anything about white or colored. It just said 'staff NCOs.'"

"Yes, but you sit back here where the colored sit regardless of their rank."

"I'm not going to do that. I'm going to sit where it says 'staff NCOs'!" I went back and sat down.

In a few minutes, a lieutenant arrived. "I order you to go back there and sit where you belong."

"And I have to tell you right now, you don't have enough rank, Lieutenant, to give me an order that denies me my constitutional rights," I said politely.

"What do you know about your constitutional rights?" he growled.

"I spend most of my time in school when I'm not working," I said. "My constitutional rights say I'm supposed to sit here with my rank and my peers, and that is exactly what I am going to do."

"If you don't move immediately, I'm going to put you on report, and you'll have to listen to the major."

I stayed put, and he stormed out.

I tried to concentrate on the movie. Then a major appeared. "Do I have enough rank to put you out?"

"Major, you do not, unless you can *rewrite* the Constitution of the United States."

"What has the Constitution to do with you?" the major asked. "It wasn't written for you. You were a slave then."

"Sir, it was written for me, and I wasn't a slave. I wasn't born yet, Major. I'm not moving."

"Well, you'll be seeing the colonel in the morning," he said.

I sat where I was until the movie was over. When I was on the way out, two white Marines came up to me, one a corporal, the other a sergeant. "We just want to tell you that we think you're right," they said. "Don't let them move you."

I was really surprised when they said they were from Mobile, Alabama, and Jackson, Mississippi.

At my barracks, the black Marines were waiting for me. "Please, Johnny, don't do this. You'll get us all in trouble; they'll make it rough on us."

"Look," I said, "you fellows don't have to do what I do. Do what you want to do, and let me do my thing. If you don't care about your rights or freedom, and you don't fight for them, you'll lose them."

"But we just don't want to get in trouble."

"Someone has to establish the fact that we're all created equal, and unless we stand up for our rights, we're never going to gain equal respect in the Marine Corps."

They gave up talking to me, a twenty-three-year-old Marine who'd decided to defy the brass.

At 8:30 A.M. the next morning, there was a knock on my door. It was the colonel's chief clerk. "He's mad, Sergeant. You better make tracks to his office. You're really going to get it."

"Yes, sir, that's all right."

"I'd sure hate to be in your shoes. He's foaming at the mouth. What'd you do to make him so mad?"

"I just went to the movie."

"Where'd you sit?"

"Where all the staff NCOs are supposed to sit."

"No wonder. Do you know where this guy is from?"

"I couldn't care less where he is from."

"Well, he's from Mississippi."

"I don't care."

"Look, this guy is tough. Why don't you tell him you're sorry, and it's not going to happen again? This guy's crazy when it comes to the race thing. Plead ignorant, say you didn't know what you were doing; you'd had a couple of drinks."

"I don't drink. I'm sorry, gunner. I appreciate your concern. But I'm going to keep on standing up for what I know is right."

Every once in a while, I'd remind myself, "Johnny, Jesus died to set you free from every kind of slavery. It's not right for you to submit to injustice—ever. It's not fair to your oppressors, even, for you to let them get by with it."

When we arrived at the colonel's office, the chief clerk snapped to attention.

"Sergeant Johnson, I want you to march in when I say to march in, and stand in front of the colonel's desk. Is that understood?"

"Yes, sir." I marched in and snapped to attention. "Sergeant Johnson reporting, sir."

The colonel jumped out of his chair. "Take my seat."

"But Colonel, sir. That's your seat."

"Don't tell me. You're running this base. You take my seat and put your feet up on the desk. Do it now!"

"Yes, sir." I sat in his chair. But I didn't put my feet on the desk.

"Now, Colonel Johnson, what are you going to do to this sergeant who deliberately defied one of your orders and told other men what they could and could not do, or where they could sit in the movie? How many days in the brig are you going to give this sergeant Johnson for that stupid act?"

I leaned back in the huge leather chair. "Well, Sergeant, you are a most outstanding and extraordinary man, and you know your *constitutional* rights. You know this is a great country, and you are proving it by tearing down racial discrimination built up over the years. You are setting a fine example, and someday you will be a United States senator. And when we look back upon this day, we'll say, 'Now, there was a *courageous* man.'"

The colonel was taking all this in with an amazed look, and his sergeant was about to crack up.

At the top of my voice, I continued, "Sergeant, instead of you going to the brig for what you've done, I'm going to give you leave."

That was too much for the colonel. "Get out of my chair!" he yelled. "I'll tell you one thing: You're not going anywhere in this Marine Corps. You'll be blackballed the rest of the time you're in the service; you'll never get promoted again as long as I'm here."

"Is that all, sir?"

"No. You are still on report."

The sergeant and I walked out; he laughed all the way back to my office. "And that bit about being a U.S. senator!"

"I'm going to run for the U. S. Senate in 1974."

"Yeah?" the sergeant said. "We both know there won't be any Negroes running for the Senate for the next one hundred years. Not as long as you got guys like the colonel running around."

I couldn't work. I thought and thought about the silly, stupid scene, and the more I thought about it, the more determined I was to do something about the situation. Why should a Marine have to go through this? Weren't we Americans, citizens in the land of the free?

I went outside and hailed a cab. "Pentagon, please," I said to the driver.

I introduced myself to the receptionist. "I'd like to see the Secretary of Defense, Mr. Louis Johnson, please."

The woman Marine looked at me. "Sorry. There's no way you can see the Secretary of Defense."

"Why not?"

"Because he's busy."

"I'll wait!"

"It might be hours."

"That doesn't matter. I'll stay here all day if necessary." I sat down and waited. Finally the receptionist said, "Ah, I'll see what I can do." She went into an office behind her, and an Army colonel, one of the Secretary's aides, came out.

"Sergeant, what do you want?"

"I'd like to see the Secretary of Defense."

"What's it about, Sergeant?"

"I'd like to break up the discrimination in the movie theater at the Eighth and I base."

He put his hands on his hips and just looked at me. "You wait here for a few minutes. I'll see if I can find someone else to help you."

Out he went. I sat down, thinking they were going to stall me. But almost immediately a brigadier general walked out. I snapped to attention. "Can you tell me what this is all about?" he questioned.

I explained to him.

"Look, maybe we can handle it without you seeing the Secretary."

"No, sir. I want to see him. That's why I came over here."

"He's getting ready to leave right now. Maybe you could come back tomorrow."

"All right. I'll come back tomorrow."

Suddenly, aides started popping out of various offices and a loud

"Attention!" echoed throughout the building. Everyone snapped to, and I looked for the man without any hair, because I knew that would be Secretary Johnson.

When he appeared, I stood up and shouted out, "Sir, are you the Secretary of Defense?" Even as I did it, I was shocked at my action. It was almost as if I acted with a volition that was not my own.

"Yes, I am," the Secretary said.

"Sir, I have been waiting here for three hours to see you, and I would just like to talk with you for one minute."

The brigadier general said, "Sergeant, I told you to come back tomorrow, that he didn't have time for you today."

Secretary Johnson said, "What do you mean, I don't have time? What is it, Sergeant?"

"Sir, I want to talk to you about the discrimination at the Eighth and I base."

"Discrimination over at Eighth and I!" he shouted. "I put out an order ending discrimination in the military."

"Sir, I went to the movie last night, and I was told I was supposed to go to the back of the theater, where the colored sat. I was only sitting where my staff sergeant NCO rank permitted me to sit, but I was told to leave."

"Did you leave?"

"No, sir, I didn't leave."

"Good for you."

"But, sir, I am now on report." I went through the whole episode, telling him about the incident in the colonel's office.

He turned to an aide. "Get the commandant on the phone for me, will you?" Then, "Come into my office, please, Sergeant Johnson."

His office was the largest office I had ever been in. There were more telephone buttons on his phone than I'd ever seen. He could press a button and get about anybody he wanted in the Pentagon.

The colonel and the brigadier general had been invited in, as well. We all sat down on a leather sofa, while Secretary Johnson waited on the phone, then switched on a speaker so we could hear what was said.

"General?" he finally asked. "What is going on in this Marine Corps? What's this crap I hear about discrimination in the theater?"

"Oh no, sir," the general answered. "You must be mistaken. There's no discrimination here."

"I've got a man right here who was almost kicked out of the movie last night, and some idiot colonel had him sitting in his chair and putting on a phony act after he'd put him on report. I want that guy relieved today. Not tomorrow, today! And I want you over to my office in five minutes." He slammed down the phone.

When General Cates came in, there was fire in his eyes. I don't think I've ever seen a man so angry.

What happened in that office is now history. I repeated the story to General Cates. Then Secretary Johnson called all the Secretaries —Air Force, Navy, Army—and the Joint Chiefs of Staff, and said, "As of today there will be no more discrimination anywhere in the Armed Forces."

I went back to the base, very popular with members of my own race after that.

President Truman supported Secretary Johnson's antidiscrimination policy, and the Secretary's decision stood. But working conditions for me around the Eighth and I base grew worse. Even with racial discrimination outlawed, so many obstructions were put in my path that working efficiently became almost impossible. The colonel had been removed from his post, but his prophecy of doom for my career seemed about to come true, in spite of God's plan for my life.

CHAPTER

10

I was approaching Korea in a twin-engine C-19 cargo plane in the winter of 1951, worrying about war and weather. The United Nations "police forces" had been outflanked by North Koreans near Pusan. All the way north to the capital, pockets of UN forces were surrounded.

The weather was poor. I could see enormous snowdrifts surrounding the only cleared airstrip in the area, and I knew that the temperature down there was twenty-five degrees below zero.

After the worst landing I'd ever experienced, I breathed a prayer of thanksgiving when we finally jolted safely to a halt. Stumbling out with the rest of the Marines, I was hit by the piercing intensity of the bitter, bitter cold. Our winter-issue clothes weren't adequate for this kind of winter!

I could hear artillery in the distance. From news reports, we knew that the fighting was intense at this lowest point of the Korean War, when surprise attacks had chopped up South Korea badly, and UN forces had almost been pushed into the sea.

My job here was to administer supplies from a ship. I'd pitched my tent with buddies on the outskirts of Seoul between a couple of hills of snow and changed my socks a couple of times to keep my feet from freezing before I was told my ship hadn't come in.

In the small tent shared with three other men, I waited with little to do except try to stay close to a tiny heater in the tent. I tried to read *The Stars and Stripes,* paperbacks, and months-old stateside magazines by a dim lantern. I had time to read the Bible, too, in Korea, with enemy bombs shrieking and bursting over us. Korea, where I had been asked to do something for my country, only short months after I had had to play "musical bases" over resentment against my theater-integration efforts.

When the brass decided to send me back to Quantico, evidently word went ahead. I was labeled a troublemaker, and at Quantico, the commanding general called me in. "I don't want you on my base. We're sending you to Parris Island, South Carolina."

He handed me new orders.

I had a long-distance talk with Dad. "Try not to let it hurt you, Jimmy," my father said, his voice trembling. He was still calling me Jimmy, although my Marine friends all called me Johnny. "Like I said before, you have to sacrifice if you want to get ahead."

I resolved to believe that, tried to let Dad's words heal, but incident after incident kept the hurt alive.

The drive from Quantico to Parris Island with Juanita and Ken, nearly eighteen months old now, was one long slap in the face.

In Richmond, Virginia, we pulled into a gasoline station for refueling. I got out of the car and took little Ken by the hand.

"Where do you think you're going?" the pump jockey said.

"I'm taking my little boy to the restroom."

"Uh-uh, we don't allow colored to use our restrooms."

"Hold it then. Stop the gas."

"I've already put in fifteen cents' worth."

"That's all you're going to put in."

I paid him, and we drove to another station. Now both Ken and Juanita needed to use the restroom. At the next station, it was the same story. And the next. I got to where I asked them if we could use their restroom before I told them to give me gas.

Finally, the last service station before a long open road had a restroom marked *COLORED.* I led Ken toward it, but he pulled free and bolted through the door marked WHITE ONLY. Too weary to call him back, I just followed him in.

The attendant spotted us coming out. "Yer supposed to use the one marked COLORED COLORED COLORED!" he screamed. "You stupid black nigger."

"My son can't read."

The attendant's father came over. "You know, we lynch wise boys like y'all every day."

"Don't yer ever come in here again, hear?" the attendant said.

We were hungry. We drifted into a roadside coffee shop and were sitting at the counter when a fat white lady behind the counter said, "Y'all cain't sit there. Y'all got to go outside and get it through the winder, at the back."

"Thank you, ma'am, but we just aren't that hungry."

We walked out, and stopped for a drink at a drinking fountain. As I lifted Ken, the woman yelled, "Y'all cain't use that. Don't y'all know that's wrong? We got one in the back thair for y'all."

We finally arrived at Beaufort, South Carolina, near the Parris Island Marine base. There were no housing facilities on the base for Negro families. We tried a dozen local hotels, motels, apartments, and houses. "Y'all cain't stay here," they all said.

A Negro cab driver finally directed us to a Negro lady who rented rooms. "But she doesn't like kids," he warned.

We rang the doorbell. Kenneth rushed in when the door opened and said, "Hi."

A lady picked him up. "I don't usually take people with children, but I'll take you." She cuddled Ken. "Just a big room, but you can use the living room, dining room, kitchen, and bathroom."

The long, dreary trek from Quantico to South Carolina was over.

For the next year, I managed the officers' club. Letters of recommendation and commendation were written and placed in my official records file.

I was naturally proud of such recognition, and of wearing the uniform of the Marine Corps. But I wanted so much to help see that the Marine Corps lived up to the democratic ideals of America; yet I was constantly "put down" when I simply asked for all that went with my rank as a Marine and as an American. Everyone around me, hard worker or not, was getting promoted with monotonous regularity, while my own growth was slow, painful, and uncertain.

Guy after guy who had come in after me soared up in the ranks, won promotions and more pay. All I got were lofty-sounding letters stating that I was doing a wonderful job running the officers' club. Beautiful words, but no chevrons.

After I had been at Parris Island for about six months, I decided to apply for housing on the base. The small space at Daisy Brown's home was inadequate, and having to share the kitchen with others was getting on our nerves.

The housing officer said they had never had a black family aboard the base, and they thought it would cause a lot of trouble. He suggested that I find a nice place in the town's black community.

I began to tell the housing officer about my constitutional rights and that I wore the uniform of the U. S. Marine Corps. None of that cut any ice with him.

I got an audience with the general. When I walked into his office, he immediately turned to me. "I am sorry, but there is no housing available."

"I thought this might happen, sir. I took the liberty of traveling through the housing area, and I have eight empty houses listed here, complete with addresses. Also, I called the housing officer, and he says that there are eight empty houses, that there is no one on the waiting list, and that I can have a house if I so desire. Now, General, you just told me there are no houses. Someone has misinformed you, wouldn't you say?"

I had taken him by surprise. Not many Marines would have confronted him; he wasn't prepared to deal with such a situation. "Yes, er, ah, well, they are probably filled by now."

"In the last ten minutes, sir?"

"All right. Look, Sergeant Johnson, I'll be real candid with you. We're trying to get along with the local people. We're in the South, Johnson. The Deep South. If I brought you in and started mixing races on the base, I couldn't get any co-operation at all from the outside. They have a racist mayor running the town. A bigot. You know how these rednecks are down here."

He shook his head sadly and offered me a cigar, which I

declined. After a few puffs on his own, he continued, "Now, as for me, I'm from New Jersey, and I don't personally feel that way. But he's got my hands tied."

"Well, sir, I'm glad to hear you don't feel that way. I'll go see the mayor and see what I can do to change the situation."

I discovered the Beaufort city hall, a dumpy frame structure dating from pre-Civil War days, on a dismal side street, and went in. The mayor wasn't in. I found him helping a customer at his hardware store.

When his customer had left, I went up to him and said, "Mayor, Your Honor, I would like to talk to you about a matter at the base." Would the sparkly-eyed mayor kick me out, tell me to go around to the side door, or say he didn't have time?

"Why, of course, Sergeant. I'll be glad to talk to you. Come on back to my office."

In his office, I said, "You know, sir, I really love this country of mine. And all I ever wanted was my share of it, and I only want to be treated in accordance with my rank and position in life. And . . ." Something about his listening, and his gray-blue eyes, encouraged me to say, "And someday, sir, I am going to run for the United States Senate."

He raised his eyebrows. "When you going to do that? In the year 2001?"

"No, sir. In 1974."

"Why 1974?"

"That's when I will have completed my college education, my Marine Corps career, and ten years of civilian life."

"Hmmm," he mused. "That's very impressive. But why are you talking to me about the base? Why don't you go to the commanding general?"

"I went to him and told him I wanted to move onto the base with the other sergeants. The general told me it wasn't he who didn't want me to move onto the base, it was you."

"Me?" The mayor's face got cherry red. "That's a damn lie!" He started at me. "I couldn't care less what goes on at your base. My job is to take care of this here city, and what they do there is their business."

He grabbed the phone and dialed. After demanding to speak to the general, he waited, then said, "John? What's this story that I don't want this boy on your base out there just because he's colored?"

He listened for a few minutes, then said, "I've never told you that, so what gave you the idea of saying it? I bet you've been calling me a racist and a redneck, too.

"Well, I want you to know I am impressed with this boy. If you don't give him a house out there, I'm going to restrict all your Marines from coming into my town!"

He banged down the receiver. "That fixed his wagon. As a former private in the service, I've always wanted to tell off a general."

Back at the base, I knew the housing officer had already gotten the word to give me a house. I also knew he'd give me a house way in the back, overlooking a swamp. Before going to see the housing officer, I picked out a centrally located house by a beautiful lake. "Here's the address of the house the general would want me to have."

"But . . ."

"Look, if you want to call him up and argue with him . . ."

He assigned me the house. I signed the papers, and he handed me the keys. Then he said, "Did the general tell you to get that house?"

"No, he didn't tell me."

"That's what you said."

"No, that's not what I said. I said this is the house the general would want me to have."

"How do you know?"

"He's such a great guy, I just know he wanted me to have the best."

He grunted, and I departed, feeling I'd accomplished something at last for my family, in exchange for all the humiliation of the past six months.

But I was also very weary. Why did so much mental energy and physical effort have to be expended just to get what one should be entitled to in the first place?

When we moved in amid icy stares, the weariness deepened.

At work the next day, the men were quiet. I wasn't sure whether they personally disapproved of what I'd done, or were afraid they'd be criticized if they were friendly. I didn't have time to find out. Suddenly I received new orders for Korea. Miraculously, my family was permitted to remain in the house on the base.

In the frigid misery of that tent in Korea, with war roaring all around, I was haunted by questions. Why, why, why? Why wasn't I getting the promotions I deserved? Why in the land of the free did I have to fight so hard to secure full freedom that the majority could take for granted?

It didn't seem right. It didn't seem American.

Could change be effected by peaceful persistence in standing up for what I knew to be right? Or would it take violence and its awful consequences—dead bodies and savaged minds? Killing produced killers. To obtain freedom and rights, was violence always necessary?

No! I knew the alternative was the way Dad had recommended, the way I had chosen, the way of continuing sacrifice to achieve inches of progress. As long as I was headed in the right direction, I would get there someday. It was a waste of time and energy to feel sorry for myself. Yes! I had God on my side. I couldn't lose!

I had to endure life in the snowdrifts for only a few more days. As abruptly as I'd been sent to Korea, I was whisked to Japan, along with a large number of sick and wounded servicemen. And, after a short stay there, I was sent back to Parris Island.

Everything was A-okay with Juanita and Ken, and I was given a higher-level position than I had held before: administrator of the officers' club. I promptly enrolled in night school and in some correspondence courses and dug into studying.

I had enough credits to graduate, but they were scattered, not concentrated around a major. I was determined to accelerate my studies and to do all in my power to get a promotion. One day I was discussing my situation with the young chief of staff, Colonel Lanigan.

"I haven't been promoted, and everybody around me is beginning to laugh. 'You know,' they say, 'we goof off, and you work twenty-four hours a day, and we get promoted, and you don't. The best thing for you,' they say, 'is quit working, Johnson. And then you'll get promoted.'"

Colonel Lanigan stared at me. "Let me check this out with Marine Corps headquarters. Come back Thursday. I'll let you know what I find out."

That evening I phoned my dad. I told my troubles to him, reminding him that several high-ranking officers had expressed doubts about my chances of ever being promoted.

"They say it's because of my attitude about discrimination. And some of the blacks accuse me of being for the white guy, just because in some cases I've spoken out about Negro acts of prejudice. The thing is, I'm for what is right; I don't care from which direction it comes."

"You're right, son," Dad agreed. "You cannot afford to allow someone to be discriminated against because he's black, white, Catholic, Jew, or whatever. It's easy to take sides. But the important thing is to be right."

"Well, gee, Dad, am I always going to be criticized for doing the right thing?"

"Of course you are," Dad replied. He didn't sound sorry for himself, he sounded proud that it was so. "But that's going to be your sacrifice. And eventually you'll be rewarded because you have done the right thing."

That talk helped a little. I figured that there was always a price to pay, but that was all right if the goal was worth it. And I knew mine was.

On Thursday, I fidgeted in the waiting room for my appointment with the colonel.

Colonel Lanigan's expression did nothing to relieve my suspense. "Johnson, you have a few bad fitness reports. But we can give you some extra-good fitness reports to offset those."

I was baffled. "But sir, I've never received a bad fitness report. If I had had a bad fitness report, wouldn't I have known about it?"

He nodded. "You would have had to see it and sign it."

"I have never signed a bad fitness report."

He believed me. "Let me go back and look again. In fact, I'm going to gather all the information and fly to Washington myself with it and get them to pull out your complete file. We'll get to the bottom of it. Hold on for a little longer, Johnny."

A week later I received a phone call. The colonel had just returned from Marine Corps headquarters and wanted to see me right away.

I was in his office within minutes. His expression was a mixture of amusement and compassion. "You'd better sit down," he advised. "You're in for a few surprises."

He opened a folder. "There was a mistake, all right—big mistake. There's a second James E. Johnson. And another thing, he also is black. And can you guess what his birth date is?"

I shook my head.

"March 3, 1926."

I gulped. "That's my birth date." I was dazed.

"What's your serial number, Johnny?"

"You have it right there, sir, 673724."

"Guess what this other Johnson's serial number is? 673724."

"For the past six years, all your outstanding fitness reports have been going into this other Johnson's jacket. He's been promoted twice on your good fitness reports."

I sighed. The whole fiasco hadn't been an act of prejudice, just sheer error, a fantastic mistake. The other Johnson was black like me. I saw how unfair I'd been in accusing others of prejudice when I was the one guilty of projecting it. By accusing people of acting out of prejudice when they weren't, I had actually magnified prejudice, kept it alive.

"Are you prepared to take an examination for promotion?"

"Yes, sir!" I almost shouted. "Wait till my wife hears about this."

In a few days, I took the examination. Within a few months I had been promoted from staff sergeant to gunnery sergeant to master sergeant. The Marine Corps was making up for the injustice I had suffered. My spirits soared.

Also in 1952, a decision came from Washington that anyone who was a staff sergeant or higher could get a commission by applying and appearing before a screening board of two majors and a lieutenant colonel. I applied and qualified for the hearing.

When the board got to me, I walked into the conference room and heard a lieutenant colonel say to the two majors, "You two may be excused. I can handle this myself." He turned to me. "Johnny, let me tell you something. I've gone through your record, and you've got the finest record I've ever seen in my life," he said. "It's just too bad."

"What's too bad, sir?"

"Well, Johnny, nothing against you, but the time is just not right. If we made you a warrant officer, we wouldn't have any place to put you. You wouldn't have anyone to associate with, you'd be lonely. It's just too bad. One of these days you just might make it, but I think right now you'll do better just remaining a sergeant."

"Colonel, is this some kind of joke? You say I've got the best record you've ever seen, and yet you're not going to promote me."

"I can't promote you. I've got my own future to worry about, too.

If I made you a warrant officer, I would probably never make full colonel."

"You know, I'm not just going to let this lie! I'll have to report it."

"Now, wait a minute. You can't report it. It's just you and me talking. Who do you think they'll believe? I'll tell them I had a look at your record, you had a low test score, and your personality would not be representative as an officer. Who do you think they are going to believe?"

"I don't think they'll believe that, the people who know me."

"Aw, now, Johnny, don't be silly. The white man says the black man is green, and everybody believes it."

I went out of there and cried. And I went to two people I could trust, Lieutenant Colonel Harry D. Clarke and Lieutenant Colonel James A. Mitchener. They couldn't believe my story. "We'll make sure the lieutenant colonel never gets any higher in this man's Marine Corps."

Because they felt there was an injustice being done to a black Marine, these two white officers put their career on the line. They wrote a letter to Marine Corps headquarters recommending me again and again, for seven years.

Meanwhile, a lot of other events were taking place.

All had been quiet on the home front only in a relative sense. After I'd been home for several months, as spring came and went, I realized that Juanita was keeping pretty much to herself. Only one or two children ever came over to play with Ken. I made her square with me.

"It's the neighbors," she said.

Most of them had not accepted the fact that a Negro family had moved in.

Then something came along that brought our immediate neighbors and ourselves to the same level.

I'd been working hard all day at the officers' club not long after the Fourth of July, feeling depressed at the lack of progress in peace talks concerning Korea, revelations coming from Senator Estes Kefauver's inquiry into crime, and the controversy surrounding Senator Joseph McCarthy's probe into communism.

At suppertime, I went home. Juanita had been busy moving furniture, and after a quick dinner, I retired to the bedroom to crack a couple of books.

Sometime after midnight, long after Juanita had fallen asleep, I became aware that the air outside was no longer quiet. The wind had been blowing, and it was becoming more intense. Our house overlooking the charming little lake was set on pillars to afford more air circulation in the subtropical climate, and the wind was thumping up from beneath as well as rattling at the doors and windows.

Growing up in Chicago, I was well acquainted with wind, but by the time I was ready for bed, I was beginning to wonder at the ferocity of this one.

I was awakened later by Juanita's shaking, or was it the house? "We're going to be airborne in a few more minutes. I think it's a hurricane." She was holding a battery lantern. "The lights are out."

"Huh?" I rubbed my eyes, then jumped up and hurried to the window. The world was flying apart. Tree limbs, garbage cans, lumber—all creation seemed to be hurtling through the air like grotesque shapes against a strangely luminous sky. The house wobbled crazily. Juanita screamed, "The roof!"

She grabbed Ken and tried to protect him with her body. I could see only blackness over us; there were walls, furniture, and books around us, and above, nothing but clouds and rain.

I rushed Juanita and Ken into the back bedroom. "Under the bed!" I shouted. I followed and prayed desperately for our safety as we lay there, huddled together.

We spent the rest of the night under the bed, while the storm screeched and howled at the house. No debris, luckily, only rain came down from above, salt rain. We could hear it hammering down on the floor and feel water lapping in under the bed, water with a peculiar sea smell.

In the morning the wind had died down, and the house was still standing. We gave a long prayer of thanks to God, then started bailing out water, mopping up as best we could.

Tommy Stringer, who occasionally came to play with Ken, arrived and stood in our living room looking up at the morning sky. He thought it was neat to be able to see the clouds floating overhead. A few minutes later his mother came looking for him.

She breathed a sigh of relief. "In all the excitement he just slipped away from us. You really should have come over to the disaster center, you know."

"Disaster center?" Juanita looked at me. I looked back dumbly.

"Why, yes. Our roof stayed put, but there was no way of knowing it would," she commented. "We'd just left the center to check our house when Tommy ran off. It's liable to rain some more. Power lines are down all over, and broken glass is everywhere. I was worried sick when I couldn't find the little stinker."

"I don't understand," I said.

Just then Sergeant Stringer came through the open door. "Martha! Tommy!" He eyed his wife and child with disapproval. "It's dangerous to be running around the neighborhood with all this junk around." A few drops of rain came down on him, and he started. Then he looked up.

"For Pete's sake! Better get some tarp over that." He regarded Juanita and me with a puzzled frown. "Where did you take shelter? I didn't see you at the disaster center."

"We didn't know anything about the disaster center," I said.

"Didn't you know there was a hurricane coming? Didn't the adjutant's office phone you to evacuate to the large brick building? God! You could have been killed!"

He glanced down at Ken. The kids were trying to get an umbrella open. There was a light drizzle coming down, and I was wondering if it was going to start pouring rain.

"Is the phone still working?" the sergeant asked. He went to it, red in the face. "I just hope it wasn't deliberate. Even if it was just carelessness, it's bad enough." He lifted the receiver off the hook. "Still working," he said, and dialed. "Maintenance? Sergeant Stringer here. Listen, you stupid jerks, this guy Johnson wasn't warned about the hurricane last night. His roof's gone, and all of his stuff's wet. He and his family could have been killed. I'm only a sergeant, but I've got a lot of pull around this joint, and if you guys don't get a crew down here to fix things up on the double, it'll be your necks, I promise you. Bring plenty of tarp with you, too." He banged the receiver down. The sergeant and his family left. The maintenance crew, wearing guilty expressions, came to make temporary repairs and take notes on major restoration work. The people who lived next door returned from the shelter and, after surveying their own relatively undamaged home, stopped by to see what was going on. They seemed apologetic that they had hardly spoken to us since we'd moved onto the base.

"I guess we were a little standoffish," Corporal Edwards remarked. "It takes something like this to make people realize how stupid they've been. Listen, what can we do to help?"

"Yeah, it does take something like this to make us realize how much we really have," I agreed. "We weren't worried about our household goods. We're just thankful to God we came through it."

I was wondering whether God had allowed this blow at us to wake us all up to the true values of life. Was this perhaps His way of reconciling us with the people of our neighborhood?

But we soon learned that the hurricane emergency hadn't affected everyone on the base in the same way. The following day, when the Stringers told us about a summer nursery school opening in a few days, they suggested we sign Kenneth up.

Juanita phoned the principal. "Oh, you're Mrs. Johnson?" He hesitated. "Pardon me, but I do recognize your name, and I'm sorry to say we just don't have any colored children in this school."

Sensing what Juanita was hearing, I took the phone. I asked him to repeat what he'd said. Then I replied, "I guess I'll have to take this to the commanding general."

"Be reasonable, Sergeant Johnson. It's the teachers I'm concerned about."

I hung up as gently as I could.

The next day I showed up at the general's office. He remembered me. "What is it now?" he sighed.

"I just want my kid to go to nursery school." I described my conversation with the principal.

"Sergeant, I can't help you. That's a private thing. It's not an official Marine Corps activity."

"As long as it's on the base, you have authority over that school. If you tell them to get off the base, I won't say anything else about it, but as long as they are on federal land and in government quarters, *my kid has a right to go to that school.*"

By this time, I'd lost all feeling of hesitancy about claiming my rights as a free and equal human being. I was entitled to every single privilege enjoyed by anyone else, and I did not feel as though I had to back down just because standing up for what was right meant rocking the boat.

The general must have read the determination in my eyes. He nodded. "Okay, Johnson. I'll instruct the principal to integrate the nursery school. Good day, Sergeant."

"Thank you very much, sir." I pivoted on my heel and marched out.

Before the opening day of school, Juanita got several phone calls. I even got some calls at work.

"Your kid might not get home from school!" And, "If he ends up in the lake don't blame anyone; it'll be your fault!" Or, "You don't care about your kid dying."

The callers didn't identify themselves.

I prayed for strength to face the issue without fear and without anger—to let God handle it. But the last couple of threats and my wife's anxiety got to me. I went down to the provost marshal. By the time I was ushered into his office, I'd forgotten all about leaving everything to God. On the other hand, I had no way of knowing whether or not Christ was filling me with the spirit that sparked me. He had reacted violently on occasion, such as when He overturned the money tables at the temple.

"I want to tell you something, sir. I can fight discrimination politely up to a point. But not when people threaten my wife and kid."

"Well . . . ?"

"Just this, sir. I have a .22 rifle and a .30-.30 rifle and a shotgun. Also, I have an M-1 rifle with plenty of ammunition. If anything happens to my son at that nursery school, I'm going to take this base apart. That's not a threat; it's a promise!"

The PM eyed me grimly. "Well, Sergeant, I guess we had better relieve you of your weapons."

"The only way you'll get them is to *take* them," I said, regretting the tone, but compelled to emphasize that I meant business.

"We can't have this sort of trouble. . . ."

"I'm just asking you to afford me the protection guaranteed by the Constitution and the Supreme Court."

The provost marshal coughed. "If you absolutely refuse to withdraw your boy from the school, I'll have to assign some men. You're asking an awful lot."

"Just what anyone's entitled to. That's the whole point."

"There's no use discussing it any further. We'll have some MPs down there."

I hoped he meant it. Just to make sure, I went to the nursery school and waited. Four MPs showed up. Two of them were stationed in the classroom where Ken was. Another was posted out in the hall, and the fourth patrolled outside.

Again, I was sick that such measures had to be necessary in the *United States of America*. What was wrong with people? Again, why, why, why? The question buzzed in my brain.

One teacher quit the second day. By the third day, in spite of the fact so many people had seemed so afraid of this one little black child, the head teacher, Mrs. Watson, phoned Juanita to say how much she enjoyed Ken. "He's a sweet little guy, one of the most charming little boys I've ever met. The other kids seem to love him. I can't understand why there was so much fuss."

After a few more days, the MPs were withdrawn. We banked on the assumption that the callers had been a radical minority and bluffers. Surely they now realized that any violence would be speedily punished. For their own good.

Gradually, things were looking up. One by one, other Negroes moved aboard the base, encouraged by my stand. The NCO club was integrated. Negroes were allowed to work in the PX along with the whites. The separate-entrance door was boarded up. The commanding general consulted me when racial flare-ups seemed imminent, and harmony was restored. My insight into white/black relationships was growing.

I got wound up one day rapping with Colonel Lanigan about why I wasn't bitter that whites had given me a bad time on the base. I testified I couldn't hate, and lately I had learned how to make a friend each day. I told him something else I was only beginning fully to realize for myself.

"Christ told us to love one another," I reminded him, "even to love our enemies. And love isn't just a mushy, sentimental notion. Love can be harsh, too." I paused, remembering way back in boot camp, where the NCOs had turned green recruits into men.

"Love doesn't treat other people wrong," I said. "And real love for the other fellow doesn't let him get by with doing an injustice to another man."

Boy! The Lord had given me a powerful insight through which to focus all my efforts to end discrimination. No wonder I was finding myself unable to hate. No wonder I'd felt guilty about my own threats. Opening the doors of freedom was supposed to be motivated by God's own love for all concerned!

CHAPTER

11

During the summer of 1953, I received a letter that made me blink in disbelief. It was from the Marine Corps commandant, General Lemuel C. Shephard. The letter said that, in recognition of my performance as administrator of the officers' club and previous record of achievement, I had been selected, subject to my approval, to be part of a three-man investigation and inspection team. The team would tour the various bases to look into the operation of officers' clubs and determine how well they were organized and run. A giant step up.

The other two members of the team were Warrant Officer Perry S. Brenton and Gunnery Sergeant Leo McDowell.

Sergeant McDowell was an outstanding man who had done fantastic work in criminal investigations to uncover drug addicts, homosexuals, and latent psychopaths in the Marine Corps. He was not only a top investigator, but he was also black. He had a chest full of ribbons for combat service in the Navy, and later, in the Marine Corps during World War II and the Korean conflict. It was going to be an unusual team with Brenton, a white Baptist, leader over two blacks.

Juanita, Ken, and I had to move back to Washington D.C., so

that I could be closer to Marine Corps headquarters, my home base.

We made the long drive back during the night hours to avoid the midsummer heat and heavy traffic, and arrived in Washington as the rising sun silhouetted the trees. The drive into the city was quiet. I reached over and took Juanita's hand. "Do you feel as if this is home, honey?"

Juanita smiled. She knew what I meant. "If only the housing situation were like Parris Island."

"I still think of this as our honeymoon town," I said. "I guess it's appropriate we've decided to buy our first home here."

No matter what main avenue you decide to drive down in Washington, the great white dome of the United States Capitol rises above the trees. Every time I see that building, I get a lump in my throat. The structure is linked with the people and this nation's ideals of freedom and opportunity. It gives me the proof I need, in stone and marble, of the capacity of the people to govern themselves.

I always remember my dad quoting Abraham Lincoln, who said when the critics complained of the cost of the building itself, "If the people see the Capitol going on it is a sign the Union shall go on."

The housing problem wasn't easy to solve. We'd been invited to stay with Juanita's family while we house-hunted and tramped the streets after calling realtor after realtor. Since I didn't tell them over the phone we were Negro, but that I was in the Marines and wanted to buy a house, they always answered, "Oh yes, Sergeant Johnson. We have a house for you. Come right on over."

But when we got there, it was, "Sorry, Sergeant Johnson. That house has just been sold." Or, "I didn't realize you had a child. This house I had in mind would be far too small."

After two weeks, we contacted a black realtor through a friend. He sent us to a white realtor, with whom he worked, who had located a house at Fourth and Webster in Northwest Washington. "Why are you taking us in this section of town?" Juanita questioned the salesman. "I thought this was an all-white area."

"Wait till you see the house," he said, ignoring her question. "I think it will be just what you want. And if you think the payments are too steep, you can rent the upper floor. It's a solid-brick house, and the upstairs apartment is complete in itself."

Juanita was impressed by the large rooms and the cleanliness; she went through the house with a dreamy look on her pretty face. By the time the man had shown us the local school, nearest church, and the surrounding area, Juanita and I were sold on buying that house.

"Ken will have just a short walk to school, too!" She turned to the salesman. "He starts first grade this year."

We didn't take long to think about it. We bought it. By the time the paperwork was finished and we'd moved in, the Korean War had finally ended. We thought our prayers had been answered, both with the war ending and the house we wanted in our possession. But the neighborhood decided to start its own little war.

By the time we became dimly aware of this, we'd already found that realtors used unscrupulous scare tactics known as "blockbusting" to find houses for black people in Washington. They would find one vacant house in a good white neighborhood, and move in a colored family—a family with nine kids plus that many cats and dogs.

Then they would scurry around to all the neighbors to tell them they could give them a good price for their house if they sold quickly, "before the price drops," because "your new neighbors are gonna turn this into a 'colored' neighborhood."

We soon found we were the only Negroes living in our neighborhood, and we weren't welcome. The neighbors themselves tried scare tactics on the phone.

"Nigger, get out of this street or else," one guy threatened.

Another growled, "We don't want your kind here."

I was approached by quite a few home buyers, one of whom offered to buy the house for nearly double the price we had paid.

"Thank you very much, but we'll stay right here," I replied.

The day before school was to start, the telephone calls became more numerous. Now I realized how serious the situation was. I wasn't the only one involved. I had Juanita and Ken to think about. He was just a little six-year-old boy who was excited about starting the first grade. Juanita had taken him shopping for his school needs; he could hardly wait to use his new lunchbox.

In 1953, the general ruling in the area was that only those kids who lived in a particular district would attend the school in that district, the idea being to keep white schools white. The district policymakers had no idea that a black family lived in the district with a child of school age.

When a caller announced that he and his friends planned to burn a cross on my lawn, I saw red. That would be the signal for all the psychopaths in town to use our house as their proving ground—the first step to mayhem and murder. As far as school was concerned, I told the callers, "They'd better watch their step. If they harm one hair on Ken's head, I'll tear that school down brick by brick."

Juanita didn't want Ken to start school. "How do we know there won't be an accident of some kind? Why can't we keep him home for a while until this dies down?"

I couldn't take the easy way, copping out. God had given me a mission, and I meant to carry it out. I went to the police station and asked for protection. Four policemen were assigned to help us protect one six-year-old lad. One policeman walked with Ken; another stayed outside in the schoolyard. It took another in the hallway and the fourth one in the classroom, just like the MPs at the nursery school in Parris Island.

Juanita phoned me at the office about midafternoon. "Honey," she pleaded, "would you mind going over and checking on him at school?"

"I'm sure he'll be okay," I assured her. "But I'll check. I'll talk to his teacher, see how he's doing."

I hung up, then tore out for the school, praying he really would be all right.

I parked away from the school, walked over, and spotted Ken out playing.

Jeers from about twenty grown men and women hanging over the fence, pointing to Ken, sickened me. I asked the policeman guarding the playground how things were going. "Most of them are just curious, Sergeant," he drawled. "But a few of them are pretty rabid. Don't pay no attention to what they're saying."

Just then a woman shouted, "There he is, there's his nigger father. He won't ruin our school!" She went on in that vein, but the rest of the men and women around her began to drift off.

I went in to talk with Ken's teacher. She said everybody enjoyed having Ken in the class. "I'm sure this will die down, Sergeant Johnson. As long as we have police protection, parents will see we don't mean to give in."

I was grateful that she felt that way. When I went out, Ken came running at me. I had time to take a picture of him on his first day of school, neatly dressed in his new clothes. He jumped into my arms. "Come on, son. I think we'll go home now," I said, almost having to choke back tears. "You can introduce me to your new friends tomorrow."

He grabbed my hand happily, barely glancing at the people jeering at the fence. He didn't even know that all that hatred and abuse were being poured out at him. I hoped I wouldn't have to tell him that his new friends' mothers and fathers didn't want him there. Nor did I want to explain to him that he was the first Negro boy to integrate a public school in Washington, D.C.

After a few weeks, the school officials decided that three policemen could be withdrawn. The fourth remained to remind parents that the law would be enforced.

One of the first assignments of our inspection team was checking out the officers' club at a southern camp where I'd been stationed a few years before as a private. No one looked at us as being very threatening; they didn't take us seriously. We quickly established ourselves on the base and looked into the handling of funds, foods, and liquor. We soon discovered that many officers did not pay for anything at the officers' club.

We wrote up the report and presented it to Brenton.

He read it.

"I know that report is absolutely scorching," I said. "Someone is going to get fired and might even go to jail."

"I call a ball a ball, and a strike a strike," Brenton said, and I could see that he was a man after my own heart. No compromise with truth.

The next morning we went in to see the commanding general. The report was written to the commandant of the Marine Corps via the commanding general and via the quartermaster general of the base. When the commanding general looked at it, he jumped up from his chair. "What is this?"

"That is a factual document," said Brenton.

"You take this thing back and rewrite it, and this time you better write it right."

Brenton stood his ground. "General, I call a ball a ball, a strike a strike."

"Listen, if you don't change this report, I had better not find one of your men on a base where I am commanding general."

"General, I am turning in the report the way it is," Brenton concluded.

We went back to Marine Corps headquarters and turned in the report. The document went right up to the top. The commanding general was given forty-eight hours to pack up and shove off to retirement.

I was staggered. Suddenly an enormous power had been thrust into my hands.

On a couple of assignments, we were involved in breaking down covert racial discrimination, the subtle, lingering kind that is so insidious.

But we still couldn't get a haircut.

One morning, we decided to bring the issue to a head—our heads. Leo McDowell and I walked into the Cherry Point, North Carolina, Marine base barber shop. Someone was in the officers' chair, having his blond tresses trimmed. The staff NCO's chair was vacant, while a couple of people were in the "anybody's" chairs in the rear. I motioned for Leo to sit in the staff NCO's chair. He did.

The barber turned from the sink where he'd been washing his hands. "Hey, what gives, Sergeant? Hey, now, listen, you know, fella, I can't cut your hair. Why don't you wait for Willie, down there at the other end of the shop?" He pointed to a Negro barber. "He can cut colored hair."

"What do you mean, 'colored hair'?" Leo asked. "My hair isn't colored. It's black."

"No, you don't understand, Sergeant. I just can't cut your hair."

I spoke up. "Can the Negro barber cut white people's hair?"

"Of course," the barber said.

"Supposing that he couldn't cut white people's hair. Only Negroes'. Could he keep his job?"

"Uh, er, I don't think so," the barber muttered. "If he refused, he'd be fired."

"You'll have to cut Leo's hair, then. Otherwise, you'll have to be fired."

The barber got red in the face. "Oh yeah? We'll see about that!" He stalked to the door and left the shop.

Before we could decide on our next move, he returned with a young major.

"What are you two, anyway? Troublemakers?"

"Sir, we're not making trouble. Just trying to get our hair cut," I said.

"Then you just go down to that end of the shop and wait for the black barber."

"Look," I replied, "no one else had to do that. If these people are not as smart as that black barber, then they should have all black barbers in this shop. That way, you'll be able to have everybody get their hair cut in here by competent barbers on equal terms."

I sighed and turned to Leo. "Guess we'll just have to take this up with the Silver Fox."

The major and the barber winced. The Silver Fox was the chief of staff of the base, so named because of his silver-white hair.

We marched over to see the chief of staff, who certainly did not want us to go back and talk to the commandant. By now everyone knew about the general being relieved of his duty.

The chief of staff found the major and said, "Get over there and tell those barbers to cut anybody's hair who comes along. If they can't cut the hair, they had better start practicing, or pick up their tools and check out."

"Yes, sir," said the major. He left, but not before telling us, "You two are not going to go very far in this Marine Corps. You're probably as high now as you'll ever get. I'd like to see you two get off this base; you just want to start trouble."

At the barber shop, he told the barbers, "You'll have to cut their hair. The chief says so. These guys are from Marine Corps headquarters."

"I don't care if they're from Heaven," the barber said. "I'll leave first." He scooped up his personal effects and departed.

The other white barber in the shop tried to avoid the major's eye, but realized he couldn't escape. "Aw, okay, I'll cut their hair."

Leo got into the chair first. I watched closely. Then it was my turn.

We had our hair cut, but we declined letting him use the razor.

It was a poor haircut, but we went there every Friday. It was the beginning of integration in the barber shops. Theaters, officers' clubs, base housing, barber shops—what would be next? Some of the Marine base officers' clubs we inspected had no problems at all, and we could give them a clean report. One of our inspection tours took us to Hawaii.

"Honey, I can't offer you a trip to Hawaii," I told Juanita after I'd been back in Washington a few weeks, "but how about going to Florida with me, to the Opalocka Marine base near Miami for two or three weeks? We've been separated long enough."

While we were in Florida, on the way to work one morning I noticed an amusement park. A couple of days later, Juanita and Ken and I started out for the park. We moved up in a long line that crawled forward, and all the way to the ticket window no one around us spoke a word. I noted a few icy stares. I had my money ready. Finally, at the ticket window, I said, "Two adults, one child."

The man in the box said, "Don't y'all know any better'n to come here? Cain't y'all read?" He pointed to a sign. "Thursday is the day for the colored people. Now move on."

"Look, we've been waiting a long time, and my son just wants a few rides." I held up Ken so the man could see how little he was.

"If we let you in, we'll set a precedent; we'll lose all our white trade. You can understand that, I'm sure." He looked impatient.

A few of the people around us were getting impatient, too. "No, sir," I said. "I can't understand it."

A heavy hand fell on my shoulder. I swung around. Four brawny white gorillas were behind me.

"Look," one of them growled, "we want to tell ya somethin'. We are all members of the Klan here in this line, and we are tired of waitin', and we've been watchin' and listenin', and if ya see a cross burnin' on yore front lawn tonight, you'll know it was us."

Juanita gasped. I took her arm and hurried her out, holding Ken in my arms. By the time we got to our car, she was in tears.

That night we both prayed for guidance. Juanita agreed it was wrong for the owner of the place to practice discrimination, especially since the amusement park was on government land within the jurisdiction of the base.

"I'll see the commanding general," I said. "If he won't do anything, this will go in our report."

After explaining what had happened, I said to the commanding general, "If you really want to carry out the commandant's wishes, sir, all you have to do is put that place off-limits. It'll be a feather in your cap."

Later the general called me back, assured me that the discrimination problem had been solved, and I could go there any day I wanted. He even gave me some passes.

The happy look on Juanita's face was reward enough, but we even got a grudging smile from the fellow at the gate. We had such a good time I told Leo McDowell about it the next morning. He went over there that night.

The following morning he looked glum. "I'm sorry to tell you, Johnny, but that place isn't integrated. They just made a special case for you. That's what those passes were about."

We wrote it all up in our report and gave a copy to the general. It was a good thing we left for Washington right away, because as soon as that report went through channels, the general was relieved of his duties. The new commanding general put the amusement park off-limits until it integrated, which it did immediately to avoid losing business.

Some time later, our inspection team was sent to El Toro Marine base to investigate rumors that minority groups were being placed only in soft-skill jobs, and we were trying to confirm it. Word had leaked ahead of us, and someone had done a good job of planning to discredit us.

The three members of our team had had dinner, and were returning to our quarters, when we heard voices and music coming from our room. I unlocked the door, and a blast of cigarette smoke and loud music hit me. Two girls in low-necked cocktail dresses lounged on our beds. They'd made a makeshift bar out of one of our bedside tables. It was littered with overflowing ashtrays, liquor bottles, and glasses.

I started to ask what they were doing here when Leo went over, grabbed each by the arm, and pushed them out the door.

I looked out in the hall just in time to see two guys coming along with cameras.

"Back inside and close the door!" Leo shouted.

I jumped back, slammed the door shut, and leaned against it. There was a knock.

"Don't answer it," Leo warned. "It's a trap!"

"What . . . how . . . ?" I stammered.

Leo laughed. "An old married man like you wouldn't know about badgers, would you?"

"I don't know," I yelped, "but whoever went to all that trouble deserves to be mentioned in our report."

We reported the incident immediately to the CID (Criminal Investigation Division), the officer of the day, and the barracks desk man. Brenton even got on to the commanding general, accusing him of setting us up. They kindly posted a guard outside our door.

After the mess was cleaned up, I realized I had something else to be thankful about: The frameup hadn't worked.

This was our last inspection tour. Leo and Mr. Brenton decided to stay in California. I went back to Washington, of course. My family was waiting for me with open arms.

I was in the Navy Annex of Marine Corps headquarters when someone said President Eisenhower was taking a stroll through. Everybody was to be at their desks and rise when he entered the room.

The Secret Service people came first, checking our records, looking behind pictures and under our desks, inspecting everything right down to fingernails. When the President came through, he spotted me.

I snapped to attention, then shook hands with him.

"Sergeant, how are you?"

"Mr. President, just fine, sir."

"What's your job?"

"I'm one of the auditors and investigators for the Marine Corps clubs, messes, and supply areas," I answered.

"Investigator?" His voice rose.

"Yes, sir."

"What have you found?"

There was a shuffle behind the President, and I could see my commanding officer looking hard at me.

"Sir," I said, choosing my words carefully, "we've found a number of things wrong, but we promptly made them right."

"Fine, fine," President Eisenhower commented. "But have you

found anyone stealing?" He'd asked a leading question, looking straight at me. I was on the spot with a Marine Corps colonel and a warrant officer staring coldly at me.

"Yes, sir, we have."

He raised his eyebrows. "How many of those men are in jail?"

The colonel stepped forward quickly. "Sir, we have a lot of them under investigation. What Sergeant Johnson really meant was that we have some suspects who are still being investigated."

"Tell me, how did you find out these people were stealing?"

"We investigated the clubs by auditing the books, purchases versus sales, and if they didn't match, we investigated further. We talked to the people operating the clubs. Most were very honest, admitted they may have taken a few things, but named others who were big stealers."

"I don't see why you have to investigate any longer, Colonel," the President said. "I think you've got a good case now, men admitting guilt. I would expect to see them in jail."

"Yes, sir. Yes, sir. I certainly will take care of it, Mr. President."

I could see that the colonel didn't want me to say anything more, and I didn't blame him. There were some hot issues that would take a lot of explaining.

"Keep up the good work, Sergeant. You're doing a fine job," the President said.

"Thank you, sir, I certainly will."

The colonel came back later and patted me on the back. "Sergeant Johnson, that was one time I was afraid all of those courses you take might have gone to your head, and the President would have been standing here for a week, listening to you." He grinned. Then he sighed. "It's bad enough that all those cases have to be written up and names named. But we don't have to air our dirty linen before the President of the United States."

I nodded gravely. "A-men!"

CHAPTER

12

In 1956 I enrolled in the Instructors' Training School at Camp Le Jeune, North Carolina. I was learning how to speak properly, use gestures, even use my body to project what I had to say. I soon found myself doing a lot of "talking" outside of class.

This "extracurricular talking" started when Sergeant Graham Smith moved in to share my quarters.

Sergeant Smith was tall, lanky, and gaunt. His shock of red hair was dull, his eyes were red-rimmed and bloodshot. I was glad enough for the companionship, but I was uneasy about my late hours. Not only did I have a lot of studying to do, I also anointed myself with more midnight oil by reading from the Bible every night. I had made a pledge to God that I would do this, and I meant to keep my promise.

I felt so thankful for His presence in my life. Ever since I had felt His presence in the wake of that Carolina hurricane, life had been going better for me. Being appointed to the inspection team had been a miracle in itself, and being able effectively and successfully to improve the operation of the clubs I'd visited was a blessing.

As soon as Sergeant Smith moved into the quarters, I noted that he wasn't being inconvenienced by my late hours studying and reading Scripture, but his drinking problem was disturbing my concentration. The sergeant had set up a regular "bar" in his corner of our room: six ounces of vodka before bed, six ounces of Bourbon for breakfast and both of them mixed for lunch.

Every Sunday when I went to church, he remarked, "I wish I could read the Bible and understand it." I didn't realize that this was his way of crying out for help. I continued to study hard, read the Bible, and witnessed to just about everyone except my roommate. I persuaded myself that it would be unfair to impose on him at such close quarters, where he had no escape.

Gradually I became aware that he often came in late, presumably from bar-hopping, and topped off the evening with a double portion of his "secret" nightcap.

As soon as he stirred in the morning, his arm reached out and his hand curled around the bottle on his nightstand.

I ached for him, feeling that he must be suffering to be so dependent on liquor. Still, I didn't know what to do to help him.

One day one of his coworkers, Corporal Adam Jacobson, walked by me at the NCOs' club. "You know, that Sergeant Smith must be an alcoholic. Have you seen him drink in the barracks? One of the officers suspects it; he's going to have him dropped from his class and hospitalized."

"Alcoholic?" I raised my eyebrows. That really put me on the spot. I knew what would happen if he was discovered drinking in the barracks.

Adam sat down at my table. "Yeah, he shows all the signs." He went on to name a few that should have been obvious to me.

I thought about this for a couple of minutes. "Actually, then, even when he's not saying anything," I said slowly, "he's crying for help."

That hand that stretched out for the bottle every morning was a hand reaching out for help. The only thing ready to receive that grip was the neck of a fifth of vodka. Or Bourbon. Or whatever.

A hand ought to be there. I got up and went to my room.

A couple of other people were there, bending over Graham.

"What's wrong?"

"Oh, just the usual with this sort of thing," a corpsman said. He and his assistant helped my roommate out to the waiting ambulance. "We're taking him to the base hospital. We'll see if we can convince him to save his liver. He'll be shipshape in a few days after he dries out."

I felt guilty. Maybe I could have helped him.

They kept him in the hospital for only three days. He came back and said, "I think I can make it this time, and the Corps isn't pressing any charges."

He spread out the medical literature he was reading. I noticed a picture of a lousy-looking liver. "That's what happens to me when I tank up." He punched a fist into the palm of his hand. "I'm going to stop. I mean it this time," he almost sobbed.

Two nights later, when I came in from a Bible study at the chapel, Graham wasn't home yet. I prepared for an examination the following morning, read a few pages in the Book of Ephesians, then turned off the light, said a prayer, and went to sleep. Sometime during the night my dreams were cockeyed. I awoke and heard, "Glug, glug, glug, glug."

I squinted in the darkness. The hand was clasped around a bottle. It all seemed like a nightmare, and it was. His nightmare.

I knew what I had to do. For so long, I had been praying for myself. I had been witnessing to strangers around the base, to those who weren't too close to me. Now I had to witness to someone very close to me. It might be less convenient to me, might take more effort, cause problems. But I had to do it.

The next morning, after the examination, I hurried back to my quarters, skipping my next class. Something else was suddenly more important. I found him there, all right—just coming out of his stupor.

"That medical literature didn't work, did it?" I asked.

He shook his head, crying, "I just can't leave it alone. I'm just caught up in it. It's a physical thing. I've had it!"

"It's more than a physical thing," I said. "And it's hard to cure it at the hospital. Or even in the mental ward."

He sighed. "They wouldn't be able to do it, either. I just can't be cured, that's all. There's just no hope. I just can't stop."

I got my Bible and sat down beside him. I knew what I was looking for, Philippians 4:13: "I can do all things through Christ, which strengtheneth me." I said, "Read it aloud, Graham."

He read it.

"Read it again."

He read it again.

"Now you have just committed yourself to the truth that you can do all things through Christ." I waited for him to say something, then went on, "What is the first thing you should do?"

"Stop drinking, I guess."

I shook my head. "No. The first thing you have to do," I said, "is to be in favor with Christ."

He looked forlorn. "Jesus doesn't like me. I'm a drinker. A gambler. You name it, I've done it."

"If you could help yourself, would you do it?"

"Of course I would."

"It's so simple and so easy, you won't believe it can be done."

"What's so simple?"

"Accepting Christ. All you have to do is to believe that Christ died on the cross to save you and to eliminate your sins. 'Believe in the Lord Jesus Christ, and you will be saved.'" I quoted Acts 16:31.

"That's too simple for me to believe. What will happen?"

"All I can tell you is this," I answered. "Christ said every word of the Bible is true, and it will never fail."

"I'll give it some thought," he said. It was time for my next class. Maybe I'd given him enough to think about.

When I came back from class, I found him still sitting on his bed, his face in his hands, crying like a baby. "I just can't do it. I just can't do it."

"What's this you can't do?"

"Give up drinking. But I can't go on like this; it's killing me."

"Has anyone ever explained to you about salvation?" I found a passage from Psalms 13:5. "'But I have trusted in thy steadfast love; my heart shall rejoice in thy salvation.'" I showed him the words.

"You know, most people think I have had everything easy in the Marine Corps," I said. "That's not true. But I realized things would not come easy until I recognized Christ was everything, and things would not be the way I wanted them to be until He came first. When I put Him first, things began to change."

I told Graham about my parents' deep Christian feelings and my own imperfect stumblings toward the truth.

"It takes something to make us wake up to our failings and our need for Him," I said. "It took a hurricane to wake me up. It's taking slavery to the bottle to wake you up."

I had to go off to class again, but I couldn't concentrate. The lecturer, a warrant officer, was droning on about the proper address to use with foreign dignitaries; I was thinking about the proper words to use to bring an alcoholic to God.

When the class was finally over, I went back to my quarters.

I knew what I had to do. I asked Graham, "Would you be ashamed to get on your knees and pray with me? And even if someone saw us, would you mind it? That's the first thing, not to be ashamed of the Lord Jesus Christ."

I got down on my knees. Whether he was willing or not, he couldn't stop me from praying for him. "God," I said, "come into Graham's life. Forgive him for the things he's done. Fill him with your love, in Jesus' name."

Tears filled my eyes. I wanted so much to be able to help. Suddenly Graham was on his knees, too, praying in an agonized whisper.

"Jesus Christ," I continued, "fill Graham with the Holy Spirit and make him clean. Help him accept You as his personal Savior." Finally I just knelt there silently. I waited for a long time, breathless, hopeful.

"Oh God! Oh God!" A cry between ecstasy and pain. It was Graham.

Christ was there with us; I could feel His presence.

When I got back from my last evening class, I noticed a nearly full case of liquor on his desk. "Oh Graham, not again!" I moaned.

He was quiet for a moment, then, "You're right. Not again. I had it under my bed. I wondered if you would dispose of it for me." He looked helpless as a newborn babe. He was. He'd just been born again.

I pounced on that case of liquor and took it into a shower, closed the curtain, opened each bottle in turn, and poured the contents down the drain.

Outside the shower I heard a number of guys shouting. "What is he doing in there?"

I came out with a crate of empty bottles, but didn't bother to explain.

For the rest of the time at Camp Le Jeune, while I finished my instructors' course, Sergeant Graham stayed on the wagon. When I left, I was confident he would remain so. I had a renewed faith in God's power to heal our minds and bodies.

Before I left, several people congratulated me on steering Graham away from alcohol. "It wasn't me," I said, "it was Jesus Christ." A year later, I learned that this man had become a lay minister.

In the next two years I needed all the strength and faith I could muster.

In some ways a moderate degree of success in temporal matters continued to buoy me up. After finishing Instructors' School with the highest score, I served for a short time as an instructor at Quantico.

Afterward, I was the first member of my race ever to attend the Sergeant Majors' School at Parris Island, South Carolina. The classes were the roughest I'd ever taken.

During my last week, Juanita, who was pregnant with our third child, came to visit me.

Janice Vernea, our second child, was born June 1955; she is very special (as are all of our children). I had prayed for a daughter and just knew the Lord would hear my prayer. It was six years after Ken was born before Juanita gave me the news that we were expecting another child. I was so excited the time didn't pass fast enough. I kept asking "How long now?" The Lord blessed us with a beautiful big-eyed, curly-haired daughter. I saw as much of her as I could, and as a result I missed a lot of reviewing for my examinations, making me end up third in the class. I kidded Juanita about that.

It was worth it. I missed her so much, having to transfer around to further my career, and there were times like these when I had to ask how much I must sacrifice. It was good that Juanita was with me all the way in my objective of running for U. S. Senate in 1974.

The continued rejection of my application for warrant or commissioned officer promotions was beginning to get under my skin. I became a little touchy, in spite of trying to handle the matter by holding fast to my faith in Christ's management of my life, and trying to understand His purpose in withholding the promotion from me.

An incident after I'd returned to Washington, as a supply assistant, revealed that a military-political conspiracy based on racial discrimination was responsible for the turndowns.

My job was to handle communications from Marine Corps headquarters, summarize them, and give them to Colonel Wally Green. I also had to summarize what left his office. The work was what I'd gone to Sergeant Majors' School to learn, and I was trying to do it well. When, after several months, suddenly no more work came across my desk for action, for summarizing, posting, analysis, and recommendation, which I customarily was asked to make, I started to wonder.

After a couple of weeks of this, I began to brood. "What's going on, God?" I asked, only to get no answer.

Finally, I decided the reason I was being treated like this was because Colonel Green was prejudiced. I came in as usual at six o'clock one morning and waited for him. "Colonel," I said, "I don't know what to say except to be blunt and come right out with it. I come in early and don't complain about work. I'm the first one here, the last out. I make sure all the work is done, never argue that it's too hard or too much. I've done my best. Suddenly, no work. You're not giving me work to do anymore. No one here is giving me anything to do. I . . ." The words were there, ready to be said. "All I can think, Colonel, is that you're prejudiced against me."

The colonel sat up straight in his chair. "Do you really believe that?"

"Yes, sir. I can't think of any other reason."

"I'm sorry you said that, Johnny, but since you did, maybe I can explain. Every morning, I come in and always see Johnny Johnson, man on the spot, cleaning my office, straightening things up, getting things going."

He gestured around the room. "When I get ready to go for lunch, Johnny Johnson is there, getting things worked out. While I'm gone, you come into my office, straighten my desk, make sure everything is correct and that I don't forget anything. You make sure the seals are on papers, that things are signed in the right places. When I get ready to leave at night, there's Johnny Johnson, the last person here, working, making sure everything's correct."

The colonel stood up and peered out the window at the morning sun. "I started thinking about all that. I called Sergeant Major Folsom and reminded him about how hard you worked. I said, 'From now on, we're not going to kill a good man just because he's the best doggone Marine we have here. You guys are just sitting around back here, and he's doing all the work.' I told them that from here on out, if anyone around here is going to get a break, Johnny Johnson will be the man. 'No more overloading him with work, Folsom. From now on, we'll make sure he gets out of here on time to be with his family like everybody else.'" The colonel sat down and smiled.

I could have dug a hole. Suddenly I realized how trigger-happy I had been in jumping to conclusions—not prejudice, just misunderstanding. I felt something within laughing at me, and it made me mad at myself. Actually, it was the best thing that could have happened to me. I had *needed* to put my foot in my mouth, to come down from my martyr attitude, my holier-than-thou persecution complex. I took a deep breath.

"Colonel," I finally said, "I was really stupid. I don't know what got into me. It was the dumbest thing for me to say that. Colonel, if you can ever forgive me for this, from now on, I'll never claim anyone is prejudiced against me even if they are." I had to work my throat muscles to keep talking. "Colonel, I was wrong. Dead wrong. I'm sorry."

"Don't worry about it, eh?" he said. "I didn't hear a word you said when you came in. One of these days you're going to be someone great, because you aren't afraid to admit when you're wrong."

"Colonel, you are someone great, and you'll be greater." I put my chin in the air. "You know what I think? I think you're going to be Commandant of the Marine Corps!"

I didn't know why I'd said that, but all of a sudden, I was completely turned around from the mood I'd been in. I felt filled again with love, courage—and confidence that the Holy Spirit had guided my actions and speech to make things come out right.

The colonel laughed. "Commandant of the Marine Corps? That's very flattering of you, Johnny. No, I'm at my height right now, as a colonel."

I saluted him and went out. But the idea persisted. And Wally Green *was* Commandant of the Marine Corps—from 1964 to 1968.

Just after this humbling, I was to be humbled in a far deeper way, and reminded of God's pattern of mortality.

The trouble with the colonel seemed to be a small test of my faith, which I had failed because of overwork, complete boredom, and frustration about promotion. I now asked God to keep my faith burning brightly that I might face similar tests more stalwartly. The test prepared me for something far more threatening to my spiritual resources.

I got word from South Bend, Indiana, where Mama and Dad lived, that she was seriously ill. I was startled. I'd received no fore-warning that her health was deteriorating. I took emergency leave.

In her bedroom in the old frame house, I kissed her, sat on the side of her bed to be near her and hear what she wanted to tell me.

She said more than once, "You know, I'm so glad I told everyone my baby was really going to be somebody, because the Lord has shown me you were meant to be something in this world and the next. I think He's shown me you will eventually be a minister."

"I don't know about that, Mama. But I've been witnessing a lot."

"I know He wants you to be a Christian and speak out for Him, unafraid." Her voice sounded weak, but I figured she was just tired and needed some sleep. I was sure she was already feeling better. I thanked the Lord for that.

"Whatever you do, don't ever forget to put God first," she said.

"And don't ever let anyone tell you you aren't an American, be-cause you are," she reminded me. "Your Indian ancestors have al-ways lived here."

Before I left her side, she said, "Be sure to love and respect your wife." She really loved Juanita. She had never forgotten how, when I was eight years old, I had described what I wanted my future wife to be like. "Don't forget, the Lord gave you exactly what you wanted in a wife, so you have to keep her and cherish her."

While I was getting ready to leave, I had a talk with Dad. "She certainly seems to be recovering from whatever it was."

Dad didn't answer directly. Instead, he complained about the harsh medicine the doctors were giving her for what seemed to be an ulcer. "They keep pouring it down her," he said, shaking his head.

I felt positively joyous leaving Mama. I was certain she was recovering. Her face was so radiant, so glowing. An inner light al-most seemed to animate her.

But two weeks after I'd returned home, Dad called to tell me that Mother had gone to be with the Lord.

I took bereavement leave and went back to South Bend, Indiana. I began to realize that Mama had looked full of life because she was full of *life—the eternal life of Jesus Christ.* She knew where she was going, even if we'd forgotten momentarily. She knew she would be with Him, forever.

"There is a time to live, and a time to die . . ." The words stayed with me a long time.

Mama's sudden absence from this physical planet struck my heart. Where do I turn for the love that's gone? How can I get it back? Yesterday, she was somewhere in this world, and I could have run to her if I'd felt the need. Now she was gone.

It was Juanita who reminded me that the love you receive is not really love from your parents or your wife, or other people, but love from God Himself. You should never depend upon your parents or anyone else for ultimate love, but always on God, because then you'll always have it. And the love you are called to show toward other people—that love comes from Him, too.

I continued working for the warrant officer promotion by making official application every year for eight straight years.

In 1959, the last year I applied, I scored 100 per cent on the examination; not only that, but also my two friends, Colonels Mitchener and Clarke, were appointed to the base promotion board that year. This wasn't a 100 per cent guarantee. There were still others whose votes would have to be considered, but it should have looked hopeful to me. However, I'd gone so long expecting success only to meet with failure that I wasn't able to think positively about my chances.

Against me in 1959 was the fact that 720 people had applied for the one warrant officer vacancy and 719 of them were white. I wanted to be the first black warrant officer in United States history. But maybe it was an impossible dream. The odds against me made me feel better, made it easier to resign myself to remaining an NCO.

A friend who was a sergeant also applied for warrant officer. He knew how long my battle had been going on. "Johnny, it's too bad," he said, "I know you're a better man than I am. It's too bad they're going to make only one warrant officer this year." He sighed. "If they were going to make three or four, you might sneak in. But you don't have a chance, Johnny." He patted my arm. "I know I will," he continued. "My record is almost as good as yours. But I have something you don't have."

"What's that?" I asked.

"White skin."

His remarks rankled. "All my life I've had people tell me what was impossible. How do you know it's impossible?"

"I heard some talk you were the best-qualified Marine," he explained. "They said it's too bad you're black. It's unheard-of; too many people hate the idea of a black man coming into the warrant officer field. It's a separate thing, Johnny—white, Protestant, and southern."

"Yeah," I drawled, "I'm only qualified by being a Protestant."

When I went to bed that night, I forced myself to be calm, said a prayer of thanks to God for what He had already given me, and fell asleep as peacefully as a babe.

At two o'clock in the morning the phone rang. "Johnny?" There was a burp, then, "I'm sorry to call you at this hour in the morning, but . . ."

I recognized the voice at once. It was my friend. "Say, matey, I've been drinking half the night. I've been so nervous waiting this thing out. But you know what? I just wanted to . . ." He burped again, then went on, "wanted to say I don't know what this Marine Corps is coming to."

I yawned. "Well, what happened?"

"Would you believe the Marine Corps would have the audacity to put a black man over a white man for warrant officer?"

"I don't know. Why?"

"Haven't you heard?"

"Heard what?"

"You won out! You've been selected to be a warrant officer in the Marine Corps. You know, I'm really proud of you. If it had been any other black guy, I would have hit the ceiling. Of course, I'm disappointed I didn't make it. In fact, I'm going to drink here all night until I get sloppy drunk. Hic."

By now I could hear barroom background noises. "Look, why don't you go home, get yourself a good night's rest, and call me in the morning? I appreciate you calling me and letting me know about my promotion."

After I hung up, I slipped my tongue out of my cheek. Sure. And my brother was elected President.

I went back to sleep hoping I didn't have another alcoholic on my hands. I needed a little counseling myself about now.

At a somewhat more reasonable hour later that morning, around five-thirty, the phone rang again. I grabbed up the phone. "HELLO!"

"That you, Johnny?" The voice on the other end crackled. "I couldn't wait too long to phone you. I know you get up at dawn. This is Colonel Mitchener. In about two or three days, you are going to be one awfully happy man, Johnny. Something good is about to happen to you."

My teeth began to chatter. What my drunken friend had burbled was true!

"Yes, Johnny. We made it!"

We. Johnny Johnson, Colonel James A. Mitchener, Colonel Harry D. Clarke, *and Jesus Christ!*

There was a lot of paperwork and red tape between the initial approval and the actual awarding of warrant officer status. A year's worth of paperwork, almost. Even at this point, one officer tried to dissuade me from accepting. "There's no place a black warrant officer can be assigned," he said. "You'll be lonely. Would you reconsider . . . ?"

"I've worked hard for eight years for this," I replied, "and there isn't anything you could possibly do or say to influence me to give it up."

Also, in the meantime, our son, Kurtis James Johnson—big, healthy, lovable—was born at the Quantico Naval Hospital on September 6, 1959. Juanita had suffered carrying him because of an arthritic hip. But he was a beautiful baby at six pounds, fourteen ounces. Somehow I knew he would be our football star.

At the warrant officer ceremony, Juanita pinned the bars on my shoulders. I felt strangely humble, aware of the blessings that God's love and Juanita's had brought into my life as well as my adorable children. From now on, I told myself, I would strive to deserve the faith they had in me, and to live up to what my mother had prophesied for me. I realized, more clearly than I ever had before, that it was only God's grace that could make it possible.

Colonel Stamm, from Virginia, saw to it that I was put in charge of commissary and supply at Quantico, Virginia.

Meanwhile, the world situation was becoming unstable once more. The United States was preparing to commit itself more fully in Vietnam. From what was being said on the grapevine, I knew I would have to serve overseas, somewhere. When orders came, it was Okinawa again.

I had several months to prepare for a change. Juanita and I decided to buy a house in Washington to replace the one we'd sold. She would be close to family and friends and in surroundings she liked.

I would be away for a long time. As far as Juanita and I knew, Heaven could be where we would meet again.

CHAPTER

13

My new job in Okinawa was to be the food administrator for the 3rd Marine Division, checking on all food and supply activity. The job tied in with many of the courses I had taken in the States.

I signed up to take some courses, too, and before long, much to my surprise, I seemed to be working as a missionary as well.

As soon as I had learned enough Japanese to get by, I visited a Japanese Baptist church high in the hills. It met in a little grass hut.

I needn't have worried about the way I spoke Japanese, because Rev. Osaka spoke fluent English. After weeks of attending the church, I was asked to speak to the congregation. Members started inviting me into their homes, too.

One day, Rev. Osaka broached the subject of a "real church." He had found a nice plot of land, but it was hilly.

"We need bulldozer, cement, and many pieces of tin," Rev. Osaka murmured. "We have to pray about it."

"Fine."

"But we not let Lord do it all, huh?" Rev. Osaka looked up at the sky. "Bulldozer, cement, tin, you can get? Lord will help."

I laughed. He thought I could do anything. I told him that just because I had a job in supply, it didn't mean I could obtain anything needed. But I would try.

A few days later, I had permission to borrow a bulldozer. I couldn't operate one, but I found a corporal who could.

At the site, the corporal and I went to work. We smoothed the lot and made forms for cement.

The next day I went over to the Warrant Officers' Association. "You know, I belong to the WOA, and I'm beginning to wonder why I pay my dues."

"How come?"

"When I want something, I can never get it."

"What do you want?"

"Fifty-two bags of ready-mix cement to build a church."

"Where do you want it delivered?"

I told him. Rev. Osaka called the next day. There were fifty-two bags of cement out at the site. Permission had been granted to call this a "government donation" for the sake of goodwill.

"How are you going to mix it?" I asked him.

"You let me pray about that. We won't let the Lord do it all either."

They dug a hole, poured all the bags in, added water, and then about twenty people got in and mixed with their feet. They carried it over to the foundation in buckets and dumped it in. We helped out with the rest of the materials needed.

The first church service in the new building was a smashing success. I was dubbed a miracle worker, but many people had made this possible—*and God.*

During this time, I'd been teaching Sunday school at the base chapel, and the chaplain was having difficulties: He was an alcoholic. I decided to talk to him.

"Listen, stuffy," the chaplain said, "what I do is my business. If I want to drink or play around with women, that's my business and the Lord's. If He doesn't care, why should you?"

"But you don't understand the influence you have. How can you tell people they should be morally right, and Christian, and obey the laws, when you're cheating on your wife? And how about your four kids you're neglecting back home?"

"You're a religious nut! Stop meddling!"

I went to see the commanding general, who was so incensed that he told the chaplain to be off the island in twenty-four hours.

"Don't you want to hear my side of the story?" he asked the general.

"You don't have a side," the general retorted.

Our captain had been scheduled to take a crew to Vietnam with supplies by ship, then return by air. At the time, Americans in Vietnam had been explicitly ordered not to fight back even if fired on.

I didn't relish getting shot at, but I had to go. I arrived during a short lull in the fighting—a very short one. As we drove along near Danang, with my right-hand man, Sergeant Ambrose McKinley, at the wheel, we heard the zzziiiiiiing of rifle fire. The good sergeant stomped on the brakes, and we jumped out on the double, crouching behind the tires, hoping they wouldn't go flat. I figured all we could do was pray, and I got right with it. But Ambrose came up with two .45 pistols. I heard ammo clips snapping into place.

"Sergeant! Where'd you get that ammo? You're going to get us locked up!"

"I'm going to save your life now, gunner, and when we get back we can worry about getting locked up." He handed me a clip.

But the sniper left, and we put away the guns. I knew my prayers had been heard. I had a brand-new reason to say, "Thank you, Lord."

When we got back to the base in Okinawa, it was time for exams in all three of my classes, many of which I'd now missed. But I couldn't drop the courses. "You take the test, and if you don't pass, you'll have to give up the program. If you drop, you'll get an F."

So I walked in the bitter cold and took three exams—accounting, government, political science—all in one night. I felt I had blown all three. The next day I went to the professor and asked if I could take them again under better circumstances.

She looked kind of puzzled. "But you couldn't improve on that test."

"Oh, I must have really blown it."

"Blown it! You made the highest mark that we have ever had on the island."

I was flabbergasted. I knew I couldn't have done that on my own. And suddenly I realized that the same Lord who had protected me from the sniper had been with me for the examinations, too. I was overwhelmed with thanksgiving.

The courses I was taking were aimed at that distant goal, the U. S. Senate.

Another activity related to the same goal was the Far East Toastmasters' Contest. A Marine had never once won the top prize. I was determined it was our turn. Runoffs had been going on for nearly a year, and we were now down to four from around seventy contestants. I was one of the four. The winner would be No. 1 toastmaster of the Far East in persuasive speech.

I'd practiced my talk in front of a mirror, even mumbled the words intermingled with prayers as I dropped off to sleep. I practiced on the way to work, to school, to church.

I knew I would have to use all the toastmaster's skills I'd learned over the years. On the big night, I talked about being an American.

"I was born in America, I live as an American, and I will die as an American," I said. "And at my death, I hope and pray I will have benefited mankind."

I went on to tell them how this country was built and about some of the heroes we'd had.

I ended by telling them a success story, the successes of many men, and how we had an opportunity on Okinawa. I gave them the challenge to be proud of being an American, saying we should all stand a little taller because of what America stood for in the world. When I finished I had a lump in my throat.

The house came apart. No one else had given a speech about love, God, and country.

I won first prize!

In 1961 I found myself on the USS *Pickaway*, from Okinawa, bound home after fourteen months in the Pacific. We were several days out when it dawned on someone that our flag was missing.

I suppose the fact that the flag is normally taken for granted explains why its absence hadn't been noticed sooner. In any event, this turned into a big thing with the men. There was grumbling.

Richard Jackson Johnson, father of Dr. James E. Johnson, was the spiritual fountainhead for the family, and the source for Dr. Johnson's ingrained motto, "Love's beyond defeat." (Johnson Family Collection)

A recent photo of the Johnson family, during a visit to Valley Forge Military Academy. Dr. Johnson and his wife, Juanita, stand on either side of their two sons, Kurtis (in uniform) and Juan. (Photo courtesy of U.S. Navy)

The other son in the Johnson family, Kenneth, died not long after this picture was taken at his commissioning ceremony. Pictured here are General Robert E. Cushman, Jr., commandant of the Marine Corps, and Dr. Johnson commissioning Kenneth a second lieutenant in the United States Marine Corps Reserve. (This was the first time in Marine Corps history that the Marine commandant personally commissioned a black officer.) (Photo courtesy of U.S. Navy)

Following Dr. Johnson's career service in the Marine Corps, and several years in private business, he was appointed by Governor Ronald Reagan to be director of the Department of Veterans' Affairs for the state of California. (Photo courtesy of U.S. Navy)

Commission Chairman Robert E. Hampton administered the oath
of office to Dr. Johnson, naming him vice chairman of the U.S.
Civil Service Commission, as Juanita, Dr. Johnson's wife, holds the
Bible. Others pictured are (left to right) in-laws of the Johnsons,
Mrs. Doris Austin and Mr. Lewis A. Butler; Commissioner Hamp-
ton; Dr. Johnson's daughter Janice; the Johnsons; and Commissioner
Ludwig Andolsek. (Photo courtesy of the U.S. Navy)

Former President Richard M. Nixon congratulating Dr. Johnson on the Civil Service Commission appointment. The President named Dr. Johnson Vice Chairman among the commissioners. (Photo courtesy of U.S. Navy)

Former Secretary of Defense Melvin Laird administered the oath of office to Dr. Johnson when the latter was appointed Assistant Secretary of the Navy. Pictured with the Johnsons and Secretary Laird are (left to right) Dr. Harold Quase, Secretary John Chafee, and the Johnsons' four children. (Photo courtesy of U.S. Navy)

A White House conference with black American leaders during President Nixon's administration. Among the black leaders are, in the bottom center of the picture (left to right), Washington, D.C., Mayor Walter E. Washington, George Haley (brother of Alex Haley), and Dr. Johnson. (Photo courtesy of U.S. Navy)

Dr. Johnson and his wife, Juanita, chatting with Dr. Billy Graham. Both Dr. Graham and Dr. Johnson were participants in the 1973 presidential national prayer breakfast. (Photo courtesy of U.S. Navy)

The United States Naval Sea Cadets passed in review before Dr. Johnson in Los Angeles at Dodger Stadium, while he served as Assistant Secretary of the Navy. (Photo courtesy of the U.S. Navy)

Former President Richard M. Nixon and former Secretaries of Defense and the Navy, Melvin Laird and John Chafee, respectively, with the then Assistant Secretary of the Navy, Dr. Johnson, at a White House conference. (Photo courtesy of U.S. Navy)

On a good-will trip to the Far East representing the United States, Dr. Johnson spoke to political and religious leaders in the Philippines, Taiwan, and Korea. Here he is pictured with Dr. Warren Walker of Los Angeles Union University as they greet Mrs. Park of Korea. (Johnson Family Collection)

The absence of the flag bothered me too, although I was sure that a search would turn it up. We'd had a hurried departure; things like this were bound to happen.

One morning after my daily jog, I was greeted by a message coming over the speakers: "All hands, all hands, assemble on the afterdeck, assemble on the afterdeck."

I hurried astern. Men were lining up in confusion, sailors forming up ahead of the Marines, when the thin, shrill notes of a bugle sounded. Before I recognized the all too familiar strains, I saw a flash and a flutter of red, white, and blue, and slowly, majestically, Old Glory ascended the pole at the stern.

I could feel the excitement of the men around me. By the time the flag had reached the top of the mast, and the bugler had ceased reveille, tears were streaming down my face.

What's a big Marine like you, Johnny, doing crying over a mere piece of cloth? I felt somewhat ashamed, and turned to see dozens, even hundreds, of others with wet eyes.

Most of these guys were kids, of a generation I had supposed no longer felt pride in nationhood, affection for the red, white, and blue.

The Marine bandleader came up front. The band started playing. We began to sing "God Bless America." The noise was deafening and beautiful. When the song was over, the men burst into cheers, shaking hands, patting each other on the back.

In the midst of all the patriotic emotion, I realized I was homesick.

The reunion with Juanita and the three children in Washington was worth a hundred Waikikis. Ken, who was twelve and attending junior high school, won the race at the airport to greet me and take my airline bag.

Vernea, now six, got to me next, and jumped into my arms, to be carried back to the main building. On the way, I bumped into Juanita, grabbed her with my free arm, and hugged her and kissed her. "I missed you like crazy!"

Juanita had left two-year-old Kurtis home with a baby-sitter. Kurtis had been less than a year old when I'd left for Okinawa in 1960. When I came into the house, he just looked at me, hung back, and stared. My youngest kid didn't even recognize his own father!

He went upstairs, and in a few minutes he toddled back with a picture in his hand. He pointed to me, then at the picture.

"Yes," his mother said, "that's Daddy." Kurtis would kiss his father's picture every night before retiring.

"Daddy!" he cried. He dropped the picture, ran to me, and I swooped him up. My tears felt warm as he pressed his cheek against mine.

In the following weeks I kept thinking of that homecoming; it had reminded me what was of major importance in my life.

CHAPTER

14

Time seemed to be moving faster; changes clipped off like machine-gun bursts. Events piled one on top of another.

It was a big shock to come back to the States and find that not only did we have a war in Vietnam, we also were having what amounted to a civil war at home. It seemed the nation was threatening to rip apart.

During the autumn of 1963, I was the adjutant of the five-hundred-man Service Maintenance Squadron, which kept the flying Marines in the air at El Toro Marine base, fifty miles down the freeway from Los Angeles. Earlier in the year, I had completed Naval Justice School. I was looking forward to being a defense counselor.

On a colder than usual November day I was at my desk when Corporal Chuck Callahan literally flew into the room.

"The President's been shot!"

I stared at Callahan. Ice started to freeze my scalp. My hand moved toward the phone just as it rang. It was the commanding general.

"President Kennedy was riding in a motorcade through Dallas," he said in a crisp, urgent tone. "There were shots. He's been rushed to the hospital. We're on full alert. There might be planes on the way to attack the United States. The Russians may be starting a war. Approve all requisitions and shoot them through on priority. We've got to have all aircraft ready at a moment's notice. Make sure all the birds in for repair are checked over on the double!"

"Yes, sir!" One part of my mind raced pell-mell: What were the immediate things to be done by my squadron? Another part tried to grapple with the news.

"One other thing," the general interrupted. "Besides what this shooting means concerning an overseas attack, there might be internal revolution in the making. We're doubling the guard at the gates. Cancel all leaves." He hung up.

During the ensuing hours and days, the situation proved to be both better and worse than we'd feared. President Kennedy died. But no bombs fell on the United States. Reaction was violent. A high degree of nervous tension gripped the nation.

Vice President Lyndon B. Johnson was swiftly sworn in as President and had his hands full keeping the nation together at this moment of crisis.

Some, including U. S. Supreme Court Chief Justice Earl Warren, appeared convinced that the President's assassination was the work of a nut working alone. Others, including myself, were just as persuaded that the act was deliberately planned by a group working together to accomplish some end that to this date has remained unclear.

Eventually, Americans recovered from the shock. But other problems came along to command their attention. The death of our President made me acutely aware of the turmoil dividing our nation. I felt that our problems stemmed from an increasing tendency to *despiritualize Christianity*. While church attendance had not dropped enough to alarm religious people, churches were increasingly instruments of social action, rather than meeting places for individuals to come face to face with Jesus Christ.

The murder of President Kennedy made me look back at the immediate past to see if I, too, had been guilty of *spiritual negligence*.

The air was full of criticism. It seemed to me that if Americans were any worse than they had ever been, it was the direct result of everyone convincing them that they were bad, sick, decadent, hate-filled.

If there was anything seriously wrong with Americans, it was weakness in allowing themselves to be persuaded of unworthiness.

In former generations, people somehow got through their youth with a fair degree of equanimity. But now modern child psychologists were telling parents and, through them, the kids themselves, that they were supposed to be mortally worried about their psyches, and when the mass media played up to them as being so important yet fragile, teen-agers began to be self-conscious, then militant about themselves.

I had seen the terrific pride of these young aboard the USS *Pickaway*. I knew that within America's soul there was still the stuff of patriotism that had made America great.

I decided that my plans to become part of the government so that I could apply principles my father taught me must go full steam ahead. In a high position, perhaps, I could spread some Christian love around.

After winning eighteen consecutive court cases at El Toro as a defense counselor, I was told about a man in another squadron who couldn't get anyone to defend him because he had been in and out of the brig on various convictions.

He requested that I defend him. I went to his commanding officer to find out why no one would help the private first class.

"He's a loser," the commanding officer said. "Don't ruin your reputation by defending him. Just let him go to the brig and stay there."

I told the young man that I would take his case.

"I got to tell you something: I'm a loser," he moaned.

"Don't tell me about your past. Just tell me the things pertinent to this case."

He did, and we won our case on a technicality.

Soon after this, the Pfc came to our Bible class. He told his story, presenting himself as "Peck's bad boy" right up until the time I took his case. "I found Christ in the courtroom during my trial," he said. "I couldn't help thinking it was God's plan to help me out of this and for me to stay out of jail so I can help others to stay out."

Both he and his parents tried to pay me for my services, but I wouldn't accept anything.

"You've already paid me, by accepting Christ," I said. "Now let's see what you can do with your future!"

Stan didn't disappoint me. He kept on witnessing to the younger fellows with whom he came in contact, and a few weeks later, he brought me a huge package wrapped in brown paper. His face was glowing with pride. "I've done something, sir. Everybody says I don't have any talent, but here's something I did!"

It was a fine oil painting of the raising of the flag on Iwo Jima, which now hangs in my home in a prominent place.

After this experience, several of us from the chapel decided that the fellows in the brig could use more classes and more instruction in Christianity. But we weren't allowed to go in and just preach about Christ. We had to go in as instructors; since I had had quite a few classes in psychology, no one questioned my right to be there.

I was determined to get to some of these soldiers. We had one Marine private in our class who looked about twenty-four or twenty-five because he was so big. He was only nineteen. He would kick the guards, spit in their faces, hang from the bars, burn his mattress. No one could do anything with him. As I was teaching, he would lean back in his chair, almost to the point where it would tip back. He knew it bothered me.

Week after week, I tried to figure a way to get through to him. When the guards would come to take the men back, he'd give them such a bad time, they'd have to put the cuffs on him.

One night we were talking about love. Along with the psychology, I taught that the real miracle to bring about change is Jesus Christ, and that is love, and God is love.

"You say you love your girlfriend. Why? How do you know you love her?"

"I just feel it," someone would say.

"That's the answer: You just feel it. You can't explain it, but you know it is there. God is love."

Enough in the class asked questions about love and the Bible for me to get some strong points across. I forgot about my heckler in the corner and threw myself into telling them that any problem can be conquered if we love God enough.

It wasn't long before the heckler decided to pay attention to what was being said, and when the guards came to take them back, the private asked one of the guards, "Sir, may I just stay here for a few minutes and talk with Warrant Officer Johnson?"

The guard looked surprised. "Do you mind, Johnson? We can put the cuffs on him."

"For what?" I answered. "Of course he can stay. I've been wanting to talk to him anyway."

As soon as the guard moved out of earshot, the Marine said, "Now, don't laugh. I don't know what happened to me tonight, but when you were talking to those other guys about love, something happened to me. I feel different; I can't explain it."

I grinned at him. "What happened? How *do* you feel?"

"Like singing. I'm not even mad at those guards anymore."

"That's really great! Praise the Lord."

"I really think I believe what you said, but how can I be sure? I've been fooled so many times."

I could see that doubt still existed, and I couldn't blame him for that. "Only *you* can be sure. You have to believe. Let's just have a word of prayer, and we'll have God show you what He can do. Now, remember, you can't be ashamed of God. If you really feel the way you do, when I get on my knees to pray, with that guard down there watching us, and you don't feel ashamed to do the same thing, then you'll know."

I got on my knees. He hesitated a few seconds, then knelt beside me. I asked God to forgive him. I prayed with all my heart. I tried to think of everything this young man might be feeling, everything he might have done that he would want to be forgiven for. Finally, as I waited for some sign from him, I heard sniffling, but I caught his words. "O Lord, O Lord, O Lord, help me." It was enough for me to know that God had heard him and was speaking to him.

He fell over toward me, put his head on my shoulder, and began to cry his heart out. The guard ran up to the gate. "Do you need some help?"

"No," I said, "I don't think you'll be having any more problems from this man."

The guard didn't believe me. But the next day, the prisoner asked for clean clothes, some cleaning rags, and water. He cleaned his cell and made himself look like a Marine.

"What did you do to him last night?" one of them asked.

"It was Christ, not me," I said, "he accepted the Lord as his savior."

By the time the private appeared in court, there were several good witnesses for him, including some brig guards, because of his new record of good behavior in jail. Since he had been at the head of a ring that had stolen televisions, radios, tools, cars, and machinery, the charges were serious. He would be lucky if he was given less than three years, I told him. I prayed that he wouldn't get more.

When he told his story from the witness stand, he didn't leave out anything, and he told it straight from the heart. "What I did was wrong," he said. "But I believe that Jesus Christ has forgiven me and made me a new creature." Witness after witness told of the change that had occurred in him. By the time I talked to the court-martial board, there seemed to be only one person really negative.

The board brought back a verdict of guilty. He was sentenced to only two months at hard labor in jail. They counted the two months he had already spent in jail and let him go.

My client later became a preacher to young people in Detroit.

During a break in the trial of my twenty-first case, I grabbed a few papers and headed over to the PX coffee shop. At a table in the corner, I spread out my papers and read through word by word until I found what I was looking for.

Curly Adams, the civilian controller, made his way over. "Got room for me, Perry Mason? I understand you're working on a tough case."

"Can't you remember my name is Johnson?"

"I understand if you win this case, you'll be the Perry Mason of El Toro, never lost a case. Seriously, don't you think you might be hurting the Marine Corps by trying too hard to get those guys off?"

"Now, wait a minute, Curly," I said. "They aren't guilty until proven guilty."

On the way back to the small building we used as our "courtroom," I thought about my client, a young private first class who had been accused of falling asleep on guard duty. His commanding officer was going to give him an Article 15, a nonjudicial punishment with some restrictions, but Spencer wouldn't accept this and had asked for a special court-martial.

When I'd first visited him, I'd warned him about telling me the absolute truth. He said he couldn't stay awake during an hour's shift, or even during meals. He'd been to see the doctor, but there was no definite diagnosis that could be put in writing.

I'd checked with the doctor and the man's commanding officer. They said they thought he was one big bluff. I was still undecided about taking the case. When the private first class came into my office for our second talk, something about him made me want to trust him.

"Look, Private," I said that morning, "if I take this case, I want to be able to defend you properly, but you've got to level with me. You can't hope to be found not guilty when you were asleep on duty."

"I was asleep, all right. But you see I have this sickness."

"But the doctor won't verify it."

"I know," he said mournfully, "but he did say there was something wrong with me. I can hardly get through a meal without falling asleep. I even fall asleep when I'm standing up."

I sighed. "Anyway, assuming I did take your case, we would have to come up with something to convince the judge you did not intentionally fall asleep. Now, I'll briefly outline what the courtroom procedure will be like, and you try to tell me all of the instances when you have fallen asleep and someone has witnessed it. Bring me all of the names of people who can testify on your behalf, people who know that when you are awake, you're a good Marine. I'll see what I can do. . . . Private? Are you listening?"

He had slumped down in the chair and was sleeping as if it were midnight.

"I'll take your case," I shouted, waking him up. "I'll send you a brief of what I've told you today; we'll go over it just before your case comes up in court."

Juanita helped me research. She found a case in which a man had fallen asleep on guard duty because of some kind of sleeping sickness. When I tried to get the doctor to testify, he refused at first. "I don't think this is one of those. . . ."

"Well, if he's in court and falls asleep, will you come up and verify that he's asleep?" I pressed. "If he's faking, then I simply lose my case."

He agreed. Then, while the court judge went through the preliminaries, the young man fell asleep. I nudged him, and he awakened. A lieutenant serving as the trial counselor looked over at me.

"Gunner, this is one case you can't win. That guy is the biggest phony I've ever seen."

"Lieutenant, this man is going to be acquitted, and you are going to be the one to say whether he's asleep or awake."

We continued with the court preliminaries as the specifications were read. The president of the court said, "Will the accused stand?"

The private first class and I stood behind a table, and as the president of court read the charges, I could see my client's eyelids drooping, his shoulders slumping. He gradually crumpled down into his chair; his head went onto the table. Then he began to snore. His snoring was so loud, the president of the court banged his gavel and said, "I don't mind you sleeping, son, but don't be so loud!"

At that point, I said, "Your Honor, if you have recognized that my client is asleep, and it's been read into the record, I would now ask you to have the doctor examine him to see if, in fact, he is asleep."

The accused snored on. The physician came up, examined his eyelids, listened to his snoring, and said, "If he isn't asleep, he's the best faker I've ever seen."

I thanked the doctor. "Your Honor and members of the court, I think we can save the government a lot of money, and this court's time. I would like to make a motion to dismiss all charges and specifications against this Marine, and have him admitted to the hospital for observation and possible discharge from the Marine Corps."

The trial defense counselor jumped up. "This is all a put-on and an act. I can keep him awake. I can punch him in his sides. He won't go to sleep sitting by me."

I hopped to my feet. "I object to that. We're not here to abuse the accused. We're here to see justice done. We have a medical doctor here who has stated that the accused is asleep. I have had the experience of being with him for about a week, every day, briefing him, and right in the middle of talking to him about his own case, he has fallen asleep."

The president of the court looked over at the court-martial board. One of the older warrant officers, Renny Martin, nodded to him. Then he looked at one of the women Marines on the panel. She nodded, too.

"Subject to any objections of any members of the court, all charges and specifications will be dismissed." Down went the president of the court's gavel. "Court is adjourned."

I looked over at my client. He was still asleep.

Conditions around the nation weren't improving, and in the presidential race, Barry Goldwater was crushed by the biggest total-vote majority in any presidential election. Not only that, his defeat was underscored by huge Democratic majorities in both Houses of Congress. American voters had rejected Goldwater's "choice, not an echo." It made me sick at heart. I felt that all I stood for was somehow repudiated.

I also realized that my time in the Marine Corps was coming to a close.

Whatever civilian occupation I went into would have to support my major goal of running for the U. S. Senate, all the more important now when our political system so desperately needed new ideas, thoughts, and motivation. Meanwhile, I plugged on as a defense counsel.

After I had won thirty-eight straight cases, the battalion commander, Major V. L. Yount, called me in.

"Johnson, you've done such an outstanding job as defense counselor, we're going to change your job. From now on you will be the trial counselor." Now it was my job to find them guilty and send them to jail.

I tried to be as enthusiastic, but it was difficult. I wanted prisoners to be not guilty, and I no longer had the chance to talk with these men in a constructive way.

Studying for a test for one of my classes, I thought about some figures running through my mind. "Twenty-five hundred per week!" I said out loud. "Why, that's more than any job I've ever heard of."

"What are you mumbling about?" Juanita asked. "Did I hear you say $2,500 per week for something?"

"Yeah. Selling insurance. I had lunch with an insurance manager today, and he offered me a job. That's the figure he gave me if I just sold two $40-a-month premium policies per day."

"Just remember your political plans," Juanita reminded me. "Besides, I think they're kidding you about all that money."

A few days later, I dropped in to the insurance manager's office, and he introduced me around. Then I took a two-hour test along with eighteen other prospective salesmen. Three of us passed. The following day there were two more tests; then I met the regional director.

"Johnny," I was told, "I said to our regional director that I was testing you in preparation for working for us down here. He doesn't believe it's possible for you to sell insurance in Orange County."

"Why? What are you talking about?"

"You can't sell because you're black."

That got my hackles up. "What do you mean, I can't sell because I'm black?"

The director nodded. "There aren't enough blacks in this area; less than 1 per cent in Orange County."

"What's wrong with the whites? Don't they buy insurance?"

"Yes, but you know . . ."

"I *don't* know. I've been dealing with the whites in the Marine Corps for the past twenty years."

"Johnny, we want to hire you. You got the highest grade on the test; you're smart. We just want you to know we're going to transfer you up to Los Angeles."

"Look, I don't want to go to Los Angeles. I'm staying in Orange County. I'll find another company if I'm going into insurance."

"All right, I'll put you in anyway."

It was all settled.

The day I accepted retirement from the U. S. Marine Corps, I didn't shed a tear—until the band played "Semper Fidelis." All my family was on the drill field. I was being saluted by General Tharin, who had already made some kind remarks about me. My whole battalion marched past, 450 Marines in dress blues, saluting me along with the other officers that were retiring.

At the last minute, to keep me from retiring, the general had done some fancy paperwork, and I'd been offered a promotion from warrant officer to second lieutenant, and then a temporary promotion to first lieutenant. "We think you've earned it, Johnny," the general said.

"I'm sorry, sir, but I just can't accept it. I'm retiring."

Now, on August 1, 1965, I had put my uniform on for the last time. The band played "From the halls of Montezuma to the shores of Tripoli/We will fight our country's battles in the air, on land and sea. . . ." All the words went through my mind, and when they came to the last part, "We are proud to claim the title of The United States Marines," I looked over at Juanita and the children, and then up at the American flag, waving high in the breeze. Tears streamed down my face. I didn't bother to wipe them away.

"Thank you, Lord," I murmured, "for twenty-one beautiful years. *Let the next ones be for You!*"

CHAPTER

15

Out of the service at last. Time to take a breath and look around.
I felt that a great weight had been lifted, the responsibilities of
honorably representing the United States Marine Corps. I was in a
holiday mood. I could see things with new eyes.

Tustin, in Orange County, California, is a small town nestled
among orange groves below the Santa Ana Mountains. There was
peace and serenity, a kind of aloofness that set Tustin apart from
other Southern California communities.

I would be going to the Prudential Insurance school at the huge
Prudential building on Wilshire Boulevard, the "Miracle Mile," in
Los Angeles. I was free only long enough to find a house.

When we innocently announced we intended to buy a house in
Tustin, our friends blinked, then shook their heads. "Tustin? Listen,
buddy, buying a house in Orange County, anywhere, is uphill, man,
for a black guy." Friends warned us of dire consequences. Orange
County had the reputation of being arch conservative. Some people
in the county didn't even believe in public schools.

We found exactly the house we wanted, a ranch-style home with
a bricked patio, sunken living room, huge kitchen with a real pan-
try, four bedrooms, several baths—the works. All of this was tucked

away behind a high stucco wall and nestled among lime trees and Chinese dwarf cherry trees.

The spread was owned by a noted veterinarian, Dr. Reginald P. V. McQuire-Linton, who had received his training with honors at Oxford.

"Your friends who try to frighten you about your reception in the neighborhood are exaggerating," the distinguished animal doctor said.

We negotiated the purchase of the house, and we were ready to expect anything when we moved in. And we got it. When I looked out the window one day, there were six big men and two or three women marching up our driveway.

Juanita joined me at the large bay window. "Oh, oh."

"Better let me handle this, honey," I said. I dragged my heels all the way to the door. Making sure the chain was in place, I opened the door just enough to look, ready to slam it shut.

"Hi," one of the ladies said. "You're Mr. Johnson, I presume?"

"Ahhh, yeah, I think so," I responded.

"Aren't you going to open the door for us? We're your neighbors."

Someone nudged my elbow. I nearly jumped out of my skin. It was Ken. "Open up, Dad. They'll think we're antisocial. She won't hurt you."

I unchained the door and opened it.

A tall, red-headed man stepped forward. "Hello, there, Mr. Johnson. We're your new neighbors."

"Can—can I help you?" I said.

"We'd like to help you! If there is anything that needs to be done in the house—washing dishes, hanging pictures. You just moved in, right? We would like to help you in any way possible."

I opened the door wide. "My wife has made a pot of coffee, and if you're brave enough to wade through all this chaos, come and help us drink it," I said enthusiastically.

They came in. They were warm, friendly people who seemed interested in my experiences and views on life, politics, and the U. S. Marine Corps.

The next day, bright and early, a priest appeared on our porch and invited us to attend services at his church. He had no sooner left than a Methodist preacher arrived. He, too, welcomed us at his church services.

By the time a Baptist minister appeared, I had our calendar unpacked and was scheduling engagements, including those we'd made last night with our neighbors. We were booked for the next six Sundays and several evenings.

Meanwhile, there was insurance school in Los Angeles.

As I neared the end of the second three weeks of on-the-job training, my sales figures passed the $1 million mark. Between August and October, I had sold $1.5 million worth of insurance, had become a "Million-dollar Round-table Member," and a member of the "President's Club."

From the beginning, I had had reservations about selling insurance. It hadn't seemed to relate much to my goal of the U. S. Senate.

But it wasn't long before I found that selling insurance did give me an opportunity to help people, to share love and Christianity.

When I rang one doorbell and said I was from Prudential Insurance, and wanted to talk about updating her insurance, the lady said, "You can't do anything for me now. My daughter was caught with some kids trying to rob a liquor store. She's out of jail and staying here. I don't feel like talking to anyone about anything."

"Maybe I can talk to her for you."

The daughter had come to the door. "What do you want to talk to me about?"

"I'd like to talk with you and your mother. Maybe, among the three of us, we could solve some of your problems."

We began to talk. "The only thing that matters in this world is the magic of love, and without it you are in serious trouble," I said.

"Nobody loves me, and I don't need anyone," the daughter retorted. "I don't love anyone else, either."

"You know, I've heard a lot of people say that, but let me tell you, we need each other, just like you need your mother, and your mother really needs you, too."

She walked out of the room. I asked the mother if we could have a word of prayer before I left.

"You must be some kind of a preacher. You're not an insurance man!"

"No, ma'am, I'm not a preacher, but I hope I'm some sort of a teacher."

I began to say a very simple prayer that I thought had some meaning. "Dear Lord, just come into this home and begin your wonderful power, which is known as love."

I went on to talk about love. Then I turned to I Corinthians, Chapter 13, and read slowly about love. I felt someone watching me—the daughter had come back into the room.

"I don't believe that's in the Bible," she mumbled.

I gave the Bible to her. "You can love," I told the daughter. "'Love isn't puffed up. Love never fails.'"

I was ready to go. At the door, the daughter said, "Mister, would you just pray with us one more time?"

I began to pray. I asked God to come into their home and to please take over. The girl began to cry, then went over and threw her arms around her mother's neck. They wept together.

I walked out of there, knowing the Lord had reunited a family.

By the time all the sales results were in for the first full year, I'd sold $5 million worth of insurance. During my second year, I sold $13 million worth, ending with a 26-month career record of $19.5 million. My largest individual policy had been for $2.5 million, in addition to three $1 million policies in the same year. I ended up top rookie in the Prudential Insurance Company.

During this time Juanita and I were taking part-time courses at Chapman College and Santa Ana College. With 160 college credits behind me, I was studying law, psychology, and real estate.

In my college classes, I tried to clear up some misconceptions among the students and faculty about the role of the military. And I always stressed that the people *are* the government. If anything goes wrong, it's the fault of the people, because they're the ones who voted for the people managing the country.

A black Orange County conservative Republican was something of an oddity for these predominantly white classes. Several of the more extreme students were trying to state their case when one decided to use me as an example.

"Yeah, man, look: Let's take Johnny Johnson here, for example. Downtrodden, struggling, kicked around. There's just no chance, man, for him, just because he's black. That's why he's a Democrat and is fighting all this crap from the establishment. . . ."

"Yeah," another chorused. "Ain't that right, Johnny?"

"Well, if you'd give me a chance," I said quietly, "I'd like to speak for myself, if you don't mind."

"Yeah, hooray," they said, shouting and clapping and looking at the instructor as though to say, "You'd better let this man speak out or else."

I told my classmates, "In the first place, I am not one who says that all blacks are alike, downtrodden, Democrats, and have a rough time. I want to be like anyone else. I want to be taken on my own merits. Furthermore, I happen to be a Republican and a conservative."

I could see it was hard for them to believe, at first, that I was leveling with them.

I was working hard, too, trying to sell my next million dollars' worth of insurance. I had set myself a high standard following Dad's advice of long ago: *Try to beat your own record.*

I was trying also to spend some time with my family, which by Christmas 1965 consisted of Juanita; Ken, now sixteen and attending Tustin High School; Vernea, ten; and six-year-old Kurtis James. And I was writing to Dad, now one hundred years old!

I had stopped worrying so much whether selling insurance was taking me from my long-range goals. But when political discussions at the colleges got hotter and world events likewise, I wondered again how I could more fully prepare myself for the time nine years hence when I planned to be in the political arena.

Then Ken came home from school one day and told us he was running for student body president. He had been president of his class in his junior year at Tustin High School. In his last year, he wanted to become student body president.

Juanita and I didn't want Ken to feel too let down if he didn't win. We pointed out that there were only 3 black students out of 2,300 on the campus, and he had 3 competitors for the office.

One was a very handsome chap, a quarterback on the football team; one was a beautiful and very articulate girl; and one boy, from a wealthy family, could throw around a great deal of money.

"Now, when you lose, son," I said, trying to prepare him for what I felt was ahead—

"Who's going to lose, Dad?" He gave me a wide-eyed, confident look. "I'm going to win. The football player is not going to work; he thinks his fame will win him the election.

"My female competitor won't get many votes because the girls don't like her. The rich guy is disliked because he has too much money and flaunts it. Then there's me. I'm going to have a girl and a boy in each class be my campaign managers. I'll write speeches for them and tell them when to talk."

Ken went on, "I'll have a tent put up on campus for my campaign headquarters. Mr. Cushman, our shop teacher, will make buttons for me and fly over Tustin and do some skywriting. It'll say, 'VOTE FOR KEN JOHNSON.'"

Ken reminded me of the positive outlook my dad always had, and the kind of advice he would give. Putting aside my initial pessimism, I said, "If you're sure of what you want and you know that you're going to win, then go right ahead, Ken, and you will win."

He invited his mother and me to the big campaign rally held at the high school stadium. We heard the other candidates "read" their speeches, but we couldn't see Ken anywhere on the platform. Had something happened?

Something had! Way across the field, I saw three motorcycles on each side of a black Lincoln Continental, all slowly driving toward the speakers' platform.

Two people walked on each side of the car. Inside, in the back seat, was Ken, in a black suit, sitting between two "bodyguards."

When the car stopped near the speakers' platform, the crowd went wild. Ken got out, and a kid up in the stands pulled a toy pistol. He fired a shot and "missed" Ken, but "hit" one of the bodyguards, who fell to the ground "dead." The attacker ran toward the platform and the car, "shooting" wildly, "hitting" another bodyguard.

By the time he'd approached Ken, Ken had turned his "cane" into a sword by a twist of the handle. He ran it through the villain, who "died" and was hoisted up onto the hood of the car. The car's occupants jumped back in and drove off. What a tremendous performance!

The crowd began screaming and clapping and stamping their feet. After disposing of the "body," the car turned and drove back. Ken, his chief campaign manager, and a couple of bodyguards marched up to the speakers' platform. The manager had on a set of tails, a long beard, and a stovepipe hat. He looked like Abraham Lincoln. He went to the mike and said, "I would like to introduce the next student body president. He is a man who is most outstanding in every endeavor. He is one of Tustin's top students and liked by everyone. He is the hardest worker. He is the best man to make this school the best in California. My fellow students, the next president of Tustin High, Kenneth E. Johnson!"

"Yes, we will certainly clean up Tustin," Ken said.

The crowd cheered.

"Tustin is great." They cheered again.

"Always will be great."

Ken's supporters jumped up and shouted and clapped.

"Only if you elect me president!"

His cheering supporters moved apart to display a huge banner stretching from one end of the bleachers to the other. Individuals had large signs, which they raised as they chanted. The signs and banner read, "VOTE FOR KEN JOHNSON."

I couldn't believe it.

During the remainder of the campaign, Ken followed up with plenty of newspaper publicity. He was fortunate in being good friends with a writer for the Tustin *News,* Bill Moses.

I had met Bill Moses in 1965. I'd read his articles and features with a great deal of approval for some time. A conservative, Bill was very candid about his opinions of candidates and community leaders in Orange and Los Angeles counties, and he "shot from the hip."

One editorial got my hackles up. While justly criticizing some very far-out left-wing black radicals in Los Angeles and condemning them for chiseling off the government while doing their best to destroy it, Bill left the impression that all black people were left-wing and chiselers.

I phoned for an appointment and went to see him.

"My name is Johnny Johnson. First of all, I didn't like that article you wrote, and I want to tell you something: All black people are not liberal, on welfare, lazy, and rioters. I am black, a conservative and a Republican. I love this country, and I don't want anyone putting me into a bag."

Apologetically, Moses said, "I didn't mean it that way, and if it sounded that way, I'm sorry. I am sure you are right; you're not the only Negro who is patriotic and hard-working. But I get fed up with these radicals, black or white; they take what America has to offer them and use it against the country. I can assure you that I'll make a retraction."

Bill did. I thanked him, and we became very good friends.

Ken won the student body election with 68 per cent of the vote.

Ken's success in high school politics stirred my own interest in the political arena. I had recently served on a team to elect John Schmitz as a California state senator and was chairing the Republican Minorities Interests Committee in Orange County. Because California's governor, Pat Brown, favored legislation to control income of insurance agents, I was personally interested. I felt it would be a strong blow against free enterprise.

There were plenty like me who'd invested time, money, sweat, blood, and tears for a future that could turn mighty dismal.

The only way to find out who supported this legislation was to fly to Sacramento and talk to Governor Brown. Representing the Insurance Underwriters of Southern California, I went to see the governor. The director of Veterans' Affairs had set up an appointment for me. The secretary ushered us in.

"Governor, this is Mr. Johnson. He just got out of the Marines after twenty-one years, worked up through the ranks to officer status." He turned to me. "Major, was it?"

I started to correct him. I was feeling a lot better. As a Republican, I'd expected a cool reception in this Democratic stronghold, but evidently the director was trying to do his job as representative of all the veterans.

"He won all kinds of medals. I remember reading about him.

He's been in Korea, Okinawa during the Japanese battle, Vietnam."
He turned to me. "How many times were you wounded, Johnny?
Anyway, as soon as he got out of the Marine Corps, he was offered
a top job with the Prudential Insurance Company; he's representing
the Insurance Underwriters here today."

Finally, the governor spoke. "Okay, okay, Joe. I'm in a hurry.
What is it you want, Mr. Johnson?"

"I would like to know your stand on this bill coming up affecting
the insurance business. I'd like to know whether you are going to
push this bill to legislate and regulate insurance commissions and
incomes."

"Oh, so you're one of those guys ripping off people with insurance rackets."

I saw red. "Now, wait just a minute, Your Excellency. Don't call
a free-enterprise business a racket. This country is based on free enterprise."

The governor was drumming his fingers on his huge, polished
desk. Now he interrupted, "You wait a minute, please. I don't have
time to talk about all that stuff now. I can save your time and mine,
too. I can answer you in one or two sentences: If there's any way I
can help push bills through to regulate some of that big stuff and
cut off some of those commissions in the insurance business, I'm
going to use all my power to do it."

I saw it was silly to let my emotions get the better of me. With
Brown, I'd be wasting valuable adrenalin. "Just let me tell you,
then, sir: I don't know how I'm going to do it, but I guarantee you
I'm going to use all the power I have to see that you are defeated
this November."

"You can't defeat me. Why, I've done so much for your race
around here . . ."

"You mean your big welfare program? What have you been
doing for my race to see that they are free to do things for themselves? No, I'm not grateful, because you're killing the only true
free enterprise I know, and that is selling, because in selling you get
paid in direct proportion to what you do."

I stormed out, and when I was halfway down the steps of the
building, I heard Joe. "Hey, Johnny. Hold it, will you? Listen, gee,
I'm sorry the boss was so irritable."

I was glad that some of the men around Governor Brown didn't agree with his approach or his ideas. But I had cooled down, and I was determined not to let it bother me. I'd been treated this way by enough officers in the Marine Corps; a mere governor couldn't keep me uptight too long. Besides, maybe this experience was part of God's master plan . . . and the next phase was yet to unfold.

CHAPTER

16

After my encounter with Governor Brown, I was interested immediately when friends told me they were thinking of supporting Ronald Reagan for governor.

"I used to see a man by that name in the movies," I said. "He drew a pistol with his left hand and wrote with his right hand." I thought a minute. "He was always a 'good guy.'"

"He's the same guy," one of the men said. "He's still a good guy."

Although I'd seen him in action in some Westerns, I didn't know what Ronald Reagan's political views were. There was one way to find out.

A small delegation of us representing the insurance industry met Ronald Reagan at the Ambassador Hotel. I did note immediately that he was a person who didn't try to flaunt himself. We had our meeting with him in a private room set up for lunch, and he seemed to invite candid questioning. He was surprised when I started talking as the spokesman for the group, and was even more so when he learned that I was not only a Republican, but also a conservative.

"Mr. Reagan, let me just ask you a simple question," I said. "How do you feel about the insurance business and the free-enterprise system?"

"I am all for the free-enterprise system," he replied quickly. "I think a man should go just as far as he can, and he should earn as much money as his ability allows him. I think the insurance industry is perhaps the last pure form of free enterprise."

I said to the others, "I don't know about the rest of you, but this is going to be my governor."

They applauded.

The meeting had been an eye opener. Reagan had come up with intelligent answers to everything anyone could throw at him. He was extremely well informed and acutely aware of the huge deficit in California's budget after the years of rule by Pat Brown. He didn't hedge about the necessity of raising taxes to whittle down this debt, despite the possibility of losing votes.

After returning to Orange County, I was appointed Southern California finance chairman of the Insurance Underwriters' committee to raise funds for Reagan's campaign.

At first, I wondered whether being black would hurt my chances, but I had no trouble: The money poured in. It was evident that Californians were eager for a change in government and were willing to pay for it.

The story was different at a small tire company, the owner of which had normally given to conservative causes. One of my people had gone out there, and the man had turned him down.

"Brown has been a louse, and I'm just not giving to any campaigns—not even to a Republican's campaign," he said.

So his name went on a list that was given to me.

"I'll go out and see this tire company owner," I told my assistant.

"No, Johnny. Don't you go out there! I hate to tell you, but he just doesn't cotton to black people at all. Some of these guys will tolerate you, but this guy won't. Stay away from him."

"Oh, don't give me all that stuff," I said, reaching for the telephone. The man should have contributed $5,000. "I'll call him right now."

"Hi, my name is Johnny Johnson. I'm chairman of a finance committee for Ronald Reagan. I want to come out and take twenty minutes of your time to tell you about the candidate. After that, you decide whether you want to contribute or participate in the campaign. Is that fair enough?"

"Confine it to ten minutes, and I'll see you."

I went out to the place, and when I walked into the plant, a foreman stopped me saying, "I'm sorry, but the job is already taken."

"What job?"

"The tire-changing job."

"Oh, I didn't come for that . . ."

"Well, the car-washing job is gone too. We don't have any more jobs."

"No—I came to see the owner."

"Look, I'm handling things here, and I tell you, there's no jobs."

"No—I don't want a job. I called him, and he told me to come to talk to him."

"Okay. Let me go in and check with him."

I could overhear the conversation from inside the office. "I ain't said anything about him comin' over to see me. I don't know what he's talkin' about."

"He insists you told him to come over."

"Ah, get rid of him!"

Just as he walked out of the office, I popped past him and stuck my hand out to the owner. "Hi—I'm Johnny Johnson, chairman of Ronald Reagan's finance committee. I called you today, and you promised me ten minutes of your time to hear about my candidate. You being a good American as you are, I know you want to hear about the candidate. *Don't you?*" I said with strong emphasis on my last two words.

He looked at the guy standing there and didn't know whether to run or listen. "We can do it over here on your counter," I said, and walked over. "I have some literature I want to leave with you, too."

He still hadn't said a word. I showed him the record of Brown in the area of increased business restrictions, his social legislation requiring more taxes, and concluded with numerous items Brown had promised to do but didn't carry through once elected.

"Now, you can have a good government *if* you are willing to participate," I concluded, thinking he was listening and taking it all in.

"Why didn't you tell me over the phone that you were colored?"

"Well, I didn't think it mattered with an intelligent man like you. You don't care about that. Are you prejudiced?"

"Oh no! Of course not. What makes you think that?"

"Why, ah—oh, just a dumb thought, I guess."

I continued to give my presentation on Ronald Reagan. "I've

finished. My ten minutes are up. I'm going to leave now. But I want to thank you for the opportunity to tell you about my candidate because I love this country so much that I'm willing to go anywhere to make sure that it works. Now that's it. Good-bye!"

"Where are you going?" he questioned.

"Well, my time is up."

"Then this is my time," he said, as he grabbed my arm. "How much money do you want?"

"Well, I know the guys at the office asked for $5,000, but we need a lot more than that. We could use at least $8,000."

"Suppose I give you $10,000. What would you say?"

"You put in $10,000, and you'll be invited to the Inaugural Ball."

"Can you be sure of that?"

"Look, if you don't get an invitation, I'll give you my ticket!"

"It's a deal."

Most of the contributions were between $1,000 and $5,000. I was amazed at the interest people were showing, and the year slipped by fast. Between June and November, our team raised $500,000, one fourth of Reagan's victory campaign budget.

I was so busy selling insurance, raising money, and studying, I sometimes met myself coming in as I was going out. But it was a challenge; it was exciting; it was what I call *really* living.

Ironically, my most difficult task was in getting support from the minorities, which I frequently addressed at political rallies. At first they booed me, thinking I was a betrayer of my race. But when I told them that their social welfare program could go down the drain if the state went broke, they sat up and took notice. If Brown's budget deficit got any worse, there simply wouldn't be any money left to finance all the welfare programs he bragged about. I told them that the only way to keep the state from going bankrupt was to have an "about-face," with new leadership.

During this period, Juanita, the children, and I had been attending a Baptist church. A few of the people were friendly; others were cold. We felt they would warm up when we got to know one another better.

One day I telephoned for an appointment with the minister. When I arrived, his secretary looked at me in surprise. It ran through my mind that she had not realized I was black when she had scheduled the appointment for me.

After disappearing into her employer's office for a moment, she returned to say, "I'm afraid the pastor is tied up; he can't be disturbed."

"Fine, how about tomorrow?"

"He's tied up tomorrow, too."

"Well, how about the next day?"

"He's tied up the next day, too."

"Next week?"

"Next week, too. In fact, he'll be tied up completely."

"Gee, is he that busy?" I said.

"Oh yeah, he's quite busy."

"Well," I said, "I can see him some Sunday right after church."

"He'll be tied up right after church, too," she said.

"Oh, you mean he's tied up as far as I'm concerned."

"That's right. I thought you'd never get it," she retorted.

"Okay."

"I'm sorry. That's what he told me to tell you," she said.

The next Sunday at the close of the service, the pastor asked all of the young boys to come forward to the altar who were giving their hearts to Christ. Ken stood up and went forward with three or four of his friends.

We noticed that the pastor asked all the other boys questions, their names, and how they felt about accepting Christ. When he got to Ken, he just said, "This is Kenneth Johnson," and went right on to the next boy.

At the end of the service, a date was announced for the boys' baptism. The following Sunday morning, I was called into the office of the assistant pastor.

"You know, I want to talk to you," he said. "You're a sensible, intelligent man, and you don't want to do anything that's against the Bible, now, do you?"

"Of course not."

"The pastor told me you'd be sensible and understand we only want to do what the Bible says, and we want to do it because the Bible is right."

"I agree with you."

"Your son went forward last Sunday."

"Yes, I'm very proud that he made a decision for the Lord."

"We are very proud, too. But you know, because the Bible pro-hibits our mixing together, you'll have to take your son to a colored church and get him baptized. After he's baptized, if you want to come sometime and listen to sermons here, that's fine. But we can't baptize him, and we can't let you join the church."

"I don't want to join your church, but I can't believe that Jesus Christ was a racist. I really feel sorry for all of you. How do you reconcile the Bible saying 'Go forth and preach the Gospel to every creature, baptizing him in the name of the Father, the Son, and the Holy Ghost.' How do you get around that?"

"He wasn't talking about blacks," the pastor's assistant countered. "I don't want to argue about it. I've got Scripture that I can show you. It's not my fault you were born black, and I was born white, and God chose to favor me and disfavor you. The curse is on you!"

"I'll stay here all day if you can prove that in the Scriptures for me."

"Well, I don't have time to look it up now, but you can see it later."

I shook my head in real sorrow for him. Then I closed my eyes and prayed aloud, "Lord, you know my heart, and you know my son's heart. We're sincere in our religious beliefs. We know that these two gentlemen cannot be on Your side under any circum-stances. So, Lord, help them to see the light, because I believe there is a lot of good in them."

It was very short and from the heart.

"One of these days, you will come to me and say you were wrong."

"I doubt that will ever happen, Johnny."

Ken's baptism was postponed indefinitely. But the Lord worked it all out a few months later in a Baptist church in Sacramento.

During all the time I was campaigning for Ronald Reagan and making the rounds as an insurance salesman, I never forgot to take time out to pray for Juanita, who was pregnant again. As Novem-ber neared, we looked forward with confidence to a new governor and a new baby.

According to my calculations, the governor would be Ronald

Reagan. And the baby would be a boy. Reagan was elected, and we named our new son Juan Eric.

After the election, I meant to dive back into my insurance selling, but Dennis Carpenter, one of my close friends and a leader in California Republican Party affairs, phoned to say that the new governor-elect wanted me to come up to Sacramento to work for the state.

"Look, I'm not going up there. I want to stay here and make some money again. He's in now, and he can do his job." I didn't feel it was time for a change of jobs when I'd been at my present job less than two years.

But then I heard from another Republican, Dave James, asking if I would join the Reagan team.

It was tantalizing, but again I declined.

I did consent, however, to attend Reagan's Inaugural Ball in Sacramento.

Mr. Reagan's inaugural address centered on the "creative society," and the need for unity in the party and unity among the people of California.

Having celebrated the victory, Juanita and I returned to Tustin, intending to resume a relatively quiet existence. But the phone started ringing again. Various people continued to call on behalf of the governor, who wanted me to come to Sacramento to join his "team." I persisted in telling them all politely that for the time being, I was going to concentrate on selling insurance.

One evening Juanita said, "Honey, I've been thinking about it. You know, if you continue like you are, all you're going to be is a rich old insurance man."

"That's all right with me," I said, but inwardly I knew that my goal was not forgotten.

"What about all those things you wanted to do in life, and how you wanted Christ to use you to help a lot of people? Government was to be the good place to do that, wasn't it?"

"I can still do that. I want to stay here and make myself a lot of money in Orange County," I teased her.

"I think the Lord would want you to go."

One evening about a week later, the phone rang.

"Yeah, yeah, of course, Denny. Cut it out, huh?"

"Denny? No, Johnny. This is really Ron. Look, can you come up to Sacramento for a talk? You and Juanita?"

I was sure it was Denny Carpenter, up to his tricks again. "Look, I'm Abraham Lincoln. I told you I wasn't going to Sacramento. Now, Denny, will you please stop this nonsense?"

"No, this is really Ronald Reagan. Wait just a minute."

Suddenly, another voice came on the line. "Johnny, this is Nancy."

Then I knew it was for real.

The job meant heading a staff of 3,600 who looked after helping 3 million California veterans get homes, farms, pensions, insurance, loans, schooling, and hospitalization. I had told the governor I'd consider it very carefully. My income would drop considerably—a pay cut hard to take at that time.

After our trip to Sacramento to discuss the job, Juanita and I got off the plane at Los Angeles and were greeted by newspaper reporters and TV cameras. "Mr. Johnson?"

"Yes."

"Are you an insurance man from Orange County?"

"Yes."

Lights flashed. "Congratulations."

"For what?"

"The governor just appointed you. You're the first black man he has appointed to his cabinet, and you're the only man appointed from Orange County."

"Oh no, you must have the wrong guy. I haven't accepted anything."

"You haven't? Look at these headlines." A newsman pushed a paper at me. "James E. Johnson, Santa Ana Negro insurance salesman, has been appointed by Governor Ronald Reagan to head the Department of Veterans' Affairs," it read.

If I could have pulled out Captain Midnight's cape, wrapped it around Juanita and myself, and flown away from those cameras, I would have gladly done so.

It is one thing to want to have your picture taken, another to be asked to comment on a job you haven't even accepted.

That night I called Denny Carpenter. "What's going on?"

"What do you mean, 'What's going on'? You accepted, didn't you?"

"No, I didn't. Now I can't reject it without embarrassing the governor. I guess I'll have to take it, but only for a year."

In February of 1967, I assumed the job. The family remained in Tustin until the school year was finished, and then we were all together again—in Sacramento.

As I drove up to the parking lot at the California Veterans' Home outside of Sacramento, a tall, wiry, tanned man in his late sixties strode over to me.

"Mr. Johnson, would you like to come over and look at my garden before going to our Bible meeting? I've got some unusual melons to show you."

For some reason, Mr. Henderson had taken a liking to me. He reminded me of an eager child. The Veterans' Home was his home, and I was part of his adopted family.

I was amazed at the activity going on. Older people were everywhere, some weeding, some just walking around looking at what others were growing. Mr. Henderson's melons were giants! I thought of what all this meant in larger terms.

These people were one of the most inspiring aspects of my new job as director of the Department of Veterans' Affairs. The self-sufficiency and independence of these senior veterans constantly amazed me.

Juanita and the children were also impressed and always willing to drop whatever they were doing to come out to the home with me on Sunday mornings for church services, or whenever we could spare the time just for visiting.

More than 1,500 people were domiciled here, supported by the state of California. If a man qualified for admission—by not having sufficient means of support and being unable to care for himself—he was given a place to live and his meals.

Those who had Social Security and a pension paid $200 a month. The men bought their own clothes at a store connected with the home. Men who became ill during their stay were transferred to the 600-bed hospital nearby.

After our Bible study, I was planning to visit some of the elderly people who couldn't come to church. Juanita thought they needed the most attention because they couldn't take advantage of all the activities planned for the more able, like swimming, bowling, bingo, cards, shuffleboard, and other games. For those with a farming background, there was even a small farm supervised by home personnel, where they could raise livestock.

"Look at my tomatoes, Mr. Johnson," Cliff Young, a little short man with a white beard, called out as we were about to leave. "I just threw the seeds in the ground, and with Mr. Henderson's help, they've turned out to be the biggest ones around."

"I don't think my advice is needed around here," I commented. "I've hardly ever stayed in one place long enough to plant daisies."

"You're from Orange County, ain't you?" Cliff asked. "My cousin runs an avocado farm down that way. Why did you want to leave that beautiful country to come up here?"

"It's a long story. Maybe I can tell you some of it on the way back to the hall."

Three of the men walked back with me, and I told them about Dad. "He'll be 101 years old this year, and when I told him about the offer of this job by Governor Reagan, he said, 'You'll do fine, son. When do you leave?'"

"Were you actually considering turning it down?" Mr. Henderson asked.

"Yes, I told Dad on the phone I hadn't planned on leaving the insurance business so soon. He reminded me about my other goals in life. And my wife, Juanita, kept asking me if all I was going to do was be a 'rich old insurance man.'"

"Are you sorry you came, Mr. Johnson?" Cliff Young inquired.

"No, when I see all the results of the vets' program, and how much you need help, I realize what a challenge it is."

"I'd like to meet your dad," Mr. Henderson said. "I think we might have a lot in common. It's just like my garden: I reap what I sow, and if I don't give those seeds the best chance for a new life that they deserve, I can't expect much, can I?"

I had to admit that he was right. I adopted Mr. Henderson as a second father. It was good to hear that kind of advice again.

About every two weeks, the governor and his wife invited members of the cabinet over to get to know each other better.

On one of these visits, I noticed that the governor had fifteen Bibles on his shelf. "Those are gifts," he said seriously. "But you really need only one. It's not important how many books you go through, but how many times the books go through you. That book, the Bible, has gone through me, and that's sufficient to get it into my heart. The Man from Galilee is always there to give you the support you need. I don't think anyone could be in government, Johnny, and make the decisions like you have to, without consulting the Man from Galilee."

When a reporter asked him, "Governor, whom are you patterning your life after?" Reagan replied, "Oh, that's very easy: the Man from Galilee."

In private, Governor Reagan loved to talk about horses and about the old days of radio in Iowa when he was a small-town announcer. One time in Iowa a black football player had come to town. No hotel would let him check in. Reagan found him trying to sleep on a bench in the bus station. He took him home, gave him a bed, and then on radio the next day, he gave the town a blistering. The following day the football player had all kinds of accommodation offers. It was one of the things I have not forgotten. Reagan did that way back when it wasn't popular to do anything for a Negro.

I had not held my position for more than six months when I discovered a big source of wasted taxpayers' money. In California, state vets were entitled to state-guaranteed home loans under the Cal-Vet Loan Program, similar to federal VA loans. For some reason, the loan administrators had been paying the property taxes rather than the borrower. The tab averaged $33 million a year. I had our department legal staff search out the authorization for permitting this practice. It could find no authority.

"We've been paying it for seventeen years," the staff reported. "When we first started, it was supposed to be done the first year, but it just kept going on."

"Unless you come up with an official document from the legislature giving me the authority to pay those taxes, I won't be paying out the $33 million."

"The veterans will rip you apart."

"Of course they won't. They don't want me to pay out money when I don't have the authority to do so."

"They'll rip the governor apart, too."

I went over and talked to the governor. "I'm going to save the state $33 million on the Cal-Vet Loan Program, which is already short of money. But I wanted you to know you are going to get blasted pretty hard for me doing this."

"What are you talking to me about it for? If it is going to save us money, go ahead and do it. I'll stand the heat," the governor assured me.

We sent out notices, 128,000 of them, with a brief letter stating, "Because there is a shortage of funds, those of you who can pay your property taxes, please do. If you cannot pay them, we will advance you the money, to be repaid to the state of California in six months."

The uproar was tremendous. When we investigated who was complaining the loudest, we discovered that it wasn't the "poor little veteran," it was restaurant owners, legislators, college professors judges, bankers, and others of the upper crust who were financially able to pay their taxes.

Threats on my life started to roll in, about twenty-five a week for a while. We had to change our home phone number. The governor assigned a uniformed policeman to stand in my office. Another policeman tailed me. I told some of the callers that the state-paid tax could be reinstated if it were approved by the state legislature, but no one attempted to pass such legislation.

My job was certainly varied! Another time, I had to force a patient to leave the California Veterans' Home because my staff found he didn't qualify. His family was well-to-do, his wife owned race horses and a $275,000 home, but because her husband was paralyzed and couldn't take care of himself, she'd arranged to have him put in the California Veterans' Home.

"Better take it easy on this one, Johnny," one of my aides warned me. "He was put in during the Brown administration, I suspect as a political favor."

"That's too bad," I replied. "He's taking up a bed badly needed by others who can't afford to go elsewhere."

I received threatening calls again, and Governor Reagan put the guard back in my office. That guard and I got to be good friends.

Then an assemblyman cursed me out on the phone one day and started an investigation of me. He even hired a private eye to shadow me, check on how much money I spent, how much time I spent in the office and at home. By the time he turned in his report, I'd worn him out.

One of my aides sneaked me a copy of his report, which had been supposed to be derogatory. It read, "After following Director Johnson around, I'm convinced of one thing: If nothing else, I believe the man is really a Christian. I've never seen a man pray so much, go to church so much." I chuckled. He'd been led to church several times, but never would come in.

I didn't know he was a detective the first time he came to see me, posing as someone who was interested in why the Department of Veterans' Affairs was going to shove a paralyzed old man into the gutter. I started talking to him about the home and the church services there. "Has anyone ever explained to you the way to Salvation?" I asked him suddenly.

"What has that got to do with the Veterans' Home?"

"Everything! Read John 1:9, then Philippians 4:13, then Psalms . . ."

"I didn't come here for a Bible lesson. I came to find out about this home."

"That's one of the reasons I'm so glad to go out there. It's part of my job, and it also gives me a chance to help those people spiritually. Two days ago, five people came to Christ, and I drove back crying with joy. When I told my wife about it, she couldn't wait to get out there to visit. When you called the other day, that's where we were."

The private eye's face lit up. "You mean you went out there on government time?"

"No, I went out there on God's time. I work from seven o'clock in the morning until about eight o'clock at night to do this, and I set aside some time for God when it's most convenient for those people out there."

He got up from his chair, shaking his head. "I'm convinced the assemblyman who sent me is wrong. You aren't what he said. You're all right."

A few days later, I noticed that no one was following me

anymore. I challenged the assemblyman's office, tried to get someone to come over and follow me, so I could show them what we
were doing, but no one would take me up on it.

In between veterans' controversies, I was surprised one day when
my secretary came to me and said there was a man outside, crying.
"He's a minister from an Orange County Baptist church."

"You've got to be kidding. Send him in."

The man walked in and fell on his knees. "Oh Brother Johnson,
how wrong I was. I've left that sinful church. I've left that man who
was an agent of Satan."

"Who are you talking about?"

"The pastor, of course—who wouldn't baptize your son, Kenneth. Lord, how wrong that man is. He's sending so many people's
souls to hell. Brother Johnson, forgive me."

"Don't you remember the prayer I prayed, Brother? That was the
end of it. I had forgiven you at that time. Get up off your knees.
Jesus Christ is the one I want you to pray to, not me."

"I'm torn up inside. My daughter has run off with some no-good
sailor, and I don't even know where she is. Could you help me,
Brother Johnson?"

I got the governor on the phone. "I'd like to use the Highway Patrol and any law-enforcement people you allow me to utilize to find
a man's daughter." I explained that she was fifteen years old and
had run off with a married thirty-year-old sailor who was AWOL.

"Johnny, you call Sullivan over at the Highway Patrol and tell
him he has my permission to do anything he can to help."

In less than forty-eight hours, the pair were found in a beachside
motel; the sailor was in custody, and the girl was back with her
parents.

After that, every time he came through Sacramento, this church-
man visited me. He always said that his former church had a lot of
good people, but as long as they were under the influence of the
pastor, they were being misled. "You know, you questioned that
Isaiah stated that blacks should not be baptized. The reason I
didn't show you that part of the Scripture then—I didn't know
where it was myself. I just believed what the pastor said. After you
had left, I tried to find it, and I haven't found it yet."

Because Mrs. Nancy Reagan took a personal interest in our Vietnam Veterans' Amputee Program, I got to know her very well. She, like the governor, was very open-minded, not prejudiced. She also was determined that all the amputees should be integrated into the community, and she visited the hospital many times to assist us in our program.

"It is the shock they experience when they first discover they've lost an arm, leg, or eye," a doctor explained to Nancy and me on one visit. "Usually they are unconscious when brought in. The next thing they know, they wake up, look at themselves, then reach for a leg or arm and it's not there. It's hard to prepare someone for this."

I found out what the doctor was talking about when several of us took Gunnery Sergeant Ross Marshall hunting with us. He hadn't spoken a word since he'd lost both legs in Vietnam. He'd shake his head, nod, make a sign, but would not speak.

We got him up in a good hunting spot in the Sierra Nevadas. One of our crew flushed a big buck. I didn't have my gun ready, but Ross did. When that buck came loping by, he raised his gun, and pow! He yelled, "I hit him, I got him, I got him! Well, what are you lookin' at me fer?" he cried. "Bring 'im in. I cain't!"

By the time we got back to town, we knew Sergeant Marshall's life history. We also knew that our program was working.

The rest of the year passed quickly, but twenty-four hours a day just wasn't enough time in which to witness for the Lord, visit with the elderly, do all the paperwork connected with the job, and have some time for honest thinking.

I'd already worked longer than the one year I'd agreed to as director of the Department of Veterans' Affairs. I felt that the $45 million worth of economic cuts and the belt-tightening we'd accomplished contributed to the success of Governor Reagan's program to bring efficiency into state government.

It all added up to a pat on the back from the governor, and a pledge from me to continue as director for a second year. But

Juanita and I were still convinced that our future lay in Orange County.

In the meantime, I kept getting telephone calls urging me to accept a position in Washington with the newly elected Nixon Administration.

When I talked to Dad about it, telling him I'd been thinking about going to Washington, he'd said, "Thinking about it? Stop thinking. When your country calls, you go and serve. What's there to think about?"

"Juanita doesn't want to leave our beautiful home here, Dad," I'd argued. "We've moved so much."

I was in the middle. Love for my country and love for my family were pulling at me. It was in the hands of the Lord. I'd wait for His answer.

And then one day the phone rang.

"President Nixon would like to speak to Mr. Johnson. Is he there?"

"Yes, this is Johnny Johnson," I said. "I hope You've got my answer, Lord. I'll need it now," I whispered.

CHAPTER

17

The next voice I heard was that of President-elect Richard M. Nixon. "How's the weather out there in California?"

"It's beautiful, and I love it out here."

"That's fine. Do you like it well enough to do some work for your state?"

"I'm doing some work now for my state, sir."

Nixon chuckled. "Yes, I know. But how about working for HEW?"

I cleared my throat. I had to be firm, even if it was the President-elect on the line. "No, sir, I wouldn't take that one at all. I don't take jobs where there is a minority. I would rather be working for all the people."

"I suppose you wouldn't take HUD either, then?"

"No, sir," I said.

"Then there's no need to talk about the OEO either," the President-elect continued. "But this other one is good. Remember, now, we have never had a black man on the Civil Service Commission. Why don't you think about that one? In the meantime, I'll have my people send you a ticket for you and your wife to come to the Inaugural Ball."

Juanita and I decided we would take the whole family. It could be a reunion with her mother and father, who were living in Virginia, and some other relatives on the East Coast.

Ken wasn't with us. He had already left to enroll at George Washington University. We would meet him there.

At Washington's Dulles International Airport, brilliant lights started to play on us. Turning to Juanita, I said, "There must be some dignitary among us. Did you see—could it be Governor Reagan?"

A reporter stuck a microphone in front of me. "How do you feel being the first and highest-ranking black to be appointed by the President-elect?"

"You must be mistaken," I answered, bewildered. "I have not been appointed by the President-elect."

The man grinned. "Oh, come on now. You have been appointed to be Vice Chairman of the Civil Service Commission." He waved a newspaper in my face. There was a terrible photo of me, with a big grin. The headline read, "BLACK CALIFORNIAN ON CIVIL SERVICE COMMISSION."

"That can't be me," I protested.

"I'm afraid it is, Johnny," Juanita said, while the kids looked, astonished to hear that bit of news.

The reporter asked, "Well, how do you feel? We understand Nixon had a hard time picking qualified men for these jobs. How did you qualify?"

I didn't really know what to say.

"How did you feel being the first black to be appointed?" he persisted.

"I don't know how I feel because I didn't know I was appointed," I replied, trying to edge away.

"Do you mean he appointed you without your knowing it?" The reporter went on. "If that's the case, are you going to accept?"

I would like to have talked to the people at the White House before answering that question, but I ended up by saying, "I'm delighted, if he has appointed me."

"Well, you will serve, then?"

What could I say? "We're not going to refuse the new President, are we?" I took Juanita's hand and gestured toward the children. "We have to go."

We had no more than gotten settled—at a Holiday Inn—when I

remembered I'd been told to go over to the White House for some preliminary instructions.

Exuberant and energetic, President-elect Nixon thanked us for all the work we had done. Fourteen of us were chatting with him, and there was a feeling of comradeship. Then in walked Lyndon B. Johnson, technically still President of the United States.

Everyone stood and applauded. President Johnson put his arm around the President-elect. "Dick, you have a fine group of people here. Are they all yours?"

"What do you mean?" Nixon asked.

Johnson laughed. "Don't make the same mistake I did. Look, you clean out every one of my appointees, and every one of the Kennedy appointments." He shook his head. "My big mistake was that I let too many people hang around. If you don't clean house, you'll make a mighty big mistake."

Nixon politely acknowledged President Johnson's advice, but we all knew he had already extended the appointments of quite a few Democrats, or had promised to do so.

Nixon welcomed us aboard and told us how pleased he was that we were joining him, making great personal as well as financial sacrifices in exchange for an opportunity to make history and to do some of the things we'd talked about.

The Inaugural Ball was a madhouse, spread out over eight hotels. There were about a million people, and to speak to even a small part of them, the new President had to travel from one hotel to the other.

Meanwhile, we were packed in like sardines at the Sheraton-Park.

We were well rewarded, however. When Richard Nixon finally arrived to speak, there was pandemonium. We had watched some of the ceremonies on closed-circuit TV. Everyone was happy about the way Nixon conducted himself and what he said: "Let's lower our voices, and join our hands, and move forward together."

Even the Democrats said this was his best speech ever, and President Nixon himself was on Cloud Nine. The newspapers commented, "If he means what he says, he will probably be the greatest President we've ever had!"

Getting my appointment confirmed resulted in so many hassles and headlines that at one point Governor Reagan called me:

"Johnny, why don't you just forget about those people and come back here, get your old job back, or any job, and join us again?"

"No, thank you, Governor. I'm going to stay here and fight this thing out."

"When those reporters get after you, don't go back and answer them. Say nothing," Reagan advised. "The best thing to do is to ask them to write out their questions and submit them to you for your answers."

I learned to do just that.

Finally there was a headline that read:

"NIXON'S BLACK APPOINTEE CLEARED"

I was to be sworn in on February 25, 1969, and I sent invitations to all of my friends on the Hill. Juanita held the Bible, and the chairman of the Civil Service Commission administered the same oath of office that the President of the United States takes, except for the words pertaining to the presidency.

Afterward there was a big cake and punch, and I made a little talk in which I said, "I hope I'm doing what the Lord would want me to do, and that is to further His work by serving Him in the way He wants me to serve."

A man by the name of Ed Penny came up. "Praise the Lord, Brother," he said. "My prayers have been answered. I wanted a person who would love the Lord first, be a Civil Service commissioner second. And you fill both prayers."

The confirmation had been tough, but the swearing-in ceremony made it all worthwhile.

While I was getting settled in my new job, Dad was getting settled in Forrest City, Arkansas, where he had gone to live. Dad had liked the surroundings and the warm sunshine. He really enjoyed himself there, getting up early in the morning and going for long walks. He was now 104 years old, but he still did his daily bend-overs and situps.

I called him quite often to see how he was. He had turned his hobby of making clothes baskets into a lucrative business, earning enough to support himself. One of the times I called him he told me about a gash on his lower leg; the hatchet he used to cut white oak had slipped. He had cleaned the wound and bandaged it. "And the good Lord will take care of the rest," he said.

I told him about a recent trip to San Francisco. "Colonel Ed Kennedy was retiring, and he asked me to come out and be the principal speaker at his retirement banquet, Dad. You'll never believe what happened."

"You'll have to tell me, son, but I bet they pinned another medal on you."

"No. Do you remember me working as a man Friday for a major general, the assistant commandant of the Washington base way back when I was called a 'dreamer' for wanting to be a U.S. senator? The one who said the Marine Corps would never be integrated?" I went on, not waiting for his answer.

"Well, I was a little late for this speech, due to plane schedules, and they were all waiting in this room—the VIP room, they called it—where all the dignitaries were assembled before we were to march in and sit at the head table. The banquet room was packed with people all waiting for the event to begin. When I walked in, the first person to spot me was this general. He shook my hand, and I thought he had been sent to greet me.

"'Well, how are you, General?' I said enthusiastically.

"'Well, uh, I'm fine,' he stuttered, looking around at the door. 'But you'll have to get out of here! This is for the VIPs. We're waiting for the vice chairman of the Civil Service Commission.'

"'You haven't read your program, have you?' I asked.

"'Listen, what has that got to do with it?' he sputtered. He seemed to be upset now. 'Where is the program chairman? I'm going to get you out of here before you start trouble again!'

"'Well, General,' I went on, 'if you would read your program, you would see that I am the vice chairman of the Civil Service Commission.'

"'You are what???' he exploded. Then he grabbed his program, opened it, and his face turned three different colors. There it was in black and white: James E. Johnson, vice chairman of the Civil Service Commission.

"I laughed. 'I guess you haven't been listening to the radio news, watching TV, or reading your newspaper anymore, eh, General?'

"'Well, I'll be darned,' he said. 'I guess I don't read enough anymore.'"

I had to wait a minute for Dad to stop laughing.

"The general stammered around for a few minutes, then I asked him about his wife and learned she had died.

"'I'm so sorry. She was a great lady, and I loved her.'

"'She loved you, too,' he said. 'She always stood up for you.'

"I gave my speech, Dad, but the whole time I was speaking, the general sat there in disbelief. Then after the speech, when I was standing there shaking hands with everyone, he came up again.

"A black second lieutenant Marine was standing nearby, and the general reached over and grabbed him and pulled him over to me. 'I'll show you what can be done in the Marine Corps. This man was under me, and you see where he has gotten?'

"Then I said as I shook hands with the young fellow, 'You can do it, but without his help.'

"'You mean he didn't help you?' he asked.

"'No, actually he was very discouraging and very negative. But remember, you have to eliminate all the negatives and emphasize the positives. Then you must sacrifice.'"

Dad seemed pleased with the whole conversation. I told him, "Take care of that leg, now."

But apparently the hatchet had been rusty. The leg started giving Dad trouble. He cleaned it out and wrapped it again, since he never believed in going to a doctor for anything. He thought if you had a wound in your body that wouldn't heal, it was your time to go.

In a later phone conversation, I sensed he wasn't telling me everything about that leg. "I'm going to take a flight out there," I told Juanita. "See how he's doing."

She urged me to go. I called a few of my sisters and told them I'd report. It was worse than we all suspected. Gangrene had set in. Dad had been limping around with it for quite a while. I insisted he see a doctor at a local hospital. Just to pacify the family, he went.

The doctor told me he was afraid my dad would die unless the leg was amputated immediately.

Dad wouldn't listen to the doctor.

"I'll talk to him," I said.

To see him lying there in bed with a white sheet over his leg was a shock. I tried not to look alarmed. "Dad, it's not bad to have just one leg. We'd rather have you, Dad, with one leg, than not at all."

"What are you talking about, boy?" He pulled the sheet up a little farther, and I could see his hands clench with pain.

"I'm talking about the doctor being able to save your life by amputating your leg."

He looked back at me with those clear eyes. "Aw, son. I'm 104, and a man has to die sometime, of something. That's what the Lord wants me to die of. But he wants me to die with both of my legs!"

"But that's the point, Dad. The doctor says you are very healthy otherwise. By removing your leg, your life will be saved. Otherwise, the gangrene will reach your heart, then your brain, and that will be it."

Dad's eyes snapped. "He doesn't know that."

"Scientifically, he does, Dad."

"If the Lord wants me to live, I will. If not . . ."

I couldn't talk him out of his decision. Later we talked about other things. He bombarded me with questions about the family and his favorite topic, Ken. "How's my Ken?"

"He's just fine."

"You know, Ken is like you, but he's almost too good to live."

"Aw, Dad, don't say that."

"No, son. You know and I know that there is something different about him. He's too good. You weren't that good."

I laughed. "Gee, thanks, Dad."

"I'm serious. When that boy talks about Christ and the things he wants to do for Him and for the world, he is just too good."

"What do you mean, 'too good'?"

"He has no evil about him. You know, when you used to steal apples . . . well, I was so happy when you got straightened out because I knew that Satan was trying to take over, but thank the Lord, He straightened you out."

"I'll be back in a while now; I've got to talk to the doctor again."

I went out of the room puzzled about what he had said about Ken. That was like Dad to be thinking about someone else at this time. I found the doctor.

"He doesn't want it off."

"I hate to suggest this, but I see it as the only way. If you sign the papers, we could put him to sleep and then remove it."

Picture after picture flashed through my mind of the amputee veterans at the California hospital, and all of the work that we had had to do with them. I couldn't do that to Dad. He would hate me until he went to his grave. I tried to explain this to the doctor. "And I think Dad is right in his own feelings. I can't make a decision like that for him. What chance does he have?" I then asked fearfully.

"What chance does a 104-year-old man have with something like this?" He said as kindly as he could, "The prognosis has to be that he will die."

I broke down and cried. I didn't know what I would do; I had always been able to call on Dad when things got rough.

"It will only be a few days," he tried to console me. "He is really strong. I don't know how he stands the pain."

I knew. I visited Dad every day. We had some time together before my brothers and sisters came, and our conversations always ended with Dad telling me that love, above all else, was the important thing in life. "If you have love, and love is God, you don't need anything else. You know how to treat your fellow man. You don't let things irritate you. I have found this is the most important thing in life, to be able to love and love my fellow man."

He smiled as he lay there, holding the Bible in one hand, grasping the sheet with the other. "Your mother is smiling down on us now, son. She was the one who prepared our food and a place for us to sleep every day, and she was the one who set us straight and kept us straight with the Lord. I know she has prepared a place for me, son, and I am anxious to be with her."

· "But, Dad," I said, trying to hold back the tears, "you'll be out of here in a few days."

"Yes, son, I will—but not in the way you're talking about. I'm not fooling myself. I'm ready."

I knew he was right. I tried to set myself for what was to come. I knew Dad's influence had been powerful in my life, and I had often been guided by his wisdom. I also knew that sometimes I had used him as a crutch, always knowing that I could go back to him. Now I would have no mother or father.

As if he knew what I had been thinking, Dad looked over at me. "Son, you will do great things in life, without me, too. But you've got to remember one thing: Don't worry about who gets the credit; just get the job done. You know, that magic I told you about, love; it doesn't just go for your people, it goes for your country, because this is a great country. This country has given me 104 years to see so many developments, and it gave me an opportunity to worship Christ in my own way."

Dad pointed a long finger. "I'll tell you like I told one of those young preachers down the road. A lot of people are going to try to tell you about the 'new religion, the new church,' and about making all kinds of changes. Now, there are three things in my mind I want you to know about: the Father, the Son, and the Holy Spirit. Son, don't you let anybody mess those things up for you. You must think about those three things."

By this time my brother Amos and all of my sisters who were able to come had arrived. We made quite a group around Dad's bed, and whenever he felt like talking, someone was there to listen. Every evening when we were ready to leave, we would all hold hands and pray. And Dad would end with, "O Lord, we sure thank You because we're all here, and we're getting along just fine, and we're sure much obliged. Amen."

The last night I knew I could be with Dad during this prayer, I almost broke down. I kissed him on the forehead, and he held my hand very tightly, as if he were saying, "This is the last time I will grip your hand, the last time I will see you in this world." Dad understood I had stayed as long as I could.

I could see as we were talking that the pains were getting more frequent. He would straighten up after one, then move around in the bed; a smile would cross his face. Sometimes he would bite his lip hard. I asked him if he would just let the doctor give him some shots to make him more comfortable.

"No, son. I want to meet the Lord with both legs, a clear head, and a clear mind. I don't want to be all doped up when I get there."

It took so much courage for Dad to go this way. I didn't know if I could have done it. Walking out the door that night, knowing that I would not see him alive again, was one of the hardest journeys I'd ever made.

Dad lasted until March 23, 1969. Ken and I flew back for his funeral. Juanita was having trouble with her arthritic hip, and we didn't think she should travel. Ken was broken up about his grandfather's death, and in consoling him, I was able to gain control of myself.

The first words my brother said were, "Dad said to tell you, 'When James hears about this, tell him I died happy. I still expect great things out of him, and he can go as far as he wants as long as he remembers Philippians 4:13. Now I'm just going to relax.' And he did. No groaning. He just slipped away."

Ken remarked how young Dad looked, even handsome. There were few lines in his face, just a few gray hairs, not even white. He didn't look like an old man, just about sixty.

As I sat in the church listening to the eulogy, I said one too. I remembered all of the times I had been able to call him and discuss my problems. Before taking any next steps, I had always called Dad.

The time I was about to accept my warrant officer commission and had had so much guff from everybody. "Remember, do all things through Christ," he had said. "If you really believe that, son, you don't have to worry at all." That had been the answer I had needed.

I remembered calling him before I went to Okinawa in World War II, feeling sorry for myself because I knew I might not come back. "Don't ever think about going over to fight; you're going over to serve your country and serve God; that is what is important, son," he had reminded me. "The Bible says, 'If you lose your life for My sake, you will find it again.'"

I had asked him to come out to visit us in California, and he'd said casually, "Oh, I'll be out there sometime."

Not until I phoned the news of a new grandson in 1966 did he get on a plane and come out. When he arrived, he'd said, "I feel like a celebrity. They were all so sweet to me, just because they found out I'm 101 years old. Everyone took turns sitting by me and shaking my hand."

Later, after we had calmed him down from the flight, he had said, "I don't want people remembering me because of my age, but because of the contributions I've made."

I sat there thinking about those contributions; he had certainly done his share.

When he was laid to rest, Ken said, "It isn't important what you do for yourself; that dies with you. It's what you do for others that lives after you are dead."

I would hear those same words spoken again four years later. Ken and I flew back to Washington, D.C., with a new determination to be a credit to Richard Jackson Johnson.

CHAPTER

18

Dad's death and his strong faith at the end renewed my own bonds with God. When I returned to Washington, I redoubled efforts to build up the prayer luncheons that Ed Penny and I had started at the Civil Service Commission.

When I first arrived in Washington, D.C., the Holy Spirit had been on my mind because of the many prayer breakfasts I had started in California. On my first morning in office I called my staff together at the Civil Service Commission and told them we were going to start a prayer breakfast.

One of my staff members jumped up. "Mr. Commissioner, you know we can't have prayer breakfasts in a government building; not here, nor in any state."

"Well, we've got this one licked because Washington, D.C., isn't a state," I replied.

The staff looked at each other for a moment. Then another member said, "But Mr. Commissioner, nobody would show up even if you had a prayer breakfast. There isn't anything you could say to get them to a prayer breakfast, particularly at six-thirty in the morning."

"Well, maybe I could write them a memorandum," I said.

"I'm sure a memorandum won't do any good," another staffer commented.

I said I'd write the memo and see. I wrote it out:

On Wednesday morning at six-thirty there will be a prayer breakfast in the conference room of the Civil Service Commission. You are cordially invited to attend. Signed, J. E. Johnson, vice chairman of the Civil Service Commission.

Right underneath this I put these words: *"The man who hires and fires."*

The place was jam-packed. There wasn't room to sit. After that, everybody came. It was sort of the "in" thing if you worked for the Civil Service Commission.

At the third meeting, we spoke on forgiveness from Matthew 18:21–22. Peter said to Jesus, "Lord, how often should I forgive my brother who sinned against me? Seven times?"

Jesus answered, "No, seventy times seven."

We talked about a forgiving heart. Many people there felt great malice toward the Nixon administration because they feared for their jobs.

After the meeting, the third-highest-ranking civil servant in the Civil Service Commission began to cry, "I now see what the prayer breakfast is all about. It's bringing people into the Body of Christ."

There wasn't a dry eye in the place when he finished giving his testimony how his whole life had been changed. He was a Catholic who felt the worst thing that could happen would be to have to attend a prayer breakfast!

At about the ninth meeting, I told this same civil servant of various things that had happened to people who believed in Word Faith. I told him what it said in Mark 11:23:

"For verily I say unto you, that whoever shall say to this mountain, 'Be thou removed, and be thou cast into the sea,' and shall not doubt in his heart, but shall believe that those things which he saith shall come to pass, he shall have whatsoever he saith."

I explained, "Whatever you said, you confess that's what will happen."

Afterward, the civil servant came up to me. "Johnny," he said, "you've got to go back and tell those people that you didn't mean what you said."

"What does it mean?"

"Look, you didn't mean literally that a mountain would move. You meant that as a figure of speech."

"No," I replied, "that's not what I mean. I mean *literally*."

"That's impossible."

"No, no! Nothing's impossible," I answered. "It says in Matthew that nothing's impossible with God. And when the Word says it will be moved, it will be moved."

Then he questioned, "I've got a hole in my backyard about 4½ feet deep. I've got a pile of dirt right beside that hole. I've got a back problem and can't fill it. Do you mean to tell me that if I pray and ask the Lord to move dirt into that hole, He's going to move that dirt into the hole?"

"Of course," I assured.

"I'm going to prove something to you," he challenged. "I'm going to pray right now, so you'll hear me."

He did: "Lord, I want You to move that dirt and fill that hole because my back is giving me all kinds of trouble. I ask this because the Word says I'll have whatsoever I saith, and I say: 'Move the dirt into the hole.'"

About ten o'clock the next day he was back. He asked me, "You heard me pray, didn't you?"

"Yes, I sure did."

"Well, just to be sure the Lord heard me, I prayed all the way home. Just to be real sure, I prayed just before I went to bed. Just to be absolutely sure He heard me, as the first thing of the day, I prayed again. Then I opened the curtains and looked out. That dirt had not moved one inch!"

He added, "I knew it wasn't going to move in the first place!"

"Well, so did I."

"Aha! I told you so!"

It was time for me to explain: "Now, wait a minute! The Bible says that if you believe in your heart, have faith in your heart, do not doubt—but you doubted."

"Okay," he countered, "you're such a great Christian. Why don't *you* pray for that dirt to move?"

"Fine," and I began to kneel.

"Let's go into the office."

"No," I said. "We'll pray right here." Then I asked the Lord very simply: "In the name of Jesus, Father, we ask that You make this manifest unto my brother and he will know the power of the Holy Spirit and that the dirt will be moved into the hole before the day is gone. Hallelujah! Praise the Lord!"

He was understandably skeptical: "Is that all?"

"That's it."

He left. But about four minutes past six o'clock that evening I overheard my secretary saying, "I'm sorry. He cannot speak to you now. He's in conference."

There was a long pause. Then she resisted, "Well, I don't care what the dirt has done! He is not to be disturbed."

I called out to her. "Hold it! Let me have that phone." I took the receiver and heard the man say, "Where've you been? I've been trying to get you all day! The dirt—it's moved!

"The people from the county came by and saw that big hole in the yard. They were afraid some kids might fall in. So they sent a crew out and filled the hole up!"

"Praise the Lord!"

"But," the man exclaimed, "you didn't tell me how the Lord was going to do it."

"The Lord didn't tell me how He was going to do it either, but the hole is filled."

"Well," the man affirmed, "I'll never doubt the faith of any person and the power of the Holy Spirit."

Another experience at the Civil Service Commission concerned an employee fired for drinking. He had been warned about his alcoholism.

One morning as my black driver and I pulled up in front of the Civil Service Commission, we saw this white man lying in the gutter, sloppy drunk.

I got out of the car and took him by the hand. "Brother, what's wrong?"

"Those doggone Civil Service commissioners fired me yesterday! I have six children. I don't know what I'm going to do."

He had vomited over all his clothing and was a mess. "Let me take you home," I said. "Maybe I can talk to the Civil Service Commission."

"Stay away from those guys! They don't like black people," he warned. "They'll throw you out."

"Why don't you let me take you home?" I asked.

He was crying as we drove him home. "You driver boys must have a hard time around here, too," he said, thinking both of us were chauffeurs. My driver tried to tell him who I was, but I interrupted.

After reaching his house, we supported him between us and walked him to the door. We were met by his wife, who screamed and cursed at him, then looked at my driver and me before scowling at her husband. "I don't know why these colored boys are doing this for you."

The alcoholic began saying bad things about the Civil Service commissioners. I turned to his wife and told her what I wanted her to do. "You clean him up and see that he gets a good night's rest. Tomorrow morning, I want him to see me."

"To see you?" she questioned. "You chauffeurs are good boys, but there's nothing that you could do for him."

My driver had enough by this time. "Lady, this man is not a chauffeur! He's the vice chairman of the Civil Service Commission."

The woman almost fainted. She began to cry and beg, "Please!"

"No, no!" I assured. "Hold it! Hold it! You take care of him. I want to see him tomorrow morning."

Before I left, I prayed for him and his wife. I then told her, "I know the Lord has touched his heart. He'll be a changed man."

Before he arrived the next morning, I went down to the printing room where he'd worked. I told them what I'd done. "Take him back," I urged, "I think the Lord has touched his heart."

When he came in, I quietly instructed him to go back to work. Later, when I saw him working in the printing room, he promised me, "I don't know how I'm going to thank you, but believe me, I pray that someday I will be able to do something for you."

Seven years later, in 1976, I was with the American Family Life Insurance Group. I had a sizable group health insurance policy under consideration by a large company, but everyone there seemed to be saying, "No, we don't want it."

A man stood up. "Dr. Johnson doesn't remember things he's done for people." Then he told his story. "I was an alcoholic. That man picked me up out of the gutter, carried me home, and gave me a job. I went to Alcoholics Anonymous and got myself straightened out. Now I'm in charge of a division in this company." He turned to the people. "I don't care what this man tells you, believe it. We're going to take this policy right now."

I didn't remember him at all. But he retold the story right there to about seventy-five people gathered in a union hall. Before I left, eight people asked me to come to speak to their groups, who wanted to know more about the Holy Spirit.

I still get chill bumps when I think about that: a little thing I had done, and the man remembered it seven years later.

I had the opportunity to start a prayer luncheon at the Cosmos Club—an organization for upper-crust bureaucrats and federal employees. The club was so exclusive that even members' wives had to come in the side entrance. Unknowingly, I walked right in the front door and waited for the waiter to seat me for our prayer luncheon —the first in a series of breakfasts and Bible study sessions for an hour every other Thursday.

The waiter stopped me. "I'm sorry, you can't come in here. We don't have any facilities for the colored."

"Well, I'm here for a specific reason," I said in surprise.

"I'm sorry," the waiter insisted, "but you just can't come in."

I looked around. All of the people serving were black. "Well, I see some other black people in here."

"Oh, that's different. Do you want a job?" He looked me over very carefully. "We could certainly use some tall waiters."

"No, thank you," I said politely.

"I'm sorry then, but you'll have to leave."

I went outside and waited for some of the other members to come along, not wishing to embarrass the waiter. When several of the members arrived and started in, I hung back.

"Aren't you coming in?"

"I've already been kicked out. I'm afraid one of you will have to go in and vouch for me," I said laughingly.

When they went in and explained to the waiter who I was, he apologized all over the place. "We've just not had Negroes in here before."

"Well, you will now," the member assured. "Johnny Johnson will be one of the first to break down discrimination in this club."

Later, the head waiter and I became very close friends, and I was able to help him make a decision for Christ.

I continued to help get the prayer breakfasts started in Washington. Then Harry Dent, counselor to the President, suggested that we begin one at the White House.

One morning Arthur Burns attended. They had invited him, but because of his Jewish religion, they were not going to talk about Jesus—only God. However, they forgot to tell me, and I was the speaker.

There I was, telling forty people packed into the room with Arthur Burns about the Lord and Savior, Jesus Christ, and how He died on the cross and saved us from our sins.

I looked toward the back of the room. Doug Coe, who for years had set up the President's national prayer breakfasts, was waving his hands. I thought he was just happy, so I beamed, "Praise the Lord, Doug!" He shook his head; then, all of a sudden, he put his head down on the table. I thought he was crying for joy.

But after the meeting, everyone was joyful, except Doug.

"Johnny, you blew it!"

"What do you mean?"

"Don't you know who was here?"

"No. Who was here?"

"Arthur Burns was here!"

"Praise the Lord!"

"Johnny, you don't understand. He's Jewish! We told him you weren't going to be talking about Jesus, and that's all you talked about."

"That's all I ever talk about."

"But Johnny, you were supposed to talk about God!"

"Listen! That *is* God."

"I think you've blown it, Johnny. I don't think we'll ever get him to come again."

But that afternoon Doug called, all excited. "Johnny, you did it!"

"I did what?"

"Guess who called me!"

"I don't know."

"Arthur Burns! He loved your speech and wants to know more about what the Bible says about Jesus!"

"Well, praise the Lord!" I rejoiced. "I'll ask him to one of our Full Gospel Fellowship meetings."

Arthur Burns not only came, but he also sat on the platform through the whole meeting, read the Scripture for us, and enjoyed every minute of the meeting.

It all happened because of the prayer breakfast. People began doing things they'd never done before. One of the things people had going for them was that they stated, over and over—at every prayer breakfast we had—it was love that was brought out in every one of us. We were able to love each other as brothers and sisters. (We did have ladies who came to our prayer breakfasts, too.)

After that White House prayer breakfast, we started three at the Pentagon: the first on the Navy side with Frank Sanders of the Navy Department; the second on the Army side; and the third for Department of Defense employees.

But the White House prayer breakfasts in the executive dining room were of particular interest because we saw people come together in Christ such as Senator Harold Hughes and Charles Colson, formerly bitter political enemies. Many congressmen and some of the President's staff attended frequently.

Redoubled efforts for the Lord meant working with and attending four prayer breakfasts and two prayer luncheons every week.

However, my satisfactions were not confined to family, prayer meetings, and my job. There were others as well. I had never left the boy scouts, having been on the board of the Golden Empire council in California. When I got to Washington, I was appointed to the fifty-eight-member national council, and a short time later to the executive board of ten members. I became the first black to serve on the executive board of the Boy Scouts of America. I took over the paraprofessional committee, which was seeking to correct the fact that not enough college-level people were applying for leadership positions in the scouting program. Solving this was a vital necessity if we were to meet the national council's goal of reaching one third of all the boys in the nation to make them good scouts and good Americans.

Also, during 1970, I had a number of speaking engagements before veterans' groups, civil service organizations, and city councils throughout the state of Maryland and Washington, D.C. area. One such invitation came from, of all places, Birmingham, Alabama. Even more unusual was the fact that it was from a union convention. Unions don't usually cotton to Republicans, especially conservative ones. And there had been much discrimination during the past thirty years against blacks in the trade union movement. *Here I was, a black conservative Republican going to speak at a Democratic-oriented union membership in "apartheid" Alabama.*

When I landed at the Birmingham airport, no one met me, so I had to catch a cab. At the hotel, I was truly astounded. That same Birmingham hotel in 1951 wouldn't have let me come inside unless I'd carried someone's bag up to their room. To be served twenty years ago, a black person had to go around to a side door and speak through a window to order a hamburger and cold drink, then had to stand out on the street to eat it. Now here I was, the vice chairman of the U. S. Civil Service Commission, coming back to all of this.

No one at the hotel knew I was a high government official, let alone the union's main speaker—only that I was black. Still, a white doorman walked up to the cab door and said, "Sir, can I help you with your bags?"

What a feeling! "You certainly can," I agreed.

Once inside I told the white bellman, "My name is Johnson, and I am the vice chairman of the Civil Service Commission."

"They've been looking high and low for you."

A lady, who had been dashing around, buttonholed the bellman. "Do you know where Mr. Johnson is?"

"He's right here."

"Oh my stars! I'm so happy to see you, Mr. Johnson. We've just heard so much about you! I'll show you up to your room."

"I'll just check in."

"You don't have to do that. We've got a nice suite for you, and you're already checked in. Come on, I'll take you up, show you around, then it will be time for the meeting."

In 1951, people who had just taken off their hoods would have come running up there with shotguns, bowie knives, tar and feathers, and ropes. But I was in a changed South, a new Dixie. The bellman brought my bag up to my room.

The banquet room was packed. The lady, who'd introduced herself as Mrs. Emily Foggarty, took my arm and led me up to the platform. The table at which I was to sit was right under a hanging chandelier. We had dinner, then I began my speech.

In the audience of fifteen hundred, only three hecklers turned up. Eight police officers kept them toned down.

I prefaced my remarks with a description of the new South and the changes I'd noticed. I told them how great I thought America was. No other country could make such a change without a tremendous amount of bloodshed. "Maybe this country won't survive forever," I said. "But the world will always remember the United States of America."

I was given a standing ovation and was busy shaking hands for nearly two hours. One woman came up to say, "I have never in my life voted for a Republican. And I just know my poor ole daddy is just going to turn over in his grave, but I'm going to vote for your President."

"You mean *our* President," I corrected her.

The speech had an interesting result. One day several months later I heard on the intercom someone asking my secretary if he could see me. "I'm the administrative assistant," I heard him say, missing part of what followed. "I've come to Washington from . . . to see Director Johnson."

I was over at the window adjusting the drapes when my secretary showed the gentleman in. He looked around, almost through me. "Where is Director Johnson?" he asked.

I strode over to him and held out my hand. "Hi. I'm Johnny Johnson, vice chairman of the Civil Service Commission."

The visitor gulped, "Well, er, uh, my boss, the governor, heard a part of your speech on the radio while driving to his office. I think it was your speech. Did you give a speech?"

"Which one?"

"In Birmingham?"

"Yes. I spoke to a union gathering."

"You said those things about America and the South?" he asked, seeming rather shocked.

"Well, I guess I did at that."

"The governor asked me to come and get a copy of your speech."

"Fine," I said. "What governor are you talking about?"

"Governor Wallace, of course. Of Alabama. He heard part of it on the radio the next morning," the aide explained. "Governor Wallace listened for a while and said, 'Say, who is that guy?'

"'Some bureaucrat from Washington, D.C.,' I told him.

"'Didn't know they had a bureaucrat in Washington with that much sense,' the governor said. 'See if you can get a copy of the speech for me.'

"I called the radio station to discover they didn't have a copy of it—only a tape. I was coming to Washington, so I'm here to pick it up."

"I would never have expected Governor Wallace to be interested in my speech."

"Well, he really is. Now . . . uh, I'm also going to have to tell him that you are black."

I smiled. "Well, I hope you do tell him I'm black! I'm very proud to be a guy who can wear his suntan the year around." He laughed and left with a copy of the speech.

Three weeks later, Governor Wallace's administrative assistant was back. "I've got a present for you," my visitor said.

"Hmmm," I responded. "Don't tell me. Let me guess: a Ku Klux Klan robe?"

He laughed. "No. Nothing like that. Governor Wallace proposed to the state militia a special recognition for you, and it was unanimously approved. You'll be the first black in the history of Alabama to be commissioned a lieutenant colonel in the Alabama militia. And here's your certificate, signed by Governor George C. Wallace."

I could hardly believe my eyes or ears.

One of the projects I was engaged in as vice chairman of the Civil Service Commission was the Affirmative-Action Program. We had found that people were discriminated against by being forced to take tests reflecting white middle-class values, to which a lot of minorities couldn't relate. Our program was designed to take the bias out of the test. Several blacks had commented that the words and sentence structures were foreign to them. Not all of those who took the tests had gone to a white school.

We were able to take out some questions we knew black schools did not normally use, and add some, more in line with their experience, changing the tests enough to give everyone a fair chance without lowering standards.

We also relaxed the program so that if some people could not pass the exam, they had a chance for a ninety-day-to-six-month trial period to prove their capabilities by performance. In 95 per cent of the cases, these people did better on the job than those who'd passed the test! Then those who had failed the test were given the chance to take the test over again, and most of them passed.

When I first went to the Civil Service Commission, they bragged to me that they had more than 22 per cent minorities working for the government. This sounded very good. But a closer look revealed that about 58 per cent were near the bottom of the scale, in menial task jobs, while, in the better jobs, only .05 per cent were minorities. Revamping the tests helped to achieve more upward mobility for minorities.

Another device the Johnson and Kennedy administrations used had been to encourage blacks and other minorities to accept lower-echelon jobs without taking any exam. While this sounds generous, it barred them forever from moving upward, because all other jobs above them were available only by passing exams. A huge number of minorities were trapped in static job situations and were forced to watch others promoted who had come in long after they had.

A lot of the minorities assumed that failure to be promoted was because of their color, and there were all kinds of problems in the Department of Housing and Urban Development. Minorities occupied the administrative office and demonstrated simply because they were frustrated.

Our Affirmative-Action Program was designed to identify discrimination—whether it was due to race, religion, creed, or sex—and then point out remedies.

We streamlined the personnel system, reducing the number of federal employees by more than 15 per cent (from 3 million to 2.8 million) without actually using the meat ax—we simply phased out some programs and put workers in other civil service vacancies. At the same time, we persuaded the President to set up a new board to see that women got a fair shake in the competition for upper-grade jobs.

Most of those promoted according to our merit system were

whites (twenty-eight to one), many of whom had complained that they'd been denied promotion for one reason or another, such as sex or favoritism.

In the midst of all this that was so encouraging, I was hit with discrimination on a personal level. It had to do with a college professor with whom Ken began having a conflict.

Ken had been a straight-A student all his life, but when he became a student in a political science professor's course at George Washington University, he started out on the wrong foot—the "right" one—as far as that professor was concerned.

The professor bluntly announced, "I am a liberal left-wing Democrat. If there are any Young Americans for Freedom or Republicans in here, you can be excused, because we are just not going to get along."

These were fighting words, and I wondered if Ken would try to stick it out.

Ken decided to try. Almost immediately, an issue arose over which student and teacher locked horns. The professor attacked the "radical right wing," and especially Barry Goldwater. Ken, who had written speeches for Barry Goldwater, Jr., contradicted him on nearly every point, telling him and the class how it really was.

After a few days, the professor asked Ken to see him in his office after class. "Look, Mr. Johnson. You are embarrassing me in front of my class."

"I'm sorry about that, but I feel it's my duty to tell the other side of the story."

The professor snorted. "It's your duty to sit and listen. I'm telling you now, you either quit it, or you are going to get an F."

Ken flashed back to all the work he'd already done, and his performance in other classes. "I've been doing A work all along."

"That," the professor said, "is a matter of opinion. In my book, you don't deserve an A." The professor tried to grin. "You're a reasonable and intelligent young fellow. Why don't you play it cool, Johnson? Just stay off my back, and you can have your A."

Ken came to me. "Dad, I'm still having trouble with that left-wing professor." He told me what had happened. "What do you think I should do?"

"Whatever you think your conscience tells you to do, son." I tried to remember what my dad had said on similar occasions. "If you feel you should go ahead and speak out, do so. If you want to play it safe, go ahead and leave him alone. Then you'll probably get that A."

"Would you play it safe?"

"Nope."

"Would you speak out?"

"Yep."

"Even if you thought you were going to get an F?"

"Absolutely!"

"That's all I wanted to know."

The next time the class met, the professor seemed unusually confident. He had mistaken Ken's silence. When Ken stood up to comment on something he'd said, the professor was all smiles. "Now, listen, everyone," he said, "Ken Johnson has changed his viewpoint. He now understands that the radical right is against the black people and against what is good in this country. So let's listen to what he has to say."

Ken began. "I want to tell all of you students that I hate sin. What happened in this class is worse than in Hitler's time. Our professor has threatened me. If I don't stop telling the truth in here and counteracting the lies he is telling, I will get an F. Well, before I get that 'F,' I want to say, don't listen to him! Think for yourself. Be a man. Be a woman. Stand up for what you know is right, not what someone says." He blurted it out fast but emphatically. Then he sat down.

The students applauded. The professor's jaw dropped, then he called for order, glaring at Ken. He quickly gave a homework assignment and dismissed the class. After class he told Ken not to bother to come back anymore.

Ken told me all this the next morning. I said, "Let's go and talk to the university president, okay?"

When we confronted the president with the information, he called in the professor. The president kept firm command of the conversation as the professor and Ken each told his side of the story. Then the president made his decision: Ken was to be allowed to return to the class.

When the grades came out, Ken got a C.

This was Ken's first C in his career, and it really hurt. He promptly enrolled again in the same class, but taught by another professor. When grades came out, Ken received an A.

He was learning, as I had, that standing up for what was right required a sacrifice. But it was always worth it if you kept the right goal in sight.

Not all of Ken's activities were concerned with politics. One of the by-products of his association with Barry Goldwater, Jr., was Ken's involvement in Project SAVE, a drug-abuse program. The project was designed to try to help very young addicts, average age 13.4, even kids as young as 9.

At this time, Ken was spending summers training with the Marine Corps as part of his plan to be commissioned as an officer. He worked his Project SAVE activities around this commitment. When he came home, he would go to the center first to see how the teen-agers were doing. He wouldn't get home until late at night, but came home rejoicing sometimes. "You know, Dad, they've tried everything on these addicts, but we only save 5 to 10 per cent of them. There's only one thing we've found that saves them, and when the kids get this, they never go back on drugs; no matter how badly hooked they are, they kick it."

"Gee," I answered, "what kind of drug is that?"

"It is Christ. When they become Christians, when they find the Lord, they turn out to be new people. There was one teen-ager who used to sit around like a zombie. We knew he was listening, but he never made any sign. Methadone hadn't helped him. It really hasn't helped any of them to speak of. Anyway, this kid one time suddenly opened his eyes while we were praying. The majority of the group thought we were nuts, Dad, our little bunch kneeling and praying. Anyway, suddenly he said, 'I feel good . . . all over.' "

"I explained it to him," Ken went on. "I said, 'The Holy Spirit came, that's what happened.' " He grinned. "You know, after that he started right away to be a real worker for us and a good Christian."

During the months of Ken's involvement with this group, we estimated that he touched at least five hundred teen-agers for Christ.

We had our second real Christmas in our new home in 1970, and it was a typical Johnson celebration. On Christmas morning, nobody ran to the tree and grabbed gifts and started tearing them open. We all waited until everyone was up, then went into the living room together. And had a service, prayers and rejoicing, and remembering that Christmas is the celebration of the birth of Christ. Everyone in the family participated.

Juanita and I were especially touched by the prayers of the youngest two children. Kurtis didn't ask God for anything. He just expressed his love for Jesus. Juan Eric came out with "Lord, if I don't get what I asked for, I still love you!" And our daughter, Vernea, always prayed with great humility and love.

Yet it seemed that Ken, of all the family, was in my mind these days, just as he had been on Dad's. I didn't understand why.

For the past two summers, he'd gone to the Marine Corps basic school for training. This year was the time appointed for him to join a nine-month, full-time training program leading to a commission.

By April 1971, Juanita and I thought it was time to start getting ready to go back to California to build a base for my campaign for the United States Senate in 1974. I went to the White House to see Fred Malik, Nixon's personnel aide.

"Johnny, I don't think they want you to leave just yet."

"That's very kind. I've enjoyed being the vice chairman of the Civil Service Commission, but it's time to go."

"We've got something good for you; only thing is I can't tell you what it is right now."

The next time he called me on the phone, he confirmed, "Johnny, the guy is delighted to have you."

"What guy?" I asked, tired of playing games.

"Melvin Laird," he went on. "We had to see whether or not he wanted you over there."

My heart skipped a few beats. "Doing what?"

"Assistant Secretary of the Navy, that's what." He sounded as though he had invented the job.

"Why didn't you tell me this before? I would just love it."

"Johnny, it's just so great to have you with us," Melvin Laird said. "We have a great team here, and that's how we want to work, as a team. We want to work together to make the Defense Department the greatest agency in government."

"We can do it," I assured him.

"You'll have to clear out of the Civil Service Commission; we can use you right away."

But it didn't happen like that. An appointment had to be made, and it took a while for Senate confirmation.

The swearing-in ceremony in Melvin Laird's office was a moving one. More than two hundred guests crowded into the spacious office. As I looked around at all my friends, our pastor, and at my family, it was difficult to believe that more than twenty years ago, I had been in this very same office with Defense Secretary Louis Johnson over a discrimination matter at a base theater. I could even remember the feelings I had had when I saw all of those buttons on the telephone, knowing that with a flick of a button he could be connected to the President, all of the chiefs of the Army, Navy, and Marine Corps, or anywhere in the world, if need be.

Melvin Laird spoke briefly; then my wife moved over to stand beside me and was given a Bible on which she and I would place our hands. It was wonderful that they had included Juanita, for I felt that this honor was hers, too. After I was given the certificate, I thanked my friends and family for making this occasion possible.

Laird surprised everyone by asking my pastor to close with a word of prayer.

That evening a reception was held at Fort McNair—fifteen hundred people and a band. But our children seemed to have the most fun. Kurtis ran around inspecting everything. Vernea, however, was a perfect little lady, as she and Ken stayed close to their mother in case she needed anything. Four-year-old Juan had more fun than anyone, being allowed to take over the drums. I was startled at how well he handled them.

Later, when it came time for autographs, I noticed my line was suddenly diminishing. Juan was on the band platform signing everybody's program!

CHAPTER

19

We had prayer breakfasts on all sides. Everything was going great. Then I received a call from Secretary of Defense Laird's office.

I asked the caller, "What does the Secretary want to see me about?"

"I don't know."

"Can't you give me some idea?"

"Yeah. He received a letter from the White House with a memorandum attached. Some woman from Baltimore is complaining about having prayer breakfasts in the Pentagon Building. She wants it stopped."

I asked, "Well, why does he want to see me about it?"

"There's a rumor that you're the person starting the prayer breakfasts. You'd better come immediately."

I said, "Okay," and hung up the phone. Then I prayed. "Lord, You know I'm not smart enough to start prayer breakfasts. You did it. If there's any credit, it all goes to you. I'm just going to stand on the Word."

Immediately, the Lord revealed to me the words, *"Didn't I tell you I would be with you to the end of the world?"*

I left my office on the first floor, walked down the hall, down two flights of stairs to the Secretary's office. It wasn't very far, yet I think it was probably the longest walk I've ever taken.

In a few minutes, the inner door opened and Laird, with a cigar in his mouth, motioned me to come in and close the door. "Johnny, are you having prayer breakfasts in the Pentagon Building?"

"Yes, sir. In your conference room, sir."

"In *my* conference room?"

"That's right, sir."

"When do you hold them?"

"Six-thirty Wednesday mornings."

"Well, praise the Lord!" the Secretary exclaimed. "I'll be there for the next one myself!"

I almost fell over. I just said, "Praise the Lord!" that he had paid no attention to the lady's protest letter.

I later noticed he was the only Secretary that, when a new appointee was sworn in, asked someone to pray before and after the ceremony.

I was so thrilled going back to my office that I decided to make a new friend—something I tried to do every day. I saw this fellow coming down the hall, and when I got to him, I said, "Pardon me, sir, I'd sure like for you to be my friend."

His response was startled. "Why? What for?"

"Because Jesus Christ and I make a new friend each day."

The man said, "Oh! Are you one of those guys?"

"What guys?"

"One of those Holy Rollers?"

"No, sir."

"Are you one of those charismatics?"

"No, sir, I'm not."

"What are you? Some kind of . . ."

"I'm just a fanatic," I interrupted.

"What does *that* mean?"

"I just believe in Jesus Christ."

He said, "Oh no!"

"Seriously," I assured, "I want to be your friend. I make a friend each day."

"Okay, friend; friends are supposed to help each other."

"That's right."

"Well, let me tell you: I just lost my job. You get my job back, friend."

"Well, I'm sure . . ."

"Wait a minute! That's not all! My creditors are closing in on me. My wife is divorcing me. Now, *friend*, see what you can do to help me."

"The first thing you have to do is to accept the Lord."

"What?"

"Accept the Lord—make a decision to live for Him. Then we will pray for you, and all these things you're talking about will be taken care of. We'll pray about it right *now*."

"What? Right here in the hall?"

"Yes, sir. Right in the hall."

I laid my hands on him and began to pray. Heads popped out of offices along the hallway. I was praying out loud, and people were looking at us.

I saw a hand come over my shoulder and rest on my new friend's shoulder. I saw braid on that arm and knew it was one of the admirals who had been in on our prayer breakfasts. He began to pray with us. Then another hand came over and rested on the man's shoulder. The second hand belonged to one of the assistant secretaries. He also began to pray.

This man turned out to be the personnel director for the Defense Department. These "big shots" were coming, putting their hands on him, and praying for him. We were praying that the Lord would open his heart, that the man would confess his sins and let the Lord take the burdens away.

As all those prayers were joined, he sank down on the floor, sobbing.

As more people popped their heads out of doors, we heard someone say, "Hey! They got him down on the floor! Call the police!"

The security guard came up. "What did they do to you?" he asked the man.

"They haven't done anything. They have cleared up my problems."

The guard asked, "What problems?"

The man said, "You wouldn't understand. I have found Jesus Christ."

The guard said, "Praise the Lord! I found Him, too!"

It was a beautiful situation. I told my friend, "I want you to go right now and tell your boss—whatever he wanted you to do, you'll do it. Tell him that you met this crazy guy in the hall who said, 'You will have whatsoever you sayeth.' You tell him you love him, and you want your job back—and you'll have your job back."

"What about my creditors?" he asked.

"Call them. Tell them you can't pay all of it, but you'll pay some of it. And tell them what the Lord has done to your life."

"That's good, but what about my wife?"

"The wife is very easy to please. Wives are the easiest people in the world to please. All they want are three little things from us: No. 1, they want to be respected as a person, not just be someone around the house; No. 2, they want to be appreciated for the things they do for us; and No. 3, they want to be loved, but they want to be told that we love them, over and over again.

"Now you do that, and I guarantee things will be great in your life."

The man went to see his boss.

I left that same afternoon for two weeks to inspect the Seventh Fleet in the Pacific.

My personnel director, Robert Wiley, and I wanted to update our file of information on the fleet's activities. We intended to gather information on the current status of aircraft carriers, supply ships, frigates, and other vessels. We also needed to find out how the people at the various bases were living and what their problems were. In addition, I wanted to develop friendly relations with all the commanders so I could pick up the telephone at any time and feel comfortable discussing needs and problems.

The headquarters for the Seventh Fleet was Honolulu. The area included Guam, Okinawa, Japan, Korea, Hong Kong, and other Pacific areas throughout which American bases were scattered. This fleet patrols and protects the Pacific area. As long as our ships are in control of a particular sea lane, other ships cannot come through unless they want a war with the United States. And our ships are armed. They aren't bluffing. They have to be ready at all times for hostile acts.

The first stop of our inspection team was Hawaii. There I learned that I was the first black man ever to inspect a U.S. fleet.

Admiral McKane briefed me on the problems he was having, what was out there in his fleet of ships, what he needed help with, and the status of the supply lines stretching over his vast realm. Out of the briefings came my information on racial problems among the personnel.

From Hawaii, we flew to Guam. There, following the usual protocol—that the most senior official on a military aircraft alights first —I dutifully walked to the door and down the ramp. On the airstrip, officials were lined up expectantly—the admiral resident on Guam, two captains, three commanders, and a host of junior officers.

I walked along the whole line of officials, shaking hands and saying to each, "Hi. My name is Johnny Johnson." Each gave me a brief glance, mumbled a greeting, then shifted their gaze to the next person to come off the plane.

Having come to the end of the line, I stood there and waited as they greeted each debarking passenger, their bewilderment increasing. Finally, when the last person came off, the resident admiral asked my senior aide, Frankie, "Are you the Secretary?"

Frankie shook his head. "No, sir." He pointed toward me. "That's the Secretary, standing over there."

The admiral hesitated; then seeing that I wasn't budging, he started slowly in my direction. When he got to me, he said, "I am so sorry, Mr. Secretary. They didn't tell me that . . . that . . ."

"That I was black?"

"Uh, yes."

"That doesn't hurt. But don't you remember that the highest-ranking official departs military aircraft first? Also, you have got to stop thinking in that stereotyped fashion. You have to think positive; anything is possible now."

We were driven to headquarters. Information was exchanged concerning the itinerary. Every time the admiral came near me, he would say something like, "Please don't report that incident at the airstrip, Mr. Secretary. It was stupid of me."

"Who did you think I was?" I asked once.

"I'm afraid to tell you," he replied.

"Don't be."

"I, er, thought you were one of the stewards and had come to help serve."

I spent a couple of days inspecting the base and planning the next leg of the tour.

By the time we got to Okinawa, everybody knew not only that I was black but also a former Marine. They knew my history and achievements, and they said right away, "How are you, Mr. Secretary? Or should we say, 'Gunner'?"

"Fine," I replied. "That is very sharp of you to know I was a gunner."

After Okinawa came Japan, and finally we were ready to return to Washington. At every place we'd stopped, there had been problems of some kind—human problems, social, racial, manpower, financial, or community. But we had a prayer breakfast on every ship I'd been on. It had been a great time.

Back in Washington, I filed a report, predicting racial troubles as a result of the present recruiting methods and the lack of effective policies for rotation of men and balancing of activities. Even if there were no racial discrimination, present policies had led to dissatisfaction. Men were crowded on ships that stayed out at sea too long.

Because of recruiting methods and better schooling and background, white personnel aboard a vessel got the good, clean jobs in air-conditioned places; they got the interesting, challenging work, such as electronics and radar. Minorities, however, did most of the menial tasks: painting and scrubbing floors, lugging huge bags around the ship, doing most of the so-called dirty work.

A stepped-up effort was needed to find and motivate more highly qualified blacks to join the Navy so that they could have good jobs. Also, undereducated blacks needed more training, enabling them to take on jobs once reserved for the whites. If the Navy would encourage more white men in semiskilled jobs to join up, it would help, too. We could realize a more balanced personnel set up, and blacks could see that those of their number who had the skills were allowed to exercise them, that anything to the contrary wasn't an example of prejudice.

The problems were aggravated by the fact that a lot of the blacks who found themselves doing menial tasks in the Navy had been recruited from neighborhoods in urban centers where, although conditions were substandard, they had status with their own people. Some of the leaders of racial flare-ups were the ones who at home in civilian life had organized gangs and ruled them unchallenged. When they entered the Navy and saw that they were no longer "Kings," but instead cleaned up after white "Lords," blacks reacted by doing what they were able to do best, fight.

Naval policy had to be changed so that no one in the service felt he was being put down.

I predicted that if we did not change the policies immediately, racial violence would erupt. While my reports were being mulled, that very thing happened aboard the USS *Kitty Hawk*.

Only then was action taken.

One morning one of my aides stopped me at the office door. "Don't go in there now. Some nut's been trying to get to you for over two weeks. He's been screaming, 'I've just got to tell him what happened.' We asked him, 'What?' but he said, 'You won't understand.' I think the guy wants to do you some harm."

"What for? I've never done anything to anybody."

The aide replied, "Well, I don't know what this guy is, but he's some kind of a nut. We didn't bother you while you were away. We thought he'd probably go away. But now that you're back, we're probably going to have him locked up."

I said, "Let me see who he is."

The aide cracked open the door and I peeked in. I remembered the man. He was the one I'd met in the hall before I'd left to inspect the fleet.

He saw me. "Hey! There he is!" He started running toward me. My staff thought he was going to attack me. They tried to restrain him. He yelled, "Let me go!" He got loose, ran to me, and threw his arms around me.

I got hold of his arms. "Well, Brother, how did things go?"

"That's what I want to talk to you about! I went back to my office that day and told my boss, 'I met a guy in the hall who told me about Jesus. I don't know what happened to me, but it seemed that a ton of bricks was lifted off. A strange thing has happened. I don't hate you anymore; I just want to tell you before I leave that I just love you. Whatever I've done to you, please forgive me.'

"You know what my boss said?" the man asked me. "He said, 'Praise the Lord, Brother. I've been waiting for months for you to make a decision for the Lord. You can have your job back.'

"Then I called my creditors and told them I had my job back, and what the Lord had done. One of them said, 'Hallelujah, Brother! Don't worry about your debts. I know the Lord has blessed you, and you will pay.'

"I was so thrilled," the man exclaimed. "Then I thought of my wife, who was divorcing me. When I got home that evening I rushed into the house, hugged my wife, and said, 'Honey, I love you! I love you!' And I kissed her.

"She pushed me away. 'You've been drinking again, haven't you?' she said.

"'No, I haven't been drinking. I met this long, lanky guy in the hall, and he told me about Jesus.'"

He'd explained to his wife what the boss had said, that he had his job back, and what the creditor had said. Then the man repeated to me what he had told his wife:

"'This black man said to me that a wife wanted to be respected as a person, told me to appreciate the wonderful things you've done for me, and said to tell you that I love you.'"

"My wife lifted her hands in the air and said, 'Praise God! I've been waiting fourteen years to hear you say that. You can forget about divorce.'"

I said, "That's wonderful! That's great!"

"The next morning when I woke up, I smelled coffee and breakfast. My wife hasn't cooked my breakfast in almost ten years. On the table there was a white tablecloth, linen napkins, and orange juice. And my wife didn't have curlers in her hair! She had on a dress and wore makeup.

"I said to her, 'What goes on?' She said, 'You're one of the King's kids now, and I'm going to treat you as one.'"

The man looked at me and concluded, "That's the story. I can't tell you how wonderful the Lord has been, and the beautiful things that have happened."

It was wonderful for me, too. I believed it had all happened because of the prayer breakfasts.

The prayer breakfasts were a special joy in my life. In the senior Army prayer breakfast at the Pentagon, we had two outstanding

generals. One was four-star General Ralph Haynes, a very outspoken Christian who insisted that Christ came first, then the Army.
When he spoke to groups of Army men, he always asked, "How
many of you have made a decision for Christ?" Some of the other
officers in the Army thought this was just a little too much. But
three-star General Jack Wright thought this was fine. He explained,
"You're either saved or unsaved. If not, you should make a decision
for Christ." General Wright had found Christ at one of our Pentagon prayer breakfasts and had become an outstanding Christian.

One day, however, we were all challenged by General David
Carlings. He had made the statement that we should discontinue
our prayer breakfasts, contending that they infringed on the freedom of the people in the Pentagon.

"Let's get this guy transferred out," someone suggested.

"Oh no," I protested. "Why don't we invite him to one of our
breakfasts? Sometimes a person is talking like that because he
hasn't been invited."

"This guy is a hard drinker, an old soldier; he's not going to
change."

"I've known Dave for years," another member said, "He wouldn't
give us the time of day."

"I'll just call and invite him. I'm speaking next week; maybe I can
get to him." I was challenged now and wasn't about to give up.

"You can ask him," a major warned, "but watch out. He can be
pretty nasty."

That morning after the breakfast, I called his office and invited
him to come to the next meeting with me.

"I'd like that," he said.

"We don't embarrass anyone, we don't have them pray if they
don't want to, or read the Bible out loud."

"Oh," he affirmed, "I don't mind reading the Bible."

"Fine."

"What time's breakfast?"

"At 6:30 A.M."

"I'll try it once."

"I'd sure appreciate that." I hung up with a somewhat mystified
feeling—glad he had accepted but wondering why it had been so
easy.

When General Carlings came by my office at six-thirty, I noticed
he was carrying a black book. As we walked down the hall to the

meeting, he said, "I'm glad you're not one of those black militants! Some of those guys get on my nerves."

I agreed. We kept on walking, then I asked him, "Did anyone ever talk with you about making a decision for Christ and what the Lord can do for you?"

"They have not."

"I'll leave some tracts with you, you can read them later. They're put out by the Billy Graham Crusade, and I think they're pretty good."

I gave him the tracts, and we went in to the breakfast. Several officers looked stunned, then quickly put out their hands and gave him a warm Christian greeting.

During the time for prayers, much to my amazement and everyone else's, General Carlings began to pray when it was his turn. "Our Heavenly Father, we thank Thee for all the blessings that Thou hast bestowed upon us. . . ."

My talk was centered around I Corinthians 12 and 13, "the love chapters." But before I started, I told them about the prayer my father always said: "O Lord, we sure thank You because we're all here, and we're getting along just fine, and we're sure much obliged. Amen."

Then I went on to tell them about love. "You know, all of us are looking for something that will last forever. Your body won't last forever; your wife won't last forever; your kids won't last forever; your job (depending upon the next election) won't last forever . . . but we have love. That will last forever."

At the end, I asked General Carlings to close with prayer. He prayed one of the longest prayers we had ever had. We all felt that the Holy Spirit had been with us that morning. But General Carlings was still a mystery.

About four days later I got a call from him, asking if he could come to see me. I was delighted. He told me about his life. Then he told how much he had disliked his own formal church. He was angry because it hadn't given him an opportunity to express the love I had talked about, nor to hold hands with the Christian brothers and let himself go. "My church doesn't even let you say 'Amen' or 'I love the Lord'!" he explained. "I had to come to the Pentagon to do that!"

"I didn't know you were a Christian," I said.

"I just found the Lord."

"Wonderful. How long ago?"

"Last Wednesday."

January of 1972 wasn't over before tests at Bethesda Naval Hospital showed that surgery on Juanita's hip performed almost a year earlier had not accomplished what had been intended. My wife's arthritic hip had kept her from even one night of really good rest in fifteen years.

In 1971, the doctor thought the operation in which the bone was scraped to get rid of the soft tissue would considerably improve her condition. Juanita felt a lot better for six months, but the pain returned.

A specialist from Boston came down to look at the X rays and talk with the examiner, then told us what had to be done. "I don't know how to tell you except that you will have to have another operation," he said.

"Will she get well?"

"To be candid with you, if we operate this time, she may never walk again. The chances are about fifty-fifty."

"Then why operate?" I asked. "She can at least walk some now."

"It would alleviate the pain," the doctor explained.

We decided to go home and think it over.

"How do you feel about it?" I asked.

"I've already made up my mind, honey, to go ahead with it. I believe the Lord will certainly protect me, and I'm sure that, with faith and prayer, the operation will succeed."

It was a typical answer for Juanita. "You can cut me and do all that, but the healing comes from God," she had told a doctor once. "I lie there and wait, but it's Christ who comes and heals me."

"Okay, honey," I said. "But this will be the last. I can't let you go through any more operations after this."

We had our minister pray for her. The operation was set for February 15, 1972. That day I drove her to the hospital. She was cheerful. I held her hand while she was on the cart and down the long corridor right to the door of the operating room. When I kissed her, she looked up at me and said, "You're acting like a baby."

I realized that tears were streaming down my cheeks.

"It's going to be okay," she affirmed.

"Of course it is," I answered.

However, the operation was complicated by an infection. Everyone close to us prayed for Juanita.

Juanita was serenely unworried, but I was nearly sick with anxiety. When the doctors told her about her prospects, she'd witness to them. "If we just really believe in Christ, this leg will get well and heal," she said. "But if it is God's will not to have this happen, I believe you doctors have done all you could."

One day, Juanita said she felt a jerk in her leg. The clotted blood had somehow "pushed up" the infection, pressing it out the side of the leg. She was given a transfusion every day until the infection washed out.

We knew it was a miracle answer to prayer, because the doctors had almost given up.

Juanita was finally released from the hospital. She could get around the house on crutches, which the doctors had said she'd have to use for a year and a half. The inserted metal cup would have to grow within the cartilage.

At least she was home.

One morning when I was in my bedroom, I heard a thump. I found Juanita lying on the floor by the tub, blood gushing out of her head.

She was semiconscious, but I was able to get her downstairs, into the car, and rush her to the hospital.

The doctor put eight stitches in her head. He checked her over carefully, assured us everything was okay with her hip, as well as her head, then released her so she could return home with me.

I was sure at this point that Juanita's troubles were over for a while. I still had to take her to the hospital periodically, however, for checkups and physical therapy.

However, on one of our hospital visits, I couldn't wait for her examination. I instructed my driver to drive my personal car to take Juanita home; then I took the government car and drove to a meeting.

I was at the meeting for only half an hour when someone rushed in. "Your wife's just been in a car accident!"

Someone had run a red light and rammed the side of our car. I made a mad dash to the hospital. I found Juanita on a cart again, being prepared for X rays. But her injury was obvious: Her collarbone was sticking out. I couldn't help crying.

She was in terrible pain. She had been so brave for so long, but she'd finally broken down and cried. I couldn't blame her.

During her many problems throughout the first few months of 1972, Juanita continually urged me to keep on with my work and other activities. I was asked by President Nixon to represent him during a commemoration in the Philippines of the fall of Bataan. The late General Douglas MacArthur's deeds in the Philippines during World War II would be an important part of the celebration.

We flew to the West Coast, then boarded a Philippine Government Boeing 707 jet provided by President Ferdinand Marcos exclusively for the use of our fifteen-man delegation.

We were met at the airport by government officials and a veterans' group, the members of which wore their American Legion caps. They had found out I'd been director of the Department of Veterans' Affairs in California.

When we arrived at the Hilton Hotel, I became aware that one of the party of escorts in the limousine was my bodyguard. He had a .38, and an automatic weapon on his shoulder. Speaking beautiful English, he informed me that the Communists had made a threat on my life. "I'm to follow you everywhere, Mr. Secretary."

In a brief walk around the block, I discovered that my bodyguard never allowed anyone in the crowd to get between us. He even checked restrooms before I entered.

When I arose at five o'clock the next morning for my jog, I discovered my bodyguard sleeping outside my door. I didn't want to wake him up, so I just stepped over him. In my jogging suit, I went downstairs and jogged along the sidewalk, almost deserted at this early hour.

When I returned to the hotel, a crowd of police greeted me. My bodyguard rushed over, looking greatly relieved.

The phone in my room had started ringing shortly after I left; the guard had gone into my room to see why I hadn't answered it. Finding me gone, he nearly had a fit, thinking I'd been kidnaped by the Reds.

"Mr. Johnson," he pleaded, "please do not do that anymore. Don't ever leave me again. If you want to run, I'll run with you . . . jog, jog, jog. If you want to crawl, I'll crawl with you. If you want to stand on your head, I'll stand on my head with you. I am supposed to be with you all the time. If anything happens to you, I get shot."

"I understand," I said.

"No, sir, you don't understand. There is no trial for me. I get shot!"

We got dressed and went to the palace for breakfast with President Marcos.

We talked about the fall of Bataan. I sensed that real bitterness still lingered. The President's voice trembled when he talked about it and his experiences. He was in on that death march where those who fell were bayoneted.

President Marcos became more and more keyed up recalling the past, but Mrs. Marcos brought him back to the present with a sweet smile that said, "Enough, you are going too far."

She is a very powerful woman, perhaps the power behind the throne. Very influential, she did not talk a great deal, did not try to impress people, just let one know she was favorable toward a person by making him comfortable.

We talked about the Communist threat. President Marcos was convinced the Communists were coming in from the outside. They were strong in the Philippines and were responsible for a lot of killings, he said. He had acted firmly and strongly by creating a near-dictatorship because of the Communist threat, in addition to his feeling that he provided his people with the strong leadership they needed.

After breakfast, President Marcos invited, "Come on, let's go in my car."

One reason President Marcos stayed so close to me was his fear of my possible assassination. The Communists had let the American ambassador know they would try to kill me, to embarrass Marcos.

We went to a meeting of veterans from World War II, Korea, and Vietnam, who were pressing for more benefits. President Marcos gave a sort of State of the Union address and took the opportunity to lash out at the Communists. In English and Tagalog, he threatened an eye for an eye.

I later went yachting with President Marcos and admired his seamanship. I was shown Corregidor, that fortified island in the bay of Manila Harbor where MacArthur and his men withstood for so long the Japanese seige; then was taken up in an elevator of the Memorial there, to the Hill of Corregidor, where one can see the gun installations and signs of Japanese bombing and shelling.

Foremost in my mind, however, was MacArthur's cave, his headquarters. The tables and lamps are intact from those days.

A ceremony and speech-making commemorated the gallant resistance against the Japanese and ended with planes stunting like our Blue Angels. President Marcos spoke of his country's progress and how necessary it was to put down uprisings inspired by the Communists.

While he was grateful for U.S. aid already received, he thought it would help all the free world for aid to be increased. There was some joking that sometimes it almost seemed America's enemies got more aid than her friends, but he stressed the bond of warmth and friendship that existed between the two countries.

A final luncheon was held where President Marcos had been born. Afterward, President Marcos presented me with a plaque and gifts for President Nixon, including an ornate shell. For me, he had a beautifully carved box, and for each of us, a box of Philippine cigars in an assortment of sizes.

On the way to the airport, I took the opportunity to see the research farm that the Rockefeller Foundation had funded. Then, as I worried about getting to the plane on time for takeoff, President Marcos said, "It's my plane; I tell them when to take off."

President Nixon was pleased with my report, and, I was feeling pretty good, too.

There were several significant things that came out of the Philippine trip, I believe.

This was the first time in the history of the United States that a black man had represented the President of the United States as head of a delegation to meet the head of any official foreign government. I felt this was really a step forward. The advancement of blacks in diplomacy was substantial. The way was open.

I was also proud to represent the United States, not only as a black man, but also as an American.

The trip, I believe, was one of the factors that helped keep diplomatic relations between the United States and the Philippines harmonious. President Marcos was so impressed with the love we carried to him that he said, "If we can have this kind of love coming from the United States, our bonds will be so tightly woven, nothing can separate us."

Spiritually, I was impressed with the fact that Marcos and his wife were Christians—something I hadn't known before. I first learned it at a luncheon during which President Marcos said grace. It was a beautiful prayer. His wife told me he was a born-again Christian. I thought that significant.

Yet another opportunity came to me that year through the prayer breakfasts. I had met Billy Graham in January at an executive session of the National Prayer Breakfast. At that meeting, Senator Strom Thurmond, Senator Harold Hughes, Al Quig, and I had spoken. After my talk, Billy gave the wrap-up speech.

I told the group what the Lord had done for me and how we must love God when things are really bad. This is how to show you are a real spiritually reborn Christian.

When Billy finished his talk, he ran over and threw his arms around me. "Listen, I've got to get you on my crusade. We're having one down in Birmingham, Alabama."

In May 1972, Billy asked me to fly to Birmingham. There I told seventy thousand people how much I loved the Lord.

When we came into the stadium, five thousand voices began to sing, and I raised my head up to say, "Thank you, Lord, for bringing me here."

However, someone else didn't take my trip in the same light. A reporter working for columnist Jack Anderson called my aide to ask a few questions. I could hear him talking and had him repeat the conversation to me later.

"I'm from the Jack Anderson column, and I'd like to ask you a few questions."

"What would you like to ask?"

"I'd like to know about Secretary Johnson's trip to Birmingham."

"What about it?"

"How much did that trip cost?"

"Why, I don't know!"

"How much did Graham pay of the Secretary's travel money?"

"You know, Mr. Johnson is a little bit out of his head. You know what the guy did?"

"What'd he do?"

"The Billy Graham Crusade sent him a ticket, and he wouldn't take it."

"Oh, he took federal money?"

"You know, he could have done that. But he personally paid for the ticket, and on top of that sent a fifty-dollar donation out of his own pocket."

"Oh, you're kidding!"

"No, you know what he did when he got there?"

"What'd he do?"

"He went down there and told them all that he loved Jesus Christ! Now, isn't that stupid—spending your own money to tell people that?"

"Well, no, I guess that's okay. But what about his expenses?"

"That character even paid for all his own expenses in Birmingham. Say—that's a good story for you. Here is a guy saying he loves the Lord and spending his own money to tell seventy thousand people about it. That would be a good story for you!"

"Oh, go get some church group to write that up." The reporter had slammed down the phone in my aide's ear.

Obviously he had been trying to find out facts that would do me no credit, and my aide had made sure he heard some good news instead . . . but good things don't make news in the Jack Anderson column!

CHAPTER

20

Soon after the Billy Graham Crusade, we had some problems on the USS *Forrestal* and the USS *Trunket*.

I took a small group with me to see what was going on. It didn't take long to find the source of the trouble. It was caused by the men being at sea too long, cooped up in small compartments. Small flare-ups had become large ones.

The major dissatisfaction was with the rating system. Most of the officers were white. If a black irritated them, he ended up with a low mark. A low mark meant no promotion. This killed co-operation and incentive.

We learned that the men were more willing to talk with a senior NCO than with an officer, so we recommended a panel be set up for such talks. We also suggested an open line to the commanding officer for those problems that couldn't be solved by the panel. We recommended that they make more "strikers"—men who didn't have skills for particular jobs or promotions, but could acquire the skill while working on the job.

When we left, the commanding officer and his personnel were in a much better frame of mind.

The year 1972 was certainly filled with job and family affairs of first magnitude; it was a banner year, except that continuous misfortunes seemed to be leading to some kind of climax.

Daughter Vernea was very busy in the church: editor of the church paper, chairman of the youth group, and organizer for a camping crusade. She also taught Sunday school, and the kids loved her.

Kurtis, who wanted to go to a military academy, was to report on August 29.

Ken's letters kept us up to date on his progress as a Marine officer candidate at the Quantico basic school. He'd made a film with Lee Marvin, and five of Ken's buddies who were flirting with drugs and alcohol had found Christ because of Ken.

I asked, "Ken, why are you worrying about these guys? You could be No. 1 in your class if you concentrated on your own work."

"But Dad," he replied, "it isn't important what you do for yourself, because that will die with you. It is what you do for others that will live after your death."

I looked at him, remembering those as the very words he had spoken after Dad's funeral. They gave me an eerie sense of foreboding that I couldn't shake off.

My father and my son. How much both of them had taught me. In some strangely beautiful way that satisfied my spirit, although my mind could not describe it, they both had it all together in a way I hadn't yet attained. *All their trusting, all my striving . . .*

Ken said it was not easy to be the son of the Assistant Secretary of the Navy. Some people respected him for it, but others were resentful. He was forced to try to be the best in everything. A captain told his father, who was a general, when asked about his class, "It's a pretty good basic class, but there is one black lad named Ken Johnson who is the only one who really knows what is going on. He knows all the weapons, the material, the manual, and he's the only one to get his homework out."

"Johnson! Do you know who that boy is?"

"Naw. Who is he?"

"His father is the Assistant Secretary of the Navy."

"Why, that little carrot! He never told me that!"

Ken wanted to accomplish on his own, not live in his dad's shadow.

Near the end of summer, the whole family attended Ken's graduation ceremony, which began with a prayer and a salute to the flag led by Second Lieutenant Kenneth E. Johnson, U. S. Marine Corps! It was a very solemn moment for us as we watched our son stand proud, then walk across the stage in his white uniform, medals on his chest, to receive that hard-earned document naming him a U. S. Marine Corps officer.

Ken was to be with us for a short period of liberty, then attend communications school at Quantico. Finishing there, he was scheduled to go to Okinawa in March of 1973.

It was with some surprise, annoyance, and concern that I then learned of Ken's medical problem, the treatment of which had been delayed to permit him to go through graduation ceremonies. The problem didn't appear to be anything serious.

He had a small swelling on his neck. It looked as though he'd been hit by pieces of shrapnel while on the rifle range or throwing grenades. The doctors wanted to make sure it wasn't a cancerous growth. Tests had been inconclusive.

On October 11 he went back to Bethesda Naval Hospital for more tests, which did not satisfy anyone. Surgery was indicated.

On the morning of the thirteenth, Ken went upstairs to say goodbye to his mother. She still had a very difficult time getting around freely and could not negotiate stairs with her crutches. Ken kissed her. "Mother, good-bye. And I want you to take care of the kids for me."

"Kenny, what are you talking about?" Juanita countered. "You'll be back here in no time."

Ken smiled. "Yes, I know."

Ken checked into the hospital on the thirteenth and his room was on the thirteenth floor. I was glad I am not superstitious.

The next day I went to visit. When I walked into his room, he came over, put his arm around me, and kissed me on the cheek. Ken was a deep, sincere, and affectionate person. The sight of him in his pajamas made me think of countless times at home when, as a youngster, he'd come down to say good night.

I hugged him, then asked, "Are you afraid, Ken?"

He smiled. "It's going to be all right. How are Mom and the kids?"

"They're doing great."

"You tell Kurtis and Juan I said they have to be good boys now."

"What do you mean? Of course they're going to be good boys. Ken, is there anything you want?"

"No. No, Dad. Nothing at all."

"I'll be back tomorrow morning."

"Aw, you don't have to come back tomorrow morning. Just give me a call."

Early on the morning of the fifteenth, I called Ken. "Son, I'll be right out there as soon as the operation is over. I talked to your doctor; he said he'd call me just as soon as it is over. You'll be out of there in two or three days."

"That's just fine, Dad." He hesitated. "Dad, you take care of Mom and the kids for me, you hear?"

"Ken, stop saying that!"

"I've been praying about this. I know the Lord will make things right for all of us."

We had a briefing when I got to the office—the usual classified meeting during which we were told what was going on around the world with our armed forces, but I was still thinking about Ken. It occurred to me that my son's operation was on his grandfather's birthday and that Juanita had her surgery on her mother's birthday.

My aide, Captain Dick Powell, put his head in. "Mr. Johnson, Ken's doctor is on the phone; he wants to talk to you right away."

I hurried to the phone. "Yes, doctor? Is the operation over?"

"Ahhh, yessss, the operation is over."

"Was it cancerous?"

"Well, ahhh, yes. It was a little cancer. If he had to have cancer, it was the best one he could have had. It was all in one ball, one we could take out—and it wouldn't ever bother him again."

"Oh, that's great. . . ."

"We had a problem. Ken had a cardiac arrest on the operating table."

The doctor seemed to take forever to go on. "But we started his heart going again by shock. We don't think his heart stopped long enough to cause any serious brain damage. He is still unconscious. We have him in the intensive-care ward."

When I got to Ken's bed, I almost wept. His hands, swollen from the needles, were wrapped in bandages. His eyes were covered with cotton. Tubes from the breathing tank were in his nose and mouth, extending down his throat. A needle bandaged into his arm led up to a bottle containing glucose that bubbled, drop by drop, into his veins.

The breathing apparatus made a monotonous sucking sound as Ken's chest went up and down, up and down, up and down. His neck was clamped, not stitched.

All of a sudden I realized—realized right down to my gut—that this was my son, whom I'd known for twenty-three years. Ken Johnson! This form with the bandages and tubes . . .

Sobbing, I took his hand and held it, soothed his arm, his forehead. I prayed, "God! Please, let him live. Take my life. I have lived. He's good. He has a lot to live for. I've lived my time out."

I stayed for thirty-five or forty minutes, listening to that monotonous sucking, swelling, and watching the contraction of his chest.

The doctor asked me into a small, crowded office. The maintenance doctor, whose job it was to keep Ken alive, was there in addition to the surgeon and another doctor. The anesthesiologist was in tears. "I don't know how it happened. I had the tube in his windpipe, so air went directly to his lungs. When we noticed he was not breathing, it was . . . I don't know just what happened. Apparently, his brain wasn't getting any oxygen at all. So the cardiac arrest. We . . ." He had to pause a moment. "We tried to massage his heart, but it didn't work. The electric shock started the heart pumping again."

The surgeon continued the story. "It was such a minor operation that I thought I could leave—get ready for other surgery—and let a technician watch over everything. But apparently the technician didn't notice that your son wasn't getting oxygen. I don't know what to say except I'm sorry."

Another doctor explained. "You know, these things happen."

The fear, the anxiety, the pity I'd felt for my son erupted in fierce anger. "What do you mean, they 'happen'?" I almost screamed. "You mean you're going to try to pass this off as something that just happened?"

I saw Ken lying there, a machine breathing for him. To be in this kind of a position because of some goof by people who were supposed to know, was impossible to understand.

"Yes, I know," a doctor continued, "only once out of five thousand . . ."

What did *statistics* have to do with the human life they were talking about? Grimly, I warned, "He'd better not die, because if he does, all of you are in trouble."

"We will have to wait twenty-four hours. Then, if he starts to come around, we can tell how he is. I don't know what brain damage was done." The doctor cleared his throat. "When he does come around, I'm afraid he might not ever be able to walk, or talk, or do anything but breathe and eat. His brain may be severely damaged. We should know something in twenty-four hours."

The sudden blast of pure honesty staggered me.

The physician patted me on the shoulder. "We'll do everything we possibly can. I will be with him constantly and do everything I can to save him, to make him come out of it as well as he can."

Now I had to tell Juanita.

I sat in the back seat as my driver threaded the car through traffic, and kept asking myself, "What do I say? How do I explain to her? How do I tell her that her son may not live? How do I tell her it was a medical 'goof'?" I prayed in the midst of my tears.

As a Christian, what did I do now? "Lord," I asked, "are You testing me to see how I will react to this? How will I carry on if Ken does not come through?" I was oblivious to traffic, to stoplights, to the city sprawling around me, to everything except an answer.

I couldn't be sure I had received an answer—but I remembered Dad's counsel: *When you asked God to guide you, you had to believe that He did.*

When I arrived home, Juanita looked at me. "How's Ken?"

"Well, honey, I suppose he will be all right."

"Suppose? Is anything wrong?"

"Well, the operation was a success, but they had a problem. He had a cardiac arrest on the operating table and he's still unconscious. I've just been out to see him."

"Cardiac arrest!" She began to cry. "I've got to go see him. I've just got to go."

"You can't, honey. You're not able to go out."

"I have to."

I tried to argue, but it was useless. "All right. Get ready and we'll go. But . . ." I turned my head away. "Remember, he's still unconscious."

"I know that," Juanita choked. "But I believe I can talk to him. When you're unconscious, you can still hear voices and sometimes understand what is going on. Maybe he'll hear me. Let me go and talk to him."

I phoned the hospital. They said it would be all right for her to come.

She got her crutches. Inside, I wept at Juanita's helplessness and Ken's greater helplessness. Outside, I retained a semblance of control.

Somehow, in another age, we arrived at the hospital. We were given white smocks. At Ken's bed, Juanita leaned over, kissed him, and caressed his arms. "Ken, this is Mother. Ken . . . please. We love you so." She sobbed between her words. "You've got to fight to save your life. Please, Ken. You've got to pull out. We want you back. *We love you so.*"

A scene flashed—me talking to my father, to the boy's grandfather, the man who had thought so much of him. I remembered the other sickbed conversation and my father's words. "He's too good, he's too good." Was that the possible answer to my wife's words? Would Ken fight, especially if he thought God wanted him in Heaven? Would he struggle?

Such thoughts again called forth scalding tears. I glanced at the dial of the heart machine. Even with my limited knowledge, I could see the rhythm was off. Way off.

Juanita was bending over Ken, massaging his arm, loving him. She responded to what was happening just as my eyes caught it: *His body was jerking like a dying animal.*

The doctor, who'd come in, whispered, "That's quite normal. That happens often to people who have had operations and are coming out of anesthesia."

We stayed about fifteen minutes. Then the long drive home.

I called my office. "I'm going to stay with my wife the rest of the day." No one needed or asked for any explanation.

I paced the floor, stopping to look at Juanita trying to compose herself. Finally I said, "I'd like to go back to the hospital to be with Ken." I didn't want to leave her alone, yet I felt I had to go.

"Do that, honey," she whispered. "At least one of us can be there."

The nurses didn't seem surprised to see me back. Then I was leaning over Ken's bed. "Ken, this is Dad, the one who loves you so much. Ken, don't forget that. We love you so much. We want you back."

There was no response. He lay there, chest rising and falling. He looked so limp.

DAY TWO. Saturday morning. The doctors said they'd checked him, thought they'd seen a little life in the brain. This was great news. Any little straw.

The chaplain came in, and we prayed together. Dr. Wayne Morrison, my minister, had heard and also was with me. Dr. Morrison came home with me that night to pray with us.

I couldn't bear being away from Ken several hours every day. I made arrangements for a room in the hospital where I could try to work and nap.

Many people called. All wanted to help.

DAY THREE. Sunday, I went to church to teach my Sunday school class. The kids said, "We shouldn't have regular Sunday school this morning. Let's just spend the time praying." So we did.

"My faith in the Lord is stronger than ever, and you should rejoice whatever the circumstances may be. If the Lord has allowed me to have a son as wonderful as this one for twenty-three years and we are all just praying right now, he must certainly come through," I prayed.

The members of the Sunday school took turns praying. That night all the young people had a special prayer meeting.

During the day I'd received more calls, then stayed until very late at the hospital.

DAY FOUR. On Monday, I went by early to talk with the doctors. No change. I thought I'd better go to the office.

I tried to work. What had happened to the "twenty-four-hour-period" after which we would know something? Time slipped away, as it seemed life slipped away. It was too much. Suddenly I pounded my fist on the desk, kicked over a table, and maybe I started to wail. My aides ran down the hall for Chief of Naval Operations Admiral Elmo Zumwalt, Secretary John Warner, and Under Secretary Frank Sanders. They all held me down and sat facing me. "Take it easy," one of them said. "We know exactly how you feel."

I shook my head. How could they know? But I settled down and finally assured, "I'm okay."

"Why don't you take off for the day?"

"I think I'll go over to the hospital."

Ken still had the tube down his throat. The machine was still pumping his lungs up and down. But then came a change. Ken was not tripping that machine. He wasn't breathing on his own. The machine was keeping him alive and working hard to do it.

I sat beside the machine all day. I buried my face in my hands. "If this is Your will, Lord, I'll just have to go along with it. But how could *this* be Your will?"

"Secretary Johnson," a nurse interrupted, "the President is on the phone." She handed me an extension.

"Johnny? This is President Nixon."

"Yes, sir."

"I just want you to know Pat and I are praying for you, your son, and your family. If there is anything I can do, just let me know. If you need my plane to go get a doctor, medication, anything, just let me know, and it'll be done."

"That is awfully kind of you, Mr. President. I appreciate your call."

"Here is my private number." He pronounced it carefully. "Call me at any time, day or night. If I can help, I certainly will."

For a little while, my spirits were lifted. Then Melvin Laird called. "Johnny, I feel so badly about this, I hardly know what to say. But . . . I know you're a good Christian, and I know you can get through this."

That was something to help me, to keep me on the track: bearing this all the Christian way. The stomping and the raging and the threatening I'd done was not the Christian way. Love was the Christian way, even in this. It was so easy for me to know that intellectually, yet so impossible really to live it in circumstances like this. Nonetheless, this was the very place where love, not blaming, was most needed. But how?

The phone rang again. It was John Warner, his voice warm and pleasant.

"Johnny, hang in there, boy. You can do it through Christ."

Through Christ! That was how I could do it. And that was the only way.

"You're absolutely right," I affirmed. "Through Christ I can do all things."

What would I do without such friends to keep reminding me about Christ, fortifying my faith and strength to bear whatever came . . . even a cross?

The phone calls helped me through the longest day of all. The doctors kept asking me to leave Ken's bedside and wait out of the room while they performed tests and consulted with each other. The tests were to decide whether there was any activity at all. Finally they called me in. "I couldn't see any activity in the brain." His voice was flat, emotionless. "That doesn't mean there isn't any there. It does look dim, though."

I went home. When I described the day to her, Juanita said, "I've got to go back there."

It was Monday night. At the hospital Juanita talked to Ken over and over, saying how much we loved him, how we would trade our lives for his. Juanita and I held hands and talked together. We found we both prayed the same thing.

DAY FIVE. Tuesday. I went by early. The doctor met me at the door of the ward. "We took another EEG on his brain. There was a glimmer of life."

I was happy! When I went to the office, I managed to be somewhat effective. I went back to the hospital expectantly.

They had taken another test. The flicker of life was not there.

The doctors discussed with me, through indirect hints, the idea of turning off the life-support machine. I didn't take it indirectly. I gave them a flat NO!

Then I lost track of the days . . . I stopped counting them. Counting time merely intensified my anguish. I tried to just drift, tried to keep my mind on Christ's promise that He would never leave me or forsake me.

Each day I went back. Ken's heart was still beating, but his brain wasn't functioning. A part of me could see him deteriorating.

One day, they put him in a different room. With a chill, I realized they were preparing him for death.

Every night Juanita and I prayed for hours. I sometimes felt I was talking to myself. In more lucid moments, I realized that God probably was trying to get through to me with an answer, if I could just summon up that very last ounce of faith and inner quietness, that hard-to-come-by serenity necessary for full communion. I also knew that sometimes the Lord answers in other ways than words or visions. Things that happen sometimes are the Lord's answers, if we've invited Him to take over. I thought of my dad again, of his no-matter-what faith.

Perhaps I couldn't keep my emotions quiet enough to listen, to be sensitive to God's communication.

OCTOBER 23. I told the doctor I had a speaking engagement at Wheaton College. "Will my son be alive when I come back?"

The doctor whispered, "I don't think so."

I phoned the office to tell them I couldn't make the speaking engagement. Frank Sanders went in my place.

OCTOBER 24. I went to the room they'd given me in the hospital. Dick Powell, my aide and executive assistant, my right hand, stayed with me, gave me papers to sign, counseled me, told me about all the prayers of everyone. When I cried, he cried.

I talked to the doctors again. "Is there any hope at all?"

"Secretary Johnson," the doctor finally said, "your son has been medically dead for days and has deteriorated to the point where the only thing keeping his chest moving, oxygen flowing, and blood circulating is that machine!"

I covered my face with my hands. I wanted to shut out reality—stark, naked, terrible, stabbing reality!

"His heartbeat is so low," the doctor continued, "so slow, it will also soon stop. There is no need to have the machine on. There is no brain and, medically speaking, no life. There is just air being pumped into his body. Should we remove the machine now?"

"No, no, no, NO! I want to sit with him, I want to stay right there until his heart stops."

Finally, I had to go upstairs to sign some papers. Before I left Ken's side, I could see that according to the machine, his heart was barely beating. I whispered, "I'll meet you in Heaven . . . *I promise.*"

I was upstairs for about ten or fifteen minutes, alone. I signed the papers and put them in a basket. Back on Ken's floor, I saw several people, including three doctors, standing outside his door. I knew why they were there. "He's in Heaven, isn't he?"

They nodded.

I had already cried for so long that I asked, "Let's all hold hands and pray. *O God, thank You so much for giving us the strength to withstand this great tragedy.*" Miraculously, I was able to control my voice. And I could *feel* strength in me!

We ask You, dear Father, to bless the doctors who have done all they possibly could to save my son's life. I didn't want this to end this way, but I promised You I would accept it, without crying. And I promised my son I would meet him in Heaven. Bless these wonderful people who have given their time and effort, who've tried to console me in every way. I know Your blessings will pour out on them!

I was silent for a moment, and dimly aware that I was almost crushing the hands on either side of me. Yet those hands were, in some mysterious way, radiating warmth and love and sympathy and not flinching. I was aware, too, that instead of blaming the doctors, I was asking God to bless them! Flooded with Christ's forgiving love, I felt freer than I'd ever felt before. *Through Christ*—that was the real answer to everything.

Bless my family that they may be able to withstand this, Lord—and give me the courage to take this awful message to my wife and the rest of my family.
Amen.

As I rode away, I recalled with real thanksgiving a whole series of events in Ken's life. I could just see this bright young lad who'd come to us at Bethesda Naval Hospital. We saw him as he was first born, having a hard time trying to live, an operation at 3½ days of age. Then we could see how smart he was as he was growing up; in every part of life, how good life was to him. I could remember now, when he would get himself dirty, he would hide from us so we couldn't see him.

He was the first black to do so many things! The first to attend a white school in Washington, D.C.; the first student body president in Orange County; the first in our hearts! How wonderful it was that he made straight A's in school! I could see him getting on the ship to go around the world with the Chapman World Campus Afloat.

Glimpses of him in college classrooms—a tall, handsome young man with everything to gain—flashed in my head. I saw him becoming a Marine Corps officer at the basic school graduation ceremony. I saw that his love for his family—mother, brothers, and sister—was as obvious as a fire on the hearth.

At home Juanita sat in the rocking chair the doctor had prescribed for her. I fell on my knees and put my head in her hands. "Kenneth is in Heaven."

Vernea came in as Juanita was weeping. I hugged Vernea, held her, soothed both of them. *Through Christ!* Vernea finally swallowed hard, fell on her knees, and cried, "Let's pray, oh, let's pray."

Then Juan walked in. "What is going on?"

"Ken has died."

He blinked. Then he dropped his head, turned, and went out, ducking back into his room.

I let him alone for a while. When I opened the door, he was on his knees, praying. He got up and went to Juanita's room with me. He put his arms around her. "Mommy, don't worry about Kenneth. He is better off than we are. He is with God."

Kurtis was at school at Valley Forge, so I asked my driver to pick him up. He was a warm person and offered to tell Kurtis for us. "I have two boys, and I think I know how to tell him."

We nodded our approval.

As they were driving back, the driver said, "Kurtis, I've got to tell you something. You'll have to be a big boy, Kurtis. Your big brother, Kenneth, is dead."

Kurtis sat in shocked silence for a few minutes. Then: "Well, I guess I'll have to take over as big brother."

When he finally got home, Kurtis explained, "When the Lord

goes into a garden, He picks the prettiest flower. He's taken Ken because he was a beautiful flower. He, he was that rose God wanted, and now he's with Jesus Christ . . . and we should try to be there, too."

CHAPTER

21

Ken was to be buried in the National Cemetery in Arlington, and the funeral home, located in Silver Spring, Maryland, was about two miles from our home. I stayed at the funeral home all day greeting our friends, astounded at the number who came to pay their respects.

The next three days, as hundreds of people passed by, giving their sympathy, the Lord stood right beside me. His strength was perfected in my weakness.

John Sullivan, my Christian brother who had found Christ at one of our prayer breakfasts, came by. "Oh Johnny, Johnny, what can I do? What can I say? How can you bear it?"

"Through Christ," I assured him. "Through Christ."

On Saturday, Leo McDowell and his wife, Polly, flew in from California, where Leo was setting outstanding records as a Navy Department recruiter. Leo and I had known each other for thirty-one years. In all of those years, I had never seen Leo cry.

As we stood there viewing Ken, Leo yanked the cross he was wearing from around his neck, breaking the chain, and very gently put it on Ken's chest.

I knew what that cross meant to him. Leo told me he had worn it through World War II, Korea, and Vietnam. "I'd always look at this cross, when things go rough, Johnny, and think that Our Lord Jesus Christ was hung on the cross. It would make me feel awfully humble that I had an opportunity to live in this country and that anything I may suffer is just a drop in the bucket compared with what He went through. That would make me feel good."

We had visits from the Secretary of the Navy, the Under Secretary of the Navy, Secretary of Defense Melvin Laird, and calls from Vice President Spiro Agnew.

Juanita and I prayed Sunday night, then prepared ourselves for the long day Monday, when Ken would be brought to his final resting place.

The service was scheduled for 10 A.M. Ken had already been taken to the Wheaton Baptist Church. Captain Powell arranged for the procession to travel through the streets without any stops, policemen standing at every corner waving the motorcade on. Twenty-two cars wound their way through the streets of Washington, D.C., and I can't remember one of those streets.

In church, I looked over to the dignitary section and was dazzled by bright, shiny buttons. The Secretaries of the Army, Navy, and Air Force were there, with a large number of staff from the White House.

Juanita and I had picked three songs to be played: "You'll Never Walk Alone," "Eternal Father," and, of course, "The Military Song." After the songs, the minister concluded the service by reading part of a letter we had from Ken when he had visited the Holy Land:

> I felt the presence of Jesus Christ when I walked along the path He had walked. For some reason, I had to come here. Now that I am here, I can truly say my life is complete.

That was the end of the letter and the minister's ceremony.

The pallbearers were dressed in their uniforms. Enlisted men carried the casket. Marine officers formed the arch, swords drawn. We followed the casket through the arch and stood while it was being placed in the hearse.

"Lord," I prayed, "let us get through this day."

Juanita and I couldn't have asked for a more beautiful setting for our son. As we all assembled at the graveside, I was startled to find that from there you could see the Pentagon building to the east and the Washington and Lincoln memorials to the north. There was green, green everywhere, broken only by the winding roads through the cemetery and the headstones on each grave. Marines in their blues, against the green background of the rolling hills and the blue sky, made a picture Ken would have appreciated.

The military roll began. Military pallbearers lifted the flag off the casket, the stars facing upward. It was then presented to four-star General Anderson, representing the Marine Corps. He received the flag with a salute, then brought it over and presented it to Juanita and myself.

The bugler played. A volley of rifle fire indicated that a soldier had passed beyond. Juanita and I both cried for joy. We knew our son was where the Lord wanted him to be.

Going through Ken's belongings, we found his personal Bible, underlined in many places. This was a real treasure to me because it gave me new insight into what my son had read most in the Bible. The Book of Revelation was underlined in so many places it was almost worn through.

We came across a picture he had drawn, and a prayer he had written. The picture was up on the wall. I remembered him saying that he didn't even understand why he had drawn it. It was an hourglass—the sand in it had just about run out.

Ken's prayer helped us to understand his feelings. Since then I have read it over and over:

Dear God,
Help me to be a sport in this little game of life,
I don't ask an easy place in the lineup.
Play me anywhere You need me; I only ask for the
stuff to give You 100 per cent of what I've got.

If all the hard drives come my way, I thank
You for the compliment. Help me to remember
that You won't let anything come that You and
I together can't handle.

And help me to take bad breaks as part of the game.
Help me to understand that the game is full of
knocks and trouble, and make me thankful for them.
Help me to be brave so that the harder they come,
the better I'll like it.

And, O God, help me to always play on the square.
No matter what other players may do, help me to stay
clean. Help me to study the book so that I'll know
the rules. Help me to think about the greatest
player Who ever lived, and other players
portrayed in the book. If they found that the
best part of the game was helping other guys
who were out of luck, help me to find that, too.
Help me to be a regular player and an
inspiration to all the others.

Finally, God, if fate deals me a heavy blow, and
I'm put on the shelf, help me to take this part
of the game, too. And when in the falling dusk
I hear the final bell, I ask no epitaphs, but only
to know that You judged me a good, brave guy in
the game of life. . . .

2nd Lt. Kenneth Edward Johnson
United States Marine Corps

"*Help me.*" The phrase was repeated a dozen times in Ken's prayer. It echoed in my mind.

No wonder his life had been such a blessing. Ken had continually asked for God's help, and He had always been faithful in giving it. Looking back, I could see so many times in my own life when the same thing had happened. But I was suddenly overwhelmed with the awareness that God had helped me many more times when I hadn't asked Him—or thanked Him.

"O God," I prayed, real remorse mingled with overflowing thanksgiving, "forgive me that I've thanked You so few times compared to the many times You've poured out your blessings upon me. Help me to thank You all the time."

CHAPTER

22

Life has to go on.

Less than two weeks after Ken died, the voters went to the polls in 1972 and gave Richard M. Nixon's second term their rousing approval. The next two years flew by as I was busy solving Navy racial problems—people problems, as I called them. And suddenly Watergate was front-page news.

The year 1974 loomed ahead.

Years ago I had declared I would run for the U. S. Senate in 1974.

With so much smoldering, with a major political conflagration about to flame up, I wasn't so sure that this would be the best year. But I remembered that holding to one's principles and goals was more important than winning.

The first step in fulfilling my promise was to break free from duties that left me too little time to campaign.

I would have to resign as Assistant Secretary of the Navy.

There was a chorus of sighs when I broke the news.

"At least give us time to find a replacement," Fred Malik moaned.

It was heartwarming to feel so needed, but I felt I was needed even more in the U. S. Senate.

I was thrilled with the kind words and warm handshakes. I also saw the awesome challenges. I knew my timing was right. But was it the right timing for the nation and California?

California! Beautiful, sunny California. Juanita and I felt like a couple of kids returning home. Tustin looked the same, only with more suburbs stretching farther into the hills, and orange orchards cut down. We found a home that suited us once again, and Juanita happily began to settle in.

My new business partner, Leo McDowell, my former Marine buddy, and his wife had moved to Los Angeles.

Our business, Maiden of Steel, Inc.—safes and security devices— was headquartered on Wilshire Boulevard in Los Angeles.

After I got the office set up the way I wanted it, Watergate news really began to flood. Every day, faces I knew were in the newspapers.

Some, like Dick Kleindienst, called me. I had first met him when he'd been on the committee to appoint me as vice chairman of the Civil Service Commission. I had always been struck by the wide-eyed look of this tall, heavy man with thinning hair, who always seemed to be chewing on a big cigar.

Dick was different from most of the rest. Deeply religious, he and I often talked about the Lord at social gatherings. He was a family man and proud of it. We had many meetings together, mostly at breakfast. He was always concerned about the low-income people of Washington, D.C. One day he phoned, very upset.

"Look, Johnny, I'm going to have to do something, and I want you to know, since you've been such a good friend. I'm going to have to resign."

"Oh no, Dick!" I exploded. "You're not involved in Watergate!"

"Of course not, Johnny. I wouldn't lie to you. I'm not involved in any way. I don't know this to be a fact, but I feel some of my closest associates may be involved, and I will not have any part of it at all. I don't want them to ask me to cover up for them. I don't want this to happen, so I see no choice."

"But Dick, we need you there."

It saddened me to think that a man could so easily get into such a position. Silently, I thanked Melvin Laird once again for not letting me get involved in the nitty-gritty of the 1972 Nixon campaign. I too might have been awash in Watergate.

Then there were the photographs in *Time* magazine, the lineup. I could hardly believe the number of people I had seen frequently at the White House who were involved in some way, including Dwight Chapin, Egil Krogh, and Charles Colson.

Chapin was the appointments secretary for President Nixon, a very young, tall, and handsome fellow, but one of the most insecure people I had met in Washington. He looked like the All-American "Mr. Clean," but stuck like glue to the President. He'd pace up and down in Nixon's office while someone was talking to the President and, when the time started running out, he would peer every other second at his watch, giving the President the signal. If that didn't work, he would act antsy and start shuffling papers on the President's desk as if preparing for the next appointment.

Once Chapin got himself in trouble interrupting Melvin Laird to say, "Mr. President, you do have an appointment."

"Don't you ever interrupt me again when I'm talking to the President. He has an appointment with me," Laird stormed. "Quit pacing around and get out of here."

Chapin looked startled for a moment, then shot out of the Oval Office.

It was hard to believe that he was being indicted on perjury charges before a federal grand jury about his connection with dirty trickster Donald Segretti.

Egil Krogh, Jr., I had previously met at our White House prayer breakfasts. He told us what the Lord had done for him. He seemed to be a very straight Christian. He was a nice-looking chap, tall and big-boned. But he also seemed nervous and insecure. He had been the chief assistant to John Ehrlichman and later Under Secretary of Transportation. A poor conversationalist, he seemed always to be trying to avoid answering questions. I felt that the Lord was dealing with him.

Before all of the Watergate conspirators were discovered, we had taken pictures of Krogh at a California meeting for political purposes. Krogh called for all the negatives and prints. We heard later that he had had them destroyed.

Now Krogh was being convicted of conspiring to violate the constitutional rights of Daniel Ellsberg's psychiatrist by approving the "plumbers" break-in at his office. And there were rumors of the indictment of my friend Charles Colson.

I had many talks with Chuck Colson. Knowing that he was now a dedicated Christian, I had complete trust that he would do the right thing. He always attended our prayer meetings in 1973, and I looked on him as one of the most intelligent people in the White House.

However, because he was very outspoken and candid, he was always being quoted and misquoted. Chuck would give you an opinion on anything and felt his opinion was just as valid as the next person's. He is not a big man, but a strong-looking person.

I remembered him frequently reading, for which he wore black-framed glasses. He looked very serious, professorish. He was definitely not a "yes" man. Whenever we talked politics, I truly felt Colson was concerned with saving the country, even though he had been quoted as saying he would do anything for Nixon.

I flew back on a plane to Washington with Colson early in 1974, and we had talked all the way. "Everything I have done, I have done in good faith and thought I was serving my country by my action," he remarked. "I would do anything to preserve this country of mine. I have received no money, nor did I rip off anyone. I merely wanted to see good government at work."

"I believe you, Chuck," I replied.

"I'm telling you the truth. But one of the things I'm just so thrilled about is that I have found Christ."

There had been many rumors then that he might be indicted for his role in the Watergate scandal, and I asked him about this. He didn't think he would be.

"Whatever happens, Johnny, I don't think I could carry this burden if I hadn't found Christ."

I tried to assure him of my friendship and of my intention to stand by him.

I wondered how all this was going to affect the political climate of the California election. No one could blame the people for being skeptical of every politician. It seemed that corruption in government, perjury, abuse of presidential power and privilege, and an "anything goes" policy had been prevailing in Washington, D.C., right under my nose.

"How am I going to prove to the people of the state of California that I have something different to offer?" I asked Juanita one night.

"You're not going to let all this trouble right now stop you, are you?" she countered.

A day before Valentine's Day, in February 1974, I formally announced my candidacy for the U. S. Senate at press conferences in Los Angeles, Orange County, San Francisco, and San Diego. It was the first time a political candidate ever held four such press conferences on the same day in different parts of the state.

If elected, I would be the second black ever elected to the Senate. The first had been Senator Edward Brooke, of Massachusetts. Actually, five black senators were appointed in the South right after the Civil War, but they did not go through the electoral process.

The main issues I campaigned on were beating inflation, solving the energy crisis, as well as restoring moral and spiritual values to American life. My slogan was, "Something can be done." I felt that such a positive statement would counteract gloom and hopelessness.

When people questioned me as to what one individual could do to "set things right," I was ready to cite dozens of examples of "loners" who'd made lasting impressions on world and national history.

I kept repeating that *I wanted to put back into America some of the things I'd gotten out of it.* I pointed out the positive values of our great nation; in spite of weaknesses, it was still the greatest nation in the world. I capped such talks with a brief story of my own life, how I'd risen from poverty and lack of advantage to become the first black warrant officer in the U. S. Marine Corps, and the first black in several other significant categories.

In April 1974, Chuck Colson was indicted for obstructing justice in the Daniel Ellsberg case by disseminating derogatory information while Ellsberg was under indictment for giving the Pentagon Papers to the press.

I didn't think Chuck would be indicted. In fact, the day he was indicted, I placed a call to him. His secretary said, "I'm sorry, Mr. Colson is not speaking to anyone."

"Do me a favor and tell him Johnny Johnson is on the phone."

Chuck came on the phone. "Johnny, how are you?"

My mood had changed. I was in tears. "Chuck, I wanted you to know how sick I am, hearing about you. But let me tell you, I love you as a Christian brother. Remember, if there is anything I can do to assist . . . I just wanted you to know you have a friend here. I know your feelings, what you've gone through. Juanita and I just want to let you know we're praying for you every day."

Chuck cried, too. "Johnny, you don't know how much this means to me. It's the best call I've had all day. Johnny, thanks a lot, thanks a lot."

"Chuck, remember any time you want to get in touch with me, you know you can."

"I certainly will," he promised. He was really down.

In April 1974, I had to fly to Washington, D.C., to work on a fund-raising effort for my campaign. While there, I dropped by to see some political friends.

After we'd talked a while, Dr. Ted Marr, whom I'd dropped in on at the Executive Offices, said, "Do you want to go by and say 'Hi' to the Vice President?"

"I sure would," I said.

We sat a long time in the waiting area of the Executive Office Building, across the street from the White House. After many people passed back and forth, we were finally summoned into Gerald Ford's office.

"Well, Johnny, it's good to see you," Mr. Ford said. "How are you doing?"

I told him about my company, then outlined my campaign to date.

"How's it going?"

I grinned. It was too early to have compiled a lot of statistics on the potential vote, but I tried to summarize individuals and Republican groups supporting my campaign.

"How about Ronald Reagan?" he inquired.

"He's not taking a position in this race because he also admires two of the other candidates who are close friends of his, too."

"It'll be a tough fight," Ford said, "but you have as good a chance as anyone. If God thinks it's the right time, you can't lose."

The Vice President seemed genuinely excited about my platform, especially my objective of raising moral and spiritual values.

When May rolled around with only one month before the June primary, Chuck Colson called again. "Johnny, I'm going to put this in writing to you, but I wanted to let you know why I'm going to plead guilty."

"You are going to do what?"

"Johnny, now hear me out. I'm pleading guilty, not because I really believe what I've done is totally wrong. At the time, I really believed it was for the benefit of the country. But I can't lie about the fact that I did it. I'm a born-again Christian, and I'm not worried about what other people will think."

I murmured my approval, for I knew Chuck was now a dedicated Christian, due to some of my efforts and to the fellowship of people like Senator Harold Hughes, Cliff Robinson, Doug Coe, Frank Sanders, and Dick Halverson.

"In fact," Chuck went on, "I'm glad about the fact that I'm a new Christian, because this is a real test for me in my new Christian faith. I can't fault on this. You, as a brother, have to understand and have to be able to tell the people."

"I certainly understand. You tell the truth, regardless of what it is; but remember we still love you, and we still stand by you."

"Johnny, I know that, but being a good Christian brother, I wanted you to know about it. I hope you understand."

"I certainly do."

Although I lost the battle, I counted my bid for U. S. senator from California a success. I polled 120,000 votes, an unprecedented achievement for a member of my race in any similar contest—despite major problems in the campaign, including a late start and shortage of money. The latter was no longer easy to raise, due to new state and federal legislation leveling many restrictions on potential donors.

After the campaign, I went back to my business.

Right after the California primary election, Chuck Colson was sentenced to a one-to-three-year prison term after pleading guilty, June 3, to obstruction of justice in the Ellsberg case. Chuck was also fined five thousand dollars.

After the sentencing, I called him. "Chuck, you just don't know how badly I feel about it."

"Johnny, I do know. I understand. Don't worry." Chuck reminded me that the Apostle Paul had done his best work in prison. "It teaches patience and humility," he explained. "This is a wonderful thing for a newborn Christian to have to go through. And I just thank the Lord He's given me the courage and the strength to go through it."

In August 1974, Dr. Ted Marr and presidential counselor Jack Marsh phoned, asking me to fly to Washington to discuss with them and the President the transfer of personnel occasioned by Gerald Ford's replacing Richard Nixon.

When I met with Dr. Marr, he said, "Johnny, we really need someone who knows the civil service system. It will make the transition period easier. You know the personnel, the regulations, and everything. We won't have to be constantly checking the books."

That made sense to me, too.

"You'll be the personnel director for the White House," Ted said.

"No. But I'll help you on a consultant basis and come back whenever you need me."

"Suppose the President asked you to do more than that?"

"Look!" I said in alarm, recalling many occasions when I'd been pressured into accepting something without due deliberation. "Don't get him to ask me."

"Let's just go around and talk to Jack Marsh," Ted said, a wry smile on his face.

In Jack's office, we found his son Robert, a handsome, intelligent young man.

We talked awhile and Ted said, "Look, I have another position for Johnny." He wrote something on a piece of paper and handed it to Jack.

"Hey, that's great," Jack said.

"May I see it?" I asked.

"Let us work it out, first, then we'll tell you," Jack assured.

"Look, fellows. I don't know what you're going to give me unless it would be the vice presidency. That would excite me enough to get me to come back here on a long-term basis. But I'm sure you didn't write 'Vice President' on that paper."

"How do you know?" Jack laughed. "Anyway, the President is going to talk to you."

The next morning, I found myself in the Executive Office Building again. The President hadn't moved all his things over to the White House. I wondered if the football trophies would follow him across the street. I hoped so, because I didn't want to feel that his new office would change my favorite President.

While we sat in the waiting area, Ted, Jack, and I discussed what we'd talked about the day before. "Could you consider a job on a long-term basis?" Ted asked. "Things will be wide open here. The President likes you, and you have proven yourself. . . ."

"I'll consider some jobs," I answered, "but I won't commit myself."

"You've done fine jobs in your state and here in Washington," Jack said. "We won't have to go through a lot of Mickey Mouse to get you into anything you want."

We had to wait about an hour before we got in to see the President. Mr. Ford was considering choices for Vice President. Many of the congressmen were pushing their favorites, including George Bush, Barry Goldwater, Howard Baker, Melvin Laird, Ronald Reagan, and Nelson Rockefeller.

When we were finally ushered in, the President had a big smile on his face. "Johnny! All the fellows have been telling me about you; I am so happy you've decided to come aboard. . . ."

"Wait a minute!" I interjected. "I'm not exactly aboard!"

"What do you mean?" He turned to Ted.

"What he means is, he's just helping us with this transition period."

"Don't let this guy get away. Let's work him," Ford said.

I laughed. "Oh, they are working me. I worked last night, this morning, all yesterday. And I know that you're busy, too, Mr. President. I won't take up much of your time."

"Wait a minute," the President directed. "Just sit down there. I'm sorry about the election. I still believe you would make a good senator. Now, what would you think if I were to invite the black caucus over?"

"Mr. President, I don't think I would do it if I were in your shoes, but I guess maybe politically you feel as though you have to. I would prefer having all the black senior Republicans, rather than the black Democrats, around to talk with you. It would give us the kind of thing we need most in the Republican Party—a boost, knowing that the President had asked our advice and guidance. But, in my opinion, you are not going to get anywhere politically talking to those other black guys. I know what they are going to say."

"I understand," Mr. Ford said.

"On the other hand, maybe you should call the black Democrats in separately and talk with them. Find out! Maybe they can give you some insight. We are talking from our party standpoint and they are going to be talking from the Democrat side. You should have the benefit of both sides."

"That's real great; I'm glad you said that," the President replied.

Then we talked about California and some of the jobs I'd had. He wanted to know about the Civil Service Commission, too. "How does one get through things in the civil service?"

"You have a tremendous chairman over there, Bob Hampton, and I'm sure he'll co-operate with you. Of course, he has about three million people to worry about."

Finally, I said, "Mr. President, I know you are busy and these guys want to work me a little more. The best of luck. I'll be praying for you."

"I need prayer. I need the kind of prayer that this country has never had before. Pray for us that things will work out fine." Then he paused before he continued, "I'm going to call on ministers. As many as I can get hold of, to ask for their guidance and prayer."

A few minutes later I flew to Chicago for a boy scout function. About six months earlier, I had been elected as vice president in charge of personnel for the Boy Scouts of America—the second-highest position in the scouting organization.

As always, I was inspired by talking about ways of teaching young people about "old-fashioned" values and responsibilities, and the greatness of their country.

Working for the new President of the United States was thrilling and something I would be doing more of in the near future. Also, having a greater responsibility with the scouts was heartwarming. I reflected on both of these activities as I flew home from Chicago.

Yet even more exciting events were ahead of me.

CHAPTER

23

One of the things we stress in our home is love. We taught our family that there are only two things that motivate people: One is fear, and the other is love. And we use the Scriptures to show how we can get rid of fear. Because of our teaching, our children believe that prayer is what brings love about.

One of the things our ten-year-old son, Juan, does when a difficult situation arises is to pray about it. In one instance, I was trying to repair our sink. There was a little hose that needed replacing in order for my wife to spray the dishes, and I tried for some time to repair it, without success. Finally I told Juan I was going to give up and call a plumber.

Juan said, "Dad, why don't we pray about it?"

"Son, you don't pray about things like that."

"Yes, we pray about things like that, Dad. I'll pray in love."

"What do you mean, Juan, you'll 'pray in love'?"

"Well, I love you and I love Jesus Christ, and if I pray in love, then He'll do it for me."

I consented, "Okay, I'll pray."

But Juan hesitated. "No, I'll pray," he said.

He folded his little hands in front of him. "Dear Lord, give my father the wisdom and the strength to repair this right now. In the name of Jesus."

I said, "Amen."

"Now, Dad, get back underneath the sink. Take the wrench and put it in your left hand."

"I've tried that before, Juan."

"Well, try again."

I pressed hard, and the thing came off. I put the new hose on and started the screw. Juan stopped me. "Put the wrench in your right hand now, Dad. You're going in the other direction."

I did. Juan took the spray. "It works fine, Dad."

I walked into the family room and threw my tools down. My wife asked, "What's the matter?"

I said, "That son of yours in there . . ."

"I'll bet he prayed for something and got it."

"That's right. How did you know?"

My wife continued, "That's what he does all the time. Whenever he wants something, he prays for it in love and it happens."

We taught our children that the greatest thing in life is love. Not candy. Not toys. But love. Every night, our older son, Kurtis, knocks on our bedroom door and says, "Dad, Mom, may I come in?"

He's almost 6-3 and weighs 205 pounds, but invariably explains, "I just want to kiss you two good night, Dad."

That's what so many parents have not done: They do not take their children in their arms when they grow up and tell them they love them. *Love is beyond defeat, and love never faileth.*

There are some people who say there are several kinds of love. Love of family. Love of self. Love for your wife. Love for your neighbors. We say, "There's really only one love, and they all come under the heading: 'Love of the Lord and Savior, Jesus Christ.' 'God's Love.'"

When you have that love in your heart, all of those other loves come under that. I've had some interesting experiences in my ministry that show it really works.

I was in Belgium where we were met by people who had strange-sounding names and people who spoke a different language. We conducted each prayer service with interpreters.

A lady from Communist Hungary came into one meeting where I

was speaking. She could not understand me, she explained later, but she could feel the love as it was radiated to her. So she found an interpreter to translate what I was saying. After the meeting, she asked to talk to me. Through the interpreter, she said she wanted to know about Jesus Christ and His love for her, because she'd never had love in her entire life. A woman from a Communist country, she explained, "I hate my country. I hate my parents."

She began to cry as I talked to her through the interpreter about the love of Jesus. She put her arms around me and wept. "I want to take this love back to my country," she said, "and introduce this kind of love there."

She explained that she had not been invited to the conference, but she heard me speaking. "I felt His love. It was a strange thing. Nothing like this has ever before affected me. I always thought that religion was for the poor."

Another time I was in Jerusalem for the Third World Conference on the Holy Spirit. We manifested love on the bus tour as we went from place to place. As the love grew, we felt that our bus had more love than any other bus. We began to tell the Israeli guides how much we loved them.

Finally, the bus driver came back to us and said, "All right, you Christians. You talk so much about love. You have so much love in your hearts for us, why don't you do something for us?"

We asked, "What?"

"We need rain. It hasn't rained in Israel in two years. So why don't you pray for rain?"

The Israelis laughed along with the bus driver. "If you can pray for rain, and it rains," they said, "then we'll believe in your Jesus."

A member of our group asked, "Would you believe that we love you, too?"

The driver answered, "If you pray and it rains, we'll believe that you love us, too."

So we all got together and prayed for rain. "Lord, open up the clouds and allow a downpour. Make a flood to show Your love and Your manifestation. Amen."

There was no rain for the next two days. We were almost to the airport on our return trip when one of the Israeli drivers came up to us. He was laughing. "Well, you Christians prayed, and it didn't rain. I guess your Christian prayers didn't do any good."

They laughed.

But I countered, "Listen! You just wait. The Lord's going to open up the clouds and there's going to be a cloudburst."

They laughed as we got on the plane.

A week and a half later, a Dallas, Texas, minister called me. "Johnny, are you the character who was over in Jerusalem praying for rain?"

"I sure was."

"Well, we got there one day after all of you were gone. It was as if the clouds opened up, and buckets of rain came down. They had a flood. It rained for eleven straight days. It rained so hard we couldn't even leave our hotel room. That's the most rainfall Israel's had in forty-some years."

"Praise the Lord!" I really meant it.

Then the minister asked, "Why didn't you guys let it rain while you were there and spoil your trip—instead of mine?"

But he said it in love.

At about 1:30 A.M. one night I received a long-distance phone call at my home in Washington, D.C. A man's voice said, "You don't know me, but I've been told that you're a person who has a lot of love in your heart, and that you give speeches and started a lot of prayer breakfasts around Washington, D.C. We'd like you to speak to us at the governor's prayer breakfast in Juneau, Alaska."

"I don't know if you're joking or not, but this is a bad time of night to ask me something like that," I answered, still half asleep.

"Yes, I know, but I'm the Governor of Alaska, and I want you to come."

I started to tell him, "I'm Abraham Lincoln, too, and I want you to come to Washington, D.C." But the caller continued before I said anything.

"My name is Jay Hammond, and I am the Governor of Alaska. We want you to come April 19."

"I think I have a speaking engagement that day."

"Well, I'm going to pray about it," he assured, and hung up.

The next day he called back. "I prayed about it, and the Lord wants you to come."

"I checked it out, and my wife assures me I have a speaking engagement that day. I'm awfully sorry."

"This is the first governor's breakfast we've ever had," the caller continued. "I'm going to keep praying."

Max Shulman, a friend of mine from California, came to Washington. I mentioned to him that I'd been invited to Juneau, Alaska, but wasn't going.

But Max persuaded, "Johnny! You have to go. I'm going up there. If you go, I'll pay your way, and you won't have to worry about any expenses."

"I have a speaking engagement. I can't break it."

Max said, "We're going to pray about that."

I replied, "Well, go ahead and pray, but I'm still going to keep the other engagement."

About three days later, the person who had invited me to speak in Maryland called me. "Would you forgive me?" he asked. "I made a mistake on the date. We're not going to have the April 19 meeting."

So I immediately called Max. "Do you still want to pay my way to Alaska?"

"I've already made reservations for us."

"But I didn't tell you that I was going."

"I know. But the Lord told me, so I've done everything that the Lord said."

It took some miracles to get us to Juneau. I was late getting to the airport. The plane had left the loading area. The supervisor recognized me and called the plane to wait. They drove me onto the airfield in a private car. But the captain in the plane radioed down that it was against regulations to open the door.

The supervisor replied, "I'll be responsible. Open up."

The aircraft door was open, but it was too high. So they called a food truck. I got on top of it; then they raised the rack to the top so I could walk inside the plane.

A lady was so mad she jumped up out of her seat, put her hands on her hips, and yelled, "Who do you think you are, holding up this plane for seventeen minutes?"

"I'm nobody important," I replied.

"Who do you work for, anyway?"

My answer seemed to settle her, "I work for the Lord Jesus."

The first miracle was in catching the plane from Washington to

Los Angeles. There I met Max, who rushed, "We've only got five minutes to catch the plane to Seattle."

We made it and took our seats. The doors were shut when the pilot radioed that we'd be delayed about 15 minutes.

"We've only got forty-three minutes to catch the plane from Seattle, Washington, going to Juneau, Alaska—and that's the only plane," Max fretted.

The pilot radioed again, "Sorry, but it's going to be another thirty minutes."

I told Max, "That really fouls us up. We only have forty-three minutes and we're using up forty-five right there."

We got off and asked the supervisor if he'd radio to Seattle to hold the plane. But he said, "We're not going to hold that plane for you or anybody else; we don't care who you are."

"Let's pray about it," Max instructed.

We held hands in the Los Angeles International Airport terminal and prayed. "Lord, open up a way."

When we got to Seattle someone popped her head inside the Los Angeles plane before we got off. She asked, "Is there a Dr. Johnson in here?"

"Yes!"

"Come with me." As we rushed to the next plane, she continued, "The strangest thing happened. The Juneau plane had taxied to the runway for takeoff when one of the engines failed. They had to bring it back. You can get on—but you'd have missed it if it had gone off on time."

Max and I exclaimed, "That's another miracle!"

We got to Juneau and had the prayer breakfast. I spoke on "God's love for mankind," including I Corinthians 13 and the two things that motivate people—fear and love—and why I wanted to talk of love.

After the meeting, a man came over and put his arms around my neck. He said, "That's the finest thing that ever happened to me, because I could feel your love and the love of the people here. I had told my wife earlier, 'The last thing in the world I want to do is get up at five o'clock in the morning to hear some bureaucrat from Washington, D.C., talk about Jesus.' But I wouldn't have missed it for the world."

"That's fine, sir," I said. "But who are you?"

"Oh, I'm the lieutenant governor."

"Praise the Lord! That's very kind of you to say you wouldn't have missed the meeting. But I'd like to know your name."

"I'm Lowell Thomas, Jr."

The governor of Alaska came up to me and said, "Johnny, I understand you're going to have a Full Gospel Businessmen's Fellowship International meeting tonight and a prayer service. May I come and bring my wife?"

"Sure," I said, "absolutely."

He came that night with his wife. Again I spoke on I Corinthians 13. After it was over, we asked those whose hearts were touched and who wanted to accept the Lord, or just wanted prayer, to come forward. The first two who came forward and got down on their knees were the governor of Alaska and his wife.

A similar situation happened in North Carolina at a businessmen's meeting. A construction man needed eight hundred thousand dollars but couldn't borrow it. His friends kept pushing him to talk to me after the meeting.

"I'm not sure this is going to do any good," he said after he'd explained his problem to me, "But I do believe in Christ. And if I don't get that loan . . . well, I've already had the papers drawn to declare bankruptcy. Three banks and other lending institutions have turned me down. I don't have anything else to do but declare bankruptcy."

I said, "Why don't we pray about it?"

We laid hands on the Bible and began to pray. The Lord showed me something. I turned to the businessman and said, "In three days, you'll have your money."

Three days later, one of the banks that had already turned him down called him. "We'd like to take another look at those papers you have for that eight-hundred-thousand-dollar loan. Could you take a million dollars?"

The man got his loan and more. His business was saved. He said it was all done because of the great love that was shared in the auditorium, by all the people there—in God's love.

As I've tried to explain throughout this book, love even overcomes racial situations.

Since God's great love has penetrated my life, in every incident that has come up, love overshadows everything else. I think that one of the clearest examples was when a man was being interviewed in North Carolina on television about attending a Christian businessmen's meeting.

The man told the television interviewer, "Johnny Johnson was the minister. I could just feel the love in that guy oozing out."

The man continued, "I never thought I could even hug a man, but I held so much love in my heart for him that when he asked those who love the Lord to come forth and give their life to Him, I ran up to that man and put my arms around him. I just hugged him, and I just love him. I could see Jesus in him."

The television reporter asked, "Was that James E. (Johnny) Johnson, the former Assistant Secretary of the Navy?"

"Yeah, that's the one."

"And you hugged him?"

"I sure did."

"But isn't he a black man?"

The man looked the reporter in the eye, "I really don't know. I didn't ask him."

Another time the Lord showed His love in a very special way. I was on my way to a Full Gospel Businessmen's Fellowship International meeting in New Mexico. It was a tough day for me, trying to get my bags packed and get to the airport. The plane door was closing when I got there. As I sat down I prayed, "Thank You, Jesus, for getting me on this plane. I do not know why I had to catch this plane, but I thank You, Jesus."

I opened my attaché case and was doing some reading when all of a sudden, a man about four seats in front of me let out a scream, "What in the world's going on, you clumsy broad?"

The man began to swear.

I saw that one of the women flight attendants had accidentally spilled some drinks on the man as the plane hit a downdraft. He was telling her off, and she was crying, "Oh, I'm so sorry."

The man scowled, "You had better be sorry. You're going to pay for this suit of clothes!"

The attendant assured, "I will pay for it, but please don't make a scene."

"I'll make as much of a scene as I want to. I will scream my head off, you clumsy clown! They should throw you off the plane—in midair!"

The attendant continued crying. The man's behavior made him look totally ridiculous. "You're not only going to get a bill, but I'm also going to write to the airline and have you fired!"

She protested, "But it was an *accident!*"

"This is the only suit I have, and I have a business engagement. Can you imagine me walking in and smelling of booze?"

Another woman came out to help the first attendant. The second woman also apologized. People were turning to look. The women tried to sponge the man's clothes off. But the more they tried, the louder he became. Finally the young woman who had spilled the drink went to the back of the plane, sat down, and cried aloud.

I sat there a moment. Then I prayed, "Lord Jesus, I don't know what to do, but I'd like You to touch that man's heart."

The Lord said, "I want to touch his heart. But I want you to go tell him about Jesus."

"Lord, that man's wild. I can't go talk to him. What will I say?"

Then the Lord revealed to me, "Go, and I will do the talking."

I moved toward the man. I could smell the alcohol spilled on him. "Sir?"

He looked up at me. "What do you want?"

"Sir, I want to talk to you."

"About what?"

"The young lady who spilled the drink on you."

"She'll get it, I can assure you. She'll never fly on another aircraft as long as she lives. I have influence with this airline."

I began, "That's what I want to talk to you about. In fact, I don't want to talk to you about her—I want to talk to you about yourself."

"What about me? Don't you come preaching to me about what I should and should not do!"

"No, sir," I said. "That's not what I want to talk to you about. I would like to tell you something, but I don't know why I'm telling you. I feel inside of me that you're a person who has a lot of compassion . . . that you're the kind of man who has a lot of good in you, the kind of a person who has a lot of integrity and a lot of love."

He looked at me. "Most of what you say is true. I'm not such a bad guy."

"I know that. I'd like to ask you another question: How would you like to walk off this aircraft when we get to New Mexico as the happiest man in the world—and the people on this plane will feel that you're the greatest man in the world?"

"That's ridiculous. They heard what I said. Nobody's going to say I'm a great guy. Besides, I don't care what the passengers think."

I continued, "Would you like to make someone else the happiest person in the world?"

"Well, I don't mind that—if it doesn't cost me anything."

"No, sir, it won't cost you a thing. I'm going to ask you to come to the back of the plane and tell the young lady you're sorry for what you said."

"Ah come on! I'm not sorry for what I said!"

"Maybe you're not now, but will you hear me out, sir?"

"All right, go on, fellow."

"All I ask is that you go to the back of the plane and tell her you're sorry. When she responds, I want you to tell her that you love her. I know you do, because you have a good heart. The Lord tells me you have a good heart. You're a good person, a good American."

"Of course I'm a good American."

"I believe that, sir. Now will you go back there with me?"

Finally he agreed. "But I'll not tell her I love her. I'll just tell her I'm sorry."

Everybody on the plane knew what had happened because the man had made such a fuss. Eyes followed us as we walked to the attendant. She had her head down on her lap.

"Miss?"

She sniffed and looked up. "Yes?" Then she saw him. She stood up and said, "Don't you start in on me again! I said I'm sorry, and I'll pay for your suit."

The man interrupted, "No, miss, that's not what I came to tell you."

"I don't want to hear anything you have to say!"

But I urged, "Miss, please—if you'd just let him say what he has to say."

The man was backing away, "See? She doesn't want to hear it."

"Just a minute, sir." Then I turned. "Miss, if you'll do that for me I guarantee that you'll be a happy person."

"I doubt it, but go on."

"Well," the man said, "I just wanted to tell you I'm sorry. You don't have to pay for the suit. I have another one."

The attendant began to cry. "Oh, that makes me so happy!" She put her arms around his neck and sobbed. "Thank you, sir! Thank you!"

"I don't know why I'm doing this, but I sure feel better now," the man beamed.

I urged him further, "Why don't you tell her the rest of it?"

"Rest of what?"

"Tell her what you and I talked about."

He took the flight attendant's arms and pushed her away a little. "I don't want you think anything funny about this, but I want to tell you that I love you."

She broke down. "I love you, too!" Then she looked up at him and asked, "Are you a Christian?"

"I don't know," he said. "I go to church."

"I'm a Christian, and this is the nicest thing that's ever happened. You have made me a happy person."

He looked into the attendant's eyes, and tears started running down his cheeks. "I'm a happy person, too."

"That is Jesus," she explained.

They began to fellowship. Then she said, "I don't want you to answer this unless you want to, but if you have not accepted Jesus Christ as your personal Savior . . ."

The man looked at me. "What's she talking about?"

I explained, then the man said, "I belong to a church."

"Yes," I continued, "but have you accepted Jesus? That's what she's asking you."

"I respect Him. . . ."

"But that's not enough," I said. "You must accept Him. Make a decision to *live* for Christ."

"How do you do that?"

"You confessed your sin to her and said you're sorry. Now confess your sins to Christ and tell Him the same thing. Tell Him you're sorry and ask His forgiveness—just like you asked her."

"Is that all?"

"Yes." I quoted some pertinent Bible verses, then added, "Let's pray right now."

We held hands at the rear of the plane and began to pray. I saw an arm come over mine and touch the man's shoulder. It was the captain. He didn't say anything as we continued to pray.

Then the Lord touched the passenger's heart. "Thank You, Jesus, for accepting me."

The captain, the flight attendant, the passenger, and I hugged each other. As we walked back to our seats, people reached out and shook hands with the man. Several of them affirmed, "That was a wonderful thing you did—telling that young lady you're sorry."

When the man got to his seat, all the passengers applauded him.

When we reached our destination, people on board did a strange thing. They usually get right off and walk away. But the passengers stood outside the plane and waited for the man to come down the ramp. Then they all crowded around him and again shook his hand. One lady gleamed, "Thanks for what you did; saying you're sorry to the girl. You're a great man!"

He had become the happiest man in the world. But the real reason wasn't because he had told the flight attendant he was sorry for what he'd said to her. The real reason was that he had the love of Jesus in his life. And, in my hotel room, I also was happy, praising God for the many ways He reveals His love in our lives.

In fact, the Lord was about to manifest Himself in my life in a most dramatic and unusual way—in a situation that would bring me "face to face" with the Lord.

CHAPTER

24

I had been driving a large auto from my office in Washington to Virginia with Jack Snyder, an attorney. We pulled underneath a railroad track and stopped for a five-way light. There was a little grade up to the light, so a lot of speed can be reached before you come to the stoplight.

We were listening to the radio when I suddenly heard a screeching sound of tires. I turned to Jack, "It sounds as if somebody's going to get hit."

I didn't see the car in the rear-view mirror, so I didn't have a chance to brace myself. The other car smashed into the rear of our car.

My head snapped forward. There was a second, lighter bump from behind. Then it was like somebody turned the lights off.

The other driver had hit us doing about fifty miles an hour. The impact drove my head through the steering wheel and against the dashboard. My right arm also went through the wheel, right to the shoulder. My right leg, which had been on the brake, was doubled back up under the seat. I had a moment of horrifying pain through my body. My head and right arm were locked inside the steering wheel up to my chest.

The pain stopped. It was as if I'd been going through a long tunnel, with darkness all around, and then there was a horizon and clearing ahead. It was like a sunrise in the West Virginia mountains, only much brighter—and prettier.

This was the brightest light I'd ever seen. It was like trying to look into the sun, but there was no glare. *I knew it was Christ.* There was no question about it.

It was like something very personal . . . like something I could reach out and touch. It was a part of me, a warmth I could actually feel.

Yet I was also floating over the accident scene and I could hear the conversations—*but I knew I was dead!*

I could actually see Jack running around to my side of the car. I could hear him speaking. Somebody asked about me, crumpled through the steering wheel, "Who's he?"

A number of spectators had gathered. There were men in white coats and policemen. I could see the guy in the white coat trying to move me. Someone else urged, "Don't move him! His neck's broken!"

They were talking about what to do, and I could hear them—yet I didn't hear with my ears. It was more like I could *feel* them talking.

Jack was saying, "What can I do?"

The guy in the white coat said, "Just get out of the way. I'll do it."

Someone said, "I don't know if this guy's going to make it."

They were trying to feel my heart. One man backed away, "He's dead."

Someone asked again, "Who is he?"

"The former Assistant Secretary of the Navy and vice chairman of the Civil Service Commission," Jack said.

Immediately a man instructed, "Then we should take him directly to the naval hospital in Bethesda. Radio in and tell them who we've got."

I began to pray within myself, looking down at me in the car and all the rest of the accident scene. I had no pain. I felt good. Then I floated away from the accident through this darkness toward the light.

I *knew* Who that Light was. No one had to tell me. I knew I was with Christ. Yet I knew I was *alive* with Him. The word "death" had nothing to do with it.

I had gone rapidly through the tunnel, through that blackness, toward the Light. It drew me faster and faster and faster. I loved that Light. Then I began to see people. The darkness began to leave. The Light was bright but not harsh. It was beautiful. And I saw streets as the Light illuminated them. It was like a bright city in space—totally beautiful.

I did not see an image of Christ, only the Light. But the first image I recognized was my son Ken. I could tell he was talking to me. It seemed I was trying to talk to him because I was surprised to see him. He didn't have on a uniform as he did when he went to be with the Lord. He wore a light garment.

It reminded me of when he was baptized. He and Vernea went into the water at Sacramento. Ken had on a long white gown. It was so vivid. I felt such a warm glow at the time he walked into the water and was immersed.

Above the accident, I felt the same love, the same warmth. It was as if he were talking to me. And I felt his love.

He said several times the same thing that he had before: "Take care of Mother. Take care of Mother and the children."

And then I saw the other people. The next one was my father-in-law, Louis Butler, who died in 1972. He had a way of smiling—squinching up his eyes a little bit. I could see his eyes, and I could hear him so clearly. He assured me, "You'll be all right."

Then I saw my mother, Veola Thomas Johnson, and my father, Richard Johnson. And that's a strange thing, because I saw them all *together*, though my parents had never met my father-in-law in real life. Yet they were there together—and not strangers to each other. I could feel the love among them.

And all wore the same white clothes.

My mother pointed to the Light, "Him." She wasn't talking about a person, but about the Light. She asked, "Did you see Him?"

I was sort of floating and had never felt so good in my whole life.

Then I saw my wife. She wasn't there physically, but I could see her as I could the others. That's always confused me: the fact that someone who has passed on can also see and hear someone who's alive, as Juanita was.

She was smiling and looking very beautiful. I thought she was smiling because Ken was there with my dad and mother and her own father. They were all in a beautiful ray of Light—a Light not over them, but *with* them, as if they were standing in the Light.

Later I learned that Juanita had a premonition about an accident happening to me. When I literally left my body, she was there in spirit. She later told me she had seen the accident scene in the spirit. She stood right there at the time and said a prayer that the Lord would bring me back. Apparently she'd seen these things happening in the spirit and *knew* I was going to be all right.

But I didn't want to come back. There everything was bright and shiny and pretty. It was the most peaceful place I've ever seen. It was as if I were floating on clouds. (It was not like being unconscious—I've been knocked unconscious before, but this wasn't the same.)

Then Juanita prayed again and called, "Come back. Come back to me." I felt a tug as she prayed.

Then my father-in-law urged, "Go on! Go on!" It became a chant with the others—my parents and my son. "Go on back! Go on back!"

Juanita was praying. "God, bring him back and let him stay with us. Don't leave us." And the chanting of the others continued: "Go back! It's not your time!" Nobody was harsh about it. But they were all very firm, chanting: "Go back. Go back!"

Again I felt the tug. I started seeing the accident scene again, and immediately my body felt heavy. I could feel something, as though someone had put a weight on me. Then the pain started, and it was nearly unbearable.

The white light changed into red. It flashed in my face. I opened my eyes and saw the red light flashing on top of the ambulance. I saw people with white coats on. And the pain became even stronger. It was so severe that it was going down my spine and neck, causing a terrible headache.

"Hey," someone said, "I think he's coming to."

Another asked, "Can you hear me?"

"Yes."

"Don't move your head." He was really brutal. He didn't say, "I *think* maybe there's something wrong with your neck," but blurted, "your neck's broken."

As they put me in the ambulance, I was conscious. I knew what was going on, but lay paralyzed. I prayed,

Lord, You said to ask anything in the name of Jesus, and You shall do anything we ask. In the name of Jesus, I pray that this spine will be healed, this leg will be healed today. Father, show me the sign before I get to the hospital that I will be healed.

In a few moments the attendant massaging my arm laughed as I assured the other attendant I was going to be healed that day. He almost mocked, "You must be a magician."

"No," I said, "But I'm sure my Physician will be able to heal me as soon as I get there."

The driver came back to help when we reached the hospital. The guy who'd been massaging my arm told the driver, "This guy says he's going to be healed before the day is out." To which the driver replied, "He's still out of his head."

The doctors and emergency-room people, alerted by radio, rushed out and asked, "How is he?"

"He's out of his head," the attendant said. "He says he's going to be healed today."

The doctor knew who I was. "Don't start spreading any such stuff around here, because somebody will think the Secretary is totally, completely out of his head, or he's some kind of nut."

But I knew, even as they examined me, that I was going to be healed that day.

"Send him down for X rays," the senior male doctor instructed. "Let's see what kind of damage there is to that neck, right arm, and right leg."

As they prepared me for X ray, a young female doctor came up to me alone. "Dr. Johnson, if you say you're going to be healed today, *when* are you going to be healed?"

"I do not know."

"Ah! If the Holy Spirit was really talking to you, He would tell you *exactly*, would He not?"

"I don't know. But let me pray and ask."

As I prayed, the Lord revealed to me, *"When you leave the X-ray room, you will be healed."*

The woman doctor turned away, but I called her back: "Just a moment! The Holy Spirit just revealed to me that when I leave the X-ray room, I'll be healed."

"Ah no!" She nodded, and they wheeled me off to the X-ray room.

The X-ray technician was a comfortable Christian, I learned later. He went to church or chapel on Sunday and stayed for an hour. When he left, he didn't think about church until eleven o'clock the next Sunday.

He couldn't raise me up, so he used the scan machine on my neck, shoulder, arm, and leg. When he finished, he smiled, "Don't move." He figured I couldn't move and was being funny.

As soon as he left the room, I prayed aloud. The young X-ray technician heard me. Thinking I was out of my head for sure, he ran out in the hall and yelled for the doctor.

They came running back with a nurse, who held the longest needle I'd ever seen. Upon seeing it, I promised I wouldn't pray aloud if they'd not give me that shot.

However, when the doctor and nurse left, and the technician was out of the room, I began to get a strange feeling in my right hand. Then it started to hurt. But it was the best hurt I've ever felt, because I knew the healing was beginning to take place.

Quietly, I began to quote Scripture and praise the Lord.

Gradually, the feeling came back all the way up to my elbow, then to my shoulder and along my neck. Slowly I worked my fingers, opening and closing my hand while saying, "Thank You, Lord!"

It was such a beautiful feeling—so wonderful, in fact, that I tried to jump off the roller bed they had me on. However, I went down on the floor because my leg wouldn't move. So I prayed, "Lord, heal my leg as well as my arm!"

My whole foot and leg began to feel as though they were in hot water. I could feel pins sticking in the leg. While I knew the healing was taking place, nonetheless there was such pain that I muffled a scream. Then I got up off the floor, crying, and lay down on the X-ray table. When I heard the technician running, I put my arm back in the same position it had been.

"Say," he said, "I thought I heard something in here."

I affirmed, "Yep."

"How you doing?"

"Doing fine, thank you."

"That's good." He paused, then looked me in the eyes, "You know, while I was out there finishing up your X rays, I prayed you'd be healed, too. I'm a Christian, but not a very strong one."

"You're either a Christian or you are not. So if you say you're a Christian, you are," I said. "And if you say you're a weak Christian, you are. You will have whatever you say. Now, I personally believe in healing; I don't care what the doctor said."

They wheeled me back up to the emergency room for more examinations. The young female doctor was the first to reach me. "Dr. Johnson, you're out of the X-ray room. Are you healed?"

"Yes, I am."

"All right. Close your eyes."

She put a little instrument against the back side of my hand. "Is that dull or is it sharp?"

"Wow! That's sharp!"

She took the instrument away and then touched me again. "Is that dull or sharp?"

"It's dull."

"Well," she continued, "if you can feel that, you should be able to move your hand."

"I can," and shoved my right hand up in front of her face and extended the fingers so she could see for herself. She let out a scream and ran down the hall.

In a moment I heard her coming back with another doctor, so I put my right arm back across my chest just the way it had been before. The woman doctor was explaining what I'd done, and the male doctor was saying she'd been working too hard. They entered the room.

The male doctor picked up my right hand. "Here, let me show you. This man pushed his *left* hand in front of your face because he wanted to convince you he was healed."

"Doctor," the woman physician argued, "I know my left hand from my right."

The doctor didn't say anything to me, but let my right hand loose. I just let it fall back down.

"You see?" he said to the woman doctor, "there's no life in that hand. He has a hairline fracture of the vertebrae. His right arm and leg are totally paralyzed. It'll be a year to eighteen months with good treatment from a physical therapist before there'll be any movement at all in that arm or leg."

She shook her head. "But he moved it!"

"I suppose he can move his leg, too?"

She replied, "I wouldn't doubt it a bit."

"Now, don't you start that!" he said, starting to check my right leg. I reached down with my right hand and caught him by his wrist. "Wait a minute," I said, "you're hurting my leg."

"That's your right hand!"

"Of course it's my right hand."

He paused a moment. "Who did you say your physician was when you first came into the hospital?"

"Jesus."

He said very softly, "You sure have some kind of a physician!"

He wanted to give me some medication. I told him I wouldn't need it, but he insisted. "Listen, you're going to take this medication even if God did heal you."

"Oh," I smiled, "you agree that the Lord did heal me!"

"Well," he said, "I don't know what happened, but it looks as if you're okay."

He walked out. The young woman doctor pulled the curtain around me, then asked, "How did you get this way?"

"I was sitting in my car when I heard a screeching of brakes. . . ."

"No, no! I'm talking about how you got such faith that the Lord was going to heal you, and it happened?"

"It's called Word Faith. That's standing on the Word of God that gave me the power to tell you that. I believe the Holy Scripture is true—every word of it. It says, 'They shall lay hands on the sick, and they shall recover.' So I asked God to lay His hands on me.

"In Matthew it promises, 'Ask anything in My Name'—that's Jesus talking—'and it shall be given you.' I believe that. I believe in my heart that my healing was God's doing."

She looked incredulous. "Every test we've given you proved you were paralyzed. There is no way you could possibly be healed unless there was some kind of divine healing. In other words . . . what I'm saying is: It was a miracle."

"Praise the Lord! I'm glad you understand. That's exactly what it was."

Now she was intent. "What happened in your life to cause you to have this kind of faith?"

I told her about Word Faith in more detail.

"Could I have that?"

"You certainly can."

She thought I was going to give her literature to read, or preach to her, as she later told me. But instead, I said, "The first thing you have to do is fall in love with yourself."

"Fall in love with myself?"

"The Bible says you should love your neighbor as yourself. If you don't love yourself, it's obvious that you cannot love your neighbor."

I explained that "neighbor" didn't necessarily mean the person next door, but anyone with whom she came in contact.

"But how can I find this?"

"It's very easy. I want you to repeat with me the Sinner's Prayer."

"What's that?"

"You pray, confess your sins, and ask forgiveness. Then you accept Jesus. I don't ask you to change. I don't ask you to do anything but accept Jesus as your personal Savior."

She took my hand, I led, and she followed.

"I love you, Lord Jesus. I have sinned and ask forgiveness for my sins. I accept Jesus as my Lord."

She started to cry. I asked her if she had any malice toward anyone in her life. She admitted a bad feeling for an older sister. So I urged her to forgive her sister and seek forgiveness.

"I feel God has forgiven me, and I love my sister," the doctor cried.

By then, my wife and pastor were outside the curtain. I knew they were praying too.

I laid my hands on the woman doctor to pray again. She opened her eyes and rejoiced, "Praise the Lord!"

Suddenly, a corpsman came around the curtain and interrupted, "What's he done to you?"

She smiled. "He hasn't done anything to me. But the Holy Spirit has made me a real doctor. From here out, I can give my patients the kind of service God wants them to have—spiritual service—so that they will not only be healed physically, but also spiritually."

My wife, pastor, and I hugged her. Even the hospital corpsman put his arms around her, and we all hugged together. There was peace and joy and love in that room. We could all feel God's presence.

And I walked out by myself, healed, as I knew God had promised.

Once again God's great love had helped me to go beyond defeat. Yet even greater miracles than my healing are still taking place every day in the hearts of men and women who believe His Word. These are the miracles of God's love manifested through the Savior, Jesus Christ, and the Holy Spirit.

EPILOGUE

James E. "Johnny" Johnson makes an impact on people. He did on me in 1974, when I first met him. At the time, I was twenty-nine and a successful author. My attitude was that I really had it all together. I had been in fifty countries, seen just about everything, was self-educated, and had set out on a plan to reach my goals in life. But like many people my age, I had lost faith in our government, in our country, and was wavering on an earlier commitment to Christ.

Then Johnny Johnson, a man who can influence your life and attitudes faster in ten minutes than a lifetime of living, entered my life. His conversations are full of country preaching, folk wisdom, and a success-motivation philosophy that not only inspires, but also leaves a life-changing impact.

I'll never forget some of the kernels of wisdom he dropped on me during our first conversation:

- If you keep God ahead of all things, you will succeed.
- The great American dream is still possible—I'm an example that it can still work.
- A person should go as far as his abilities will carry him.
- It's important to put back into this country some of the things that you take out of it.

- Something can be done to right wrongs, and one person can make the difference.

- It isn't important what you do for yourself, because that will die with you; but what you do for others will live on afterward.

- Make a new friend each day and be ready to help that friend in a time of need without the expectation of the favor being returned.

- When you are striving for a goal, never give up hope; keep trying and you will succeed.

- Those people who are too "dumb" to realize that something can't be done, usually do the impossible.

- You will go far in life if you don't always worry about who gets the credit for the job.

It didn't take me long to realize that what Johnson was saying had worked for him and would work for me or anyone else who would listen.

The more I talked with Johnson, the more I realized that he was a person with a unique sensitivity, a dispenser of country wisdom, a practitioner of simple Christian faith, a believer in strong patriotism, and a person who applied love to every problem. He told me many stories about his life—some had me rolling with laughter, while others had tears streaming down my face.

In 1974, I wondered if the dramatic narrative of Johnson's life could be captured in a book. I felt that if his story could be told, it would revitalize the faith of millions in God, in the great American dream, and in themselves. This book fulfills my hope of capturing Johnson's life in print.

But the book was no easy achievement for the Johnson family or myself. The first draft was 800 pages long, based on 60 hours of taped interviews. Its length was edited three times. When I tried to interest a publisher, it was rejected by thirty-six of the nation's best-known publishers, even though I was an established author with nine other books to my credit.

A few publishers said that the book was too religious. Some said that it was not religious enough. Others said that the writing lacked quality. Still others said, "Black books don't sell."

But I had confidence in the manuscript. It was my best inspirational work. Furthermore, the Lord told me while in prayer, that we would find a publisher. So I applied two of Johnson's principles in continuing the search: I was too "dumb" to listen to the critics who said it would never be published, and I never gave up hope—I kept praying and trying, knowing that someday a publisher would be found because the Johnson story was worth telling; his many achievements have made this country a little better place for all Americans.

Although during Johnson's career he has worked to serve Americans of all racial backgrounds, he has achieved nearly a hundred "firsts" for the black American heritage. They include:

- First member of the black race to become a commissioned warrant officer in the United States Marine Corps.
- First member of the black race to win the toastmasters' International Far Eastern speaking contest.
- First Marine of any race to win the Far Eastern speaking contest.
- First member of the black race to retire as an officer of the naval service.
- First member of the black race to write over $1 million worth of insurance in his first 2½ months in the insurance business.
- First member of the black race to be appointed to a governor's cabinet—director of the Department of Veterans' Affairs for the state of California under Governor Ronald Reagan.
- First member of the black race to become director of the Department of Veterans' Affairs in the state of California.
- First member of the black race to be appointed vice chairman of the U. S. Civil Service Commission—appointed by the President of the United States.
- First member of the black race to be appointed by the President of the United States to become Assistant Secretary of the Navy—Manpower and Reserve Affairs.
- First member of the black race to be on the executive board of the Boy Scouts of America.
- First member of the black race to run for the United States Senate from the state of California.

- First member of the black race to be elected vice president of the Boy Scouts of America.
- First member of the black race to represent the President and the United States in the Philippines to commemorate with the Philippine Government the fall of Bataan.
- First member of the black race to inspect the United States Naval Fleet in the Pacific as the Assistant Secretary of the Navy.
- First member of the black race to inspect the United States Naval Fleet in the Atlantic as the Assistant Secretary of the Navy.
- First member of the black race to be honored by a foreign government as Assistant Secretary of the Navy.
- First member of the black race to be awarded the Navy's Highest Civilian Achievement award.
- First member of the black race to receive the Civil Servant of the Year award.
- First member of the black race to receive from the Freedom Foundation at Valley Forge the highest award for a public address on patriotism.
- First member of the black race to receive the Presidential Appreciation award from the President of the Philippines.
- First member of the black race to be elected trustee of the Freedom Foundation at Valley Forge.
- First member of the black race to receive the Silver Buffalo award as vice president of the Boy Scouts of America.
- First member of the black race to commission a major ship, the USS *California*.

James E. Johnson has received nearly eight hundred awards during the past twenty-five years for outstanding achievement and significant service to his country at home and abroad.

Johnson's achievements will long be remembered. His influences on my life will not be forgotten, including the memorable prayer his father taught him: "O Lord, thank you because we're all here, and we're getting along just fine, and we're sure much obliged. Amen."

DAVID W. BALSIGER